THE BEST OF
TROUT AND SALMON

THE BEST OF

TROUT AND SALMON

edited by JOHN WILSHAW

Virgin

First published in Great Britain in 1994 by
Virgin Books
an imprint of Virgin Publishing Ltd
332 Ladbroke Grove
London W10 5AH

A catalogue record for this book is available
from the British Library.

ISBN 1 85227 454 9

Designed by Roger Kohn
Typeset by
TW Typesetting, Plymouth, Devon
Printed and bound in Great Britain by
Mackays of Chatham plc

CONTENTS

─── *Chapter three* ───

SEEING THE LIGHT

─── *Chapter four* ───

THE STILLWATER REVOLUTION

─── *Chapter five* ───

COPING WITH DISASTER

Chapter six

A QUESTION OF MANNERS

Chapter seven

PIONEERS AND DISCIPLES

Chapter eight

THE GREAT LURE DEBATE

INTRODUCTION

O N THE FACE of it, *The Best of Trout and Salmon* is simply a collection of what I consider to have been the best examples of angling journalism and debate produced over the past forty years. But, after browsing through over 5,000 articles, I realised that, informative and amusing as many were, those features were much more than that.

Their writers were, and still are, anglers of great commitment who have fashioned our sport into what it is today. No matter what the subject, they always obeyed the unwritten rule that gamefishing is far more than just another sport or recreation, it is a reflection of the very best in ethics and fairness. Old-fashioned words when voiced today, but they have always been highly prized by successive editors of *Trout and Salmon*.

The generations may have moved on from those early days in the fifties, but few articles were ever published without some sort of challenge from readers with other and equally strongly held viewpoints.

So, enter the Letters Page – always a keen arena for debate and never boring. You can almost hear those fast-moving pens scratching out a vitriolic reply.

Memorable conflicts number those about the new 'bubble' fly lines, which were destined to replace for ever the traditional green oiled silk; cane rods versus glass and carbon; the worth of immigrant rainbows, and pity on those who had the gall to tinker with the dressing of a much-loved fly, while still calling it by its original name!

Some of those splendid letters were penned by anglers renowned as constant seekers under stones and the magazine has been all the better for their wit, knowledge and undying enthusiasm. The articles have been selected to cover all the main aspects of fishing for salmon, sea trout, the native trout of waters running and still and of course tackle and fly dressing, that evergreen tree from which all those branches eternally spring.

We would like to thank all the writers represented here for their kind permission to reproduce their articles and letters. Every effort has been made to contact these writers: our apologies to anyone that we have been unable to reach.

Chapter one

In The Beginning

➣ *Few are lucky enough to be introduced to fishing at a tender age by a father or relative eager to keep a family tradition alive and to pass on what could well be generations of knowledge about fishing and those secret places.*
➣ *Most of us are drawn to water and all things slimy before even owning a pair of wellies that fitted, and the love affair slithered on from there.*
➣ *Others miss all those magical years and stumble into the sport in later life when the ability to run, throw and bash balls about wanes. Their learning curve has to be swift, for there's an awful lot to learn before that all-important feeling of confident competence is achieved.*
➣ *Jon Beer's own genesis followed a very different pattern . . .*

FISHING WITH FATHER
by JON BEER, *March 1990*

I HAVE ALWAYS envied people with eccentric relatives. I have a friend whose Aunt Rosalind shot a postman because she thought it was Thursday. That sort of thing. What stories I would have to tell if only my father had had the foresight and consideration to have been potty – not crouching-in-the-corner-and-drooling potty but interestingly potty in a retired-Indian-Army-colonel-using-curry-flavoured-trout-flies sort of way! This will not be that sort of story. My father has retained his marbles to this day.

Nor will it be a story of angling lore learned at my father's knee, passed down during enchanted days of childhood scrambling up the trickle of a Highland burn. In fact our angling lives have converged only slowly over the years until now we find ourselves fishing together as we might have done 30 or more years ago.

I do not say that we never fished together in those days. The first trout I ever saw hooked and landed was done so by my father. The occasion, though isolated by so many years from our more recent fishing expeditions, carried many of the hallmarks that characterised our subsequent enterprises – disaster, deliciously mingled with *just* enough meagre success.

The family was on holiday in Scotland, in a guest house on the shore of Loch Eil, west of Fort William. The previous evening we had been walking over the hillside when we passed a local lad carrying a string of trout he had wormed from 'the Black Pool'. They looked enormous to eyes used to the small roach and perch of the Grand Union Canal in Hertfordshire. Father promised that we would catch some of these creatures.

The next morning we drove to the mouth of a small river that drained into the loch over miniature sandbanks. With a tempting of fate that now makes me wince, we took out a frying-pan ready to receive the catch. Father announced that we would spin. From an ancient box, unopened I suspect since *his* childhood, he gingerly pulled out a Devon minnow. It was beautifully painted with eyes and translucent flanks of mottled green. It looked deadly – as well it might, for, in addition to the first treble-hook I had seen protruding from its rear end, there was another treble on a short length of wire sticking out from behind each of the two spinning vanes. These nine barbed hooks, whirling gaily, would carve a swathe through the Highland fauna like Boadicea's chariot through a Roman legion. What it would have done through a shoal of grayling I shudder to think.

We excitedly took turns pulling this offensive weapon through the runs and cleaning the masses of weed it collected at every murderous pass. In due season something livelier than weed was jerking at the end of the line and the first small trout was landed. I can't remember which of the hooks it fell to: I cannot believe the trout was trying to catch a minnow only marginally smaller than itself and even if it were I don't see it had a hope of getting to the tail treble without first being mown down by the other two. It didn't seem to matter at the time.

Galvanised by this success we spun all the harder, grapnelling a second beautiful but tragic fish before a wetness in the wellingtons alerted us to the fact that Loch Eil is a sea loch and that we were on a shrinking sandbank in midstream. I scrambled up on to Father's back and he splashed through the deep channel that separated us from mother and sister. We were both soaked from the waist down. Damp but delighted.

There is a sort of something on the faces of womenfolk when triumphantly presented with a 'haul' of two small trout. It is something less than a sneer – but decidedly more than a smile. Anyway, eked out with a pound-and-a-half of sausages, those fish made a good meal for the four of us. It had been a good day. And as we drove off that afternoon we crushed the frying-pan, left under the car to cool.

Our fishing paths diverged at this point. Father was increasingly busy at the Helm of Industry and I returned to real fishing, to the roach and perch of the Grand Union Canal. I was never a fishing fanatic. I continued to fish in a desultory, even furtive, way into my teens but, if the truth be told, I thought the image clashed somewhat with my prospective career of blues singer.

But around this time I met someone who was a fanatic. Where I was under the sway of Blind Lemon Jefferson and Spider John Koerner, Paul Richardson was under the sway of Mr Crabtree and young Jim. Paul was a prefect at the time. In fact nature had fashioned Paul for a prefect since he was a stickler for the propriety of things like the wearing of school caps and such. When, after university, he settled in the Derbyshire Dales it was inevitable that he would wallow in the fly fishing that he had only been able to dabble in before. And, given that streak of fanatical puritanism that marks a natural-born Head of House, it was equally inevitable that he would fish the dry fly.

I had never seen it before. We went to the Derwent at Darley Dale above Matlock. There were thick beds of ranunculus growing up from the cool depths of gravel and towing downstream into a sparkle of white flowers. I had never seen a fly dropped into a channel and a dark shape rise from the shade to sip it down. I had never seen a man smack his rod on to the water in the frustration of missing a third rise in a row, or seen that top-section shatter under such abuse. This was stirring stuff. I was captivated.

I was shown the rudiments of casting and given a Tups to drop into a tumbling run where ineptitude and arm waving would count for little. An obliging grayling hurled himself on to the fly and hung on until towed into the shallows of the lower pool. His job of captivation complete, he slipped off and disappeared. But one of us was still firmly hooked.

It was fly only for me then. This is considered eccentric on the rich waters of the Lincolnshire fens. The names of those streams I plied, the Maud-Foster Drain, the South Forty-Foot Drain, had little of the magic of the Test and Itchen – and none of the trout. But they had rudd by the million which would come at a tiny black dry fly and later, as I progressed, could be

taken on a Pheasant-Tail Nymph worked along a reed-bed. It was an excellent school for the lightning rises of the small wild trout I found on visits to wilder regions. I was starting my fly fishing at the bottom.

Father, meanwhile, had come to fly fishing by a different route. Steering the ship of industry is, by all accounts, something of a strain. A fellow captain of industry had, on retirement, acquired an interest in a famous tackle manufacturer and dealer. Father had helped in the negotiations and had taken some of his reward in a comprehensive array of tackle, mindful perhaps of the pleasures he had enjoyed fishing for trout on the soft waters of Somerset during the war: also, perhaps, mindful of the tax benefits of goods over cash. If fly fishing were to become his hobby then he would do the thing properly. He had taken casting lessons and later a rod on the serene and expensive waters of a carefully managed millstream and lake. He was starting his fly fishing at the top.

Years later we met again somewhere in the middle.

In the intervening years he had moved from Hertfordshire, I had moved from Lincolnshire and we both ended up within three miles of each other in the north of Oxfordshire. We met, we chatted, we splashed about on a mile of the upper Cherwell that a benevolent fate had dropped in our laps; we got to know each other. And then, a few years later, when Father relinquished the helm of industry we celebrated with the first of our fishing trips.

Uncle John had bought a house with frontage on the River Eamont in Cumbria. I have written before about the delights of the Eamont and I will no doubt do so again, for it has, in my opinion, some of the best brown trout fishing in England. But I knew nothing of that on this first trip.

It did not start well. It had been raining steadily on the long drive up from the south. Each brook and then beck that we crossed was fuller and dirtier than the last. On the flanks of the Pennines we could follow the silver streaks of torrents tumbling down each gully.

At the strange riverside we were cold and wet and slightly daunted. The Eamont is a big river when you are used to the softer streams of the South. Full of admirable restraint we decided to walk the water before fishing – but we would carry rods 'just in case'. And a landing-net. And everything else. The lower Eamont twists between cliffs and steep slopes. On the first of these slopes, barely 100 yards from the car, I slipped and fell on to the hand that was holding the rod and the landing-net. The rod crunched like a stick of rhubarb over the net handle. The only rod I owned that could cope with this large river had shattered an inch above the butt. The rain stopped.

In Penrith I bought Araldite, dowelling and sandpaper and spent the afternoon whittling, sanding and then glueing a dowelling plug to join the two sections. The sun came out.

The whipping of the keeper ring was extended to cover the scars of the breakage and the whole shooting match left on the radiator overnight. The first cast next morning was unimpaired – if a little nervous.

The river, thanks to the gigantic settling tank of Ullswater, was full, but not flooding, and carried just a tinge of colour from its two tributaries. It was dry fly perfection. Each walk up the river revealed rising fish in ever more lies, all, so it seemed, prepared to put on a real show for our first visit. We have visited the same spot many times since then, but never with that volume of water or with that reckless rising of fine fish. But we learned. Now we always look eagerly for white water cascading off the gaunt hills beside the M6: we always carry Araldite, dowel and sandpaper somewhere in the car – and I have given up landing-nets for river trouting.

Another trip took us to Wensleydale and the River Ure. I had visited the dale years before with a party of students and retained a vivid memory of stonewalled fields each with its square barn, stepped waterfalls in a river flowing over smooth pavements of limestone and really alarming pub-opening hours. As befits responsible staff members we had prised our students out of the pub before eleven and sent them back to the hostel. We had thought to grab a quick one ourselves just before last orders. If we finished it quickly we might get another one in before 'time'. The flaw in this plan was that 'time' was never called. We continued having just a last quick one until around two o'clock, when some of the students found a spare set of keys in my luggage and fetched us back in the college van.

In truth, we could not have walked. We couldn't stand.

I told this story to Father on the journey to Wensleydale: I'm not sure he believed me. I'm not sure I did. We arrived at the Rose and Crown in Bainbridge, HQ of Wensleydale Angling Association who control six miles of this beautiful river around the village. Father had just booked a room and I was studying the map of the association water hanging by reception when a man, chuckling heartily and wiping away tears of laughter, led another chap out of the office. The second chap wore the modest grin of one who has just told a cracking good joke.

'Heh, listen to this one, dear,' said the landlord to his wife, who had just booked us in. 'Mr Riley here says he'll be staying another week, now that we've moved him out of the punishment cell. D'you hear that? The punishment cell! Guess what room he was in?'

His wife shifted uncomfortably, but the landlord was having far too good a time to notice. 'Room Three – the punishment cell! That's a good one, eh?' He shook his head and chuckled: it was a good one, all right. We had just booked Room Three.

The meal was outstanding. Rack of lamb consisted of half a rib-cage of succulent stuff that melted as we chatted far into the evening, relishing the fishing to be done the next day. We lingered over it, the kitchen long closed and the tables set for breakfast around us. It was well past midnight when we tottered upstairs and opened the door to Room Three. Inside, the noise was deafening. Room Three was directly over the packed bar whose ancient exposed beams supported our uncarpeted floor. Lying in bed I could clearly follow a three-cornered conversation below: A was standing under my bedside table; he was telling jokes to B, who was on the other side of the bed; C was slightly to the south of B. Animated chatter from other knots of noisy dalesmen was coming up through various portions of the floorspace. We laughed – at first – and then the awful implications of my earlier story began to dawn on the two of us. I do not know what time that bar closed: around 2.30 I suggested to Father that we might as well go and join them, but I couldn't make him hear above the noise. So we lay there. I think A bored me to sleep in the end.

We didn't really do the fishing justice the next morning. But we were still learning. Father bought a camper van before the next season.

There is a great joy in rolling the camper van down a farm track and into a field beside a tumbling river. The gentle sounds of running water lull you to sleep and sunlight reflected off the rippling water dances about the roof as you wake. As you lie there you know you have only to sit up to see rises dimpling the surface of the lovely River Petteril. You are wrong. In fact you can't see a damned thing.

Every window is covered with a thick, translucent, sticky smear of cow dribble. They have coated every inch in their frantic efforts to lick God-knows-what from the bodywork. It is wonderful stuff this cow spit: if left to dry it can glue the wipers to the screen or be peeled off in a tattered sheet from the glass. When we opened the side door for an *alfresco* breakfast a chorus-line of boisterous heifers jostled in to join us. We learnt from that, all right: we now carry in the van, as essential fishing tackle, an electric fence. Connected to the battery we can enforce a 200-inch exclusion zone around our riverside residence.

It was on the River Petteril in Cumbria that we had our briefest fishing trip. The Petteril is a charming tributary of the Eden. Its source is on the north-east slopes of the Lake District and it runs for most of its length between the M6 and A6 to join the Eden at Carlisle. We had visited this stream several times but always, it seemed, during a drought, not uncommon for streams in the north-eastern rain-shadow of the Lake District. But on our route north the hills had been shining this time and we knew we would find the river at its best. Two hundred and fifty miles is ample time for two fishermen to wind up their fevered anticipation but, as old hands at the game, we knew how to play it cool. No frenzied scramble for tackle with us: first we would have a cup of tea and plan our campaign with cool heads. I boiled the kettle, stumbled, and tipped the whole thing down Father's leg and foot.

A dash to Carlisle General for emergency treatment and then the long drive home again. Two hundred and fifty miles is ample time for a silent, severely scalded fisherman to reproach his son.

We haven't visited the Petteril since then. But there have been other trips to other rivers, sometimes in the West Country or Wales or wherever we can find wild brown trout willing to come out and play.

We started from different places, Father and I, and though our tastes and tactics have converged through many miles of discussions and shared experiences, the different roots of our fishing are still visible through the later growth. Father casts better than I do: his leader unrolls and straightens in copy-book fashion to lie like a line drawn across a still pool – if you like that sort of thing. On the brooks where I first hung out you made a score of sideways flicks for every classical overhead cast you could perform: my leader always bends a lot – I call this 'creating slack to delay drag'. Father calls it something else. But we both catch fish. And, by and large, I am beginning to enjoy fishing with Father.

Look. It shouldn't be true, but it *is* true: we find it hard to say what we mean. What I have been saying is, 'Thanks, Dad'.

❧ Peter Lapsley was already a well-known game fisher when his own father took up the fly rod for the first time. It started with a thoughtful Christmas present, but the Lapsley Senior fishing story really began with a meeting over a beer in a West Country pub.

A BLOCK OFF THE OLD CHIP

by PETER LAPSLEY, *August 1978*

GOLF, ORNITHOLOGY, his family and a busy and successful career which took him on a forty-year whistle-stop tour of the world denied father the opportunity to fish seriously until he was in his late fifties. And then, quite suddenly, a number of metallic fragments in his leg, souvenirs of a meeting with an over-zealous German pilot 10,000 feet above the North African desert in 1941, began to cause trouble.

The seventeenth and eighteenth holes of the golf course became just a little more difficult and long hikes over the marshes in search of avocets and curlews produced a dull ache, sometimes even a slight limp. We began to look around for a pastime which would call for less walking than his current pursuits, and, after a little gentle persuasion, he began to show an interest in trout fishing.

A rod-kit as a Christmas present and a fly-line for his birthday, along with a couple of dozen flies tied during the winter, settled it. He bought a reel, a landing-net and a paperback book of instruction as well as an assortment of more-or-less useful paraphernalia which caught his eye in the local tackle-shop. We agreed to meet for lesson one at a charming old West Country pub.

I had been there for a couple of days when he arrived. The river, running fast and clear, was in excellent shape and the fierce little wild brownies were, as ever, rising freely to anything that looked even remotely edible.

Filled with hope, we set up father's tackle. The speed with which he reduced a 9 foot, knot-less, tapered leader to a 6 in bird's-nest was breathtaking. I winced slightly as he produced from his smart new fishing bag a salmon priest which would have transformed the local *Salmo trutta* (average, two or three to the pound) into plaice with a single blow. But soon we were ready.

Standing atop an almost vertical 10 foot bank on a bend in the river, we surveyed our beat. The upstream stretch consisted of a series of four or five smooth, slow-running, wadable pools, each connected to the next by a shallow, bubbling stickle. Here and there, a tree growing from the bank, its roots spreading out into the stream, its branches hanging low over the water, provided piscine cover from both current and sun. Father elected to work along this length, searching likely lies with a floating Blue Upright.

I sat on the high bank watching as he went. His casting was very passable for one who had done so little and, as 10–12 yards of line snaked out upstream, he looked quite the old hand.

He inched his way slowly up the river. Ill-disciplined bushes caught his back-cast a couple of times and a rogue bramble on the far side stole his fly once, but all-in-all he was doing well; fishing out the stickle from the bottom, throwing in under herbage along the pool's edge, trying the slack water above and below tree stumps or boulders.

But he wasn't catching fish.

Cautiously, I moved up until I was lying on the bank right above him as he started on the second stickle. As his fly bobbed down on the rapid water, there was a slight splash. The same thing happened when he cast again, but he did nothing. It was clear that he was not seeing the rises in the turbulent water, so, after a brief discussion, we agreed that if I said, 'Strike', he would tighten unquestioningly.

He cast again. I could not see the fly, but marked where it should have landed and followed the current with my eyes. A slight hump in the water – 'Strike!'

Like a cork from a pop-gun, the angriest little salmon parr in the south-west peninsula shot from the water and hurtled back over father's shoulder to plummet into the pool behind him. Remarkably, it was still attached when we had jointly disentangled the loops of fly-line from all those catchy places – wader straps, landing net and ears – and we released it gently.

We clambered ashore and sat by the stream for 10 minutes, smoked a cigarette and watched the current sweeping past. It was warm, but not so warm that I failed to notice the hot, sticky draught down the back of my neck or the gentle snorting in my right ear. As I turned my head, my eyes met those of a bovine mountain; head down, horns hanging over me, he pawed at the turf thoughtfully.

I was on my feet in a flash, father beside me, and we backed cautiously away until we were teetering on the brink of the precipitous drop to the river. Apparently undismayed by the sight of two grown men, fishing rods held defensively in front of them, each trying to look nonchalant but each shuffling his feet nervously, the bullock turned and ambled off to join his brethren further up the field.

Dignity restored, we returned to the task in hand. Father decided to continue his exploration of the upper length of the beat. I watched for a while and then wandered downstream to an arcade of trees which always draws me like a magnet. The fishing there is not easy but with a short brook rod and a little care, it is possible to wade slowly up it for its full 100 yards. Few people bother, and the trout lying in beneath the banks and the tangled roots are often larger than the average for the river.

Stealthily I moved up the tunnel, throwing a Pheasant Tail Nymph into likely lies and corners. I took two fish, one of them a demon of almost 1 lb and missed several more before I came out into the sunshine at the end. Time had stood still beneath the soft, green canopy, and I was startled to find that it was more than an hour since I had left father a quarter-of-a-mile away.

I came upon him quite suddenly as I rounded a bend in the river. Thigh-deep in the fast-flowing, oily-surfaced water at the foot of a stickle, rod tucked awkwardly beneath his arm, half-framed glasses perched on the end of his nose, 15 feet of fly-line trailing in the water, the butt of a new leader in one hand and the instruction book open at 'knots' in the other, he was lost in concentration.

'How are you doing?' I called.

His pink, beaming face turned towards me.

'Marvellous,' he said, 'three in the bag and two more returned.'

He's never looked back.

And then there was the flyfisher who missed out on those muddy childhood days and the inevitable telling-offs about the dangers of falling in, or straying with those bloodbrother pals whom parents always thought were unsuitable company, and only felt the magnetism of the riverbank when he sought a secret place where he could satisfy his passion for strong cigarettes.

SMOKE ON THE WATER

by LAURENCE CATLOW, *February 1991*

THE OTHER DAY I started wondering how I became a fisherman, and was forced to acknowledge that my motives were not innocent. It was no pure delight in nature that led me to the riverbank, it was no healthy and sporting impulse. It did not really happen until I was 17. Until then, although I had fished a while, it had only been when there was nothing better to do and, on the odd occasions when I did go fishing, I soon grew weary of it and never got as far as catching a fish.

But, at the age of 17, my fishing tackle began suddenly to be put to constant service and became a source of almost daily consolation. I was then a boy at Stonyhurst, a Catholic boarding school in rural Lancashire; it was a beautiful spot, and one of the chief features of the surrounding countryside was the River Hodder. We were allowed access to a long stretch of the river, which was no more than a brief stroll from the college, and so it was that I often set off down the road, wearing a pair of black waders and with an eight-foot fly rod swinging over my shoulder. I always put my rod together before leaving school, because somehow it made me feel more of a fisherman. I took a box full of flies and knew the names of some of them; I cannot remember that I ever took a landing net and it did not matter anyway because I am quite certain that I never hooked a fish. Accompanying the box of flies was a knotted tangle of nylon and a battered reel which carried an old and half-rotten silk line. I did not think I wore a hat of any sort unless it was raining and I did not bother with grease for the line, oil for the flies, scissors, a spring balance or with any of the paraphernalia which I now consider essential for a happy fishing trip. But always, whatever the weather and whatever the state of the water, without exception there was concealed in one of my pockets a box of matches and a packet of cigarettes, and always they were Woodbines.

Equipped with this gear I would amble on my way, waving my rod from time to time as though in anticipation of the first cast. Sometimes I would meet a master or a priest, who might wish me luck or perhaps remind me there was a Latin prose due the next day. On a sunny day it was a pleasant walk to the Hodder. The river itself was always very beautiful. I used to watch it from the shelter of a sycamore by Cromwell's bridge, with my rod resting against one of the branches and with a cigarette hanging between my lips.

That first Woodbine was an ecstasy of forbidden delight and was often followed by four more – I bought them in packets of five from the post office. I would watch the drifting smoke and wonder, without much concern, whether it might be visible to the probing eyes of a vigilant Jesuit: I would lie back and gaze vacantly into the sky, or lean forward and look at the river, vaguely aware of the hatching fly and the rising fish. Often, when the packet was finished, or keeping a single Woodbine as an evening indulgence, I would walk back to the college in a mood of contented fulfilment and explain to everyone who bothered to ask about my sport that the trout had not been feeding or that I had failed to find the right fly. Then I would settle down to my Latin prose.

On such days, and they were perhaps the commonest sort, I never got as far as wetting my line. But there were times when I did fish for a while. Then I enjoyed the sensation of running water against my waders and was pleased by the fortuitous elegance of an occasional cast: I was never troubled by the hopeless incompetence of most of them.

I went fishing to smoke cigarettes, and to lie in leafy sunshine as I smoked them. But I was not a complete imposter; I did, after all, fish sometimes and, as I lay in bed at night, I was often moved by the sudden longing to catch a trout; then I would resolve to smoke no more than a single Woodbine the next day – before fishing the whole afternoon with exemplary determination. Once I even got into the river as soon as I reached it and cast away quite happily for at least 20 minutes. But by then I was jaded with fishing and resigned my ambition of the night before. Retreating into the shadow of Cromwell's bridge, I settled down to a pastime that brought instant satisfaction with the striking of a match.

I troubled my confessor at the college with many anxieties and doubtless with many imaginary, as well as many grave and obvious, sins. But it never occurred to me to reveal, not even in the most guarded language, the scandal of my excursions to the River Hodder: the wilful deceit they involved and the cynical contempt I was showing for the rules of the community to which I belonged. I suppose that, had I been inspired to confess the true nature of my activity as a fisherman, I would have been obliged to put a stop to it; and, although it may seem blasphemous, I still cannot help thanking God for so wisely blinding my conscience in this respect. It was His way of turning me into a real fisherman. It must be 15 years since I last lit a cigarette and I must by now have caught at least ten trout for every Woodbine I ever

smoked beneath the crumbling stones of Cromwell's bridge.

It was God and the River Hodder that between them made me a fisherman: it was the sight of the sun on the water as I sat there smoking, it was the sound of water running between the rocks as I lay back trying to blow smoke rings, it was the gurgling motion of water beneath the arches of the old bridge, glimpsed absently as I took out another Woodbine and struck another match; it was the peace I inhaled along with all the nicotine. I never caught a trout from the Hodder at Stonyhurst and I never tried very hard. As a schoolboy angler I was a flop and a fraud; but those visits to the river opened my eyes to the magic of running water, and it was this fascination which later blossomed into the happiest obsession with which any man can be afflicted. I have been punished in the best way imaginable for the forbidden delights of my schooldays: the pretext for my excursions to the river has itself become a ruling passion which suggests, to me at least, that divine justice is tempered by a sense of humour – and by a kind heart.

Almost my last visit to the Hodder – it must be more than 20 years ago – took place just after my A-levels; it was an evening expedition and, since I had only one Woodbine in my pocket, I decided once again to go through the motions of fishing before sitting down to smoke. It was one of those summer evenings so perfect that to be out in them along the margins of a river is a foretaste of Heaven; it was an evening when every detail of the landscape, every careless detail, every colour, shape, sound and movement seemed an emphatic proof that our world is the gift of a kind creator. I was besotted with it; so transported that I abandoned my usual lair and fished upstream towards the woods round the next corner. I must, I suppose, have felt that such an evening called for a break with tradition, demanding the dignity of some special place which I would afterwards associate with that evening alone.

I did not, of course, catch a trout, nor even one of the salmon parr with which the river swarmed; and, when my fly caught an overhanging branch and was lost in the leaves, I never thought of replacing it. But still, stupefied by the beauty of flowing and shining water, I splashed upstream through the shallows, rod still in hand and with all thoughts of tobacco suspended. It was some sort of trance and it may have lasted ten minutes, it may have lasted half an hour; perhaps it was no more than a delayed and heightened sense of relief at finishing my exams. But whatever it was and however long it lasted while it held me under its strong enchantment, the soft sounds a river makes on a still evening sank quietly into me. It blended with the splashes of rising fish and the screaming of swifts, the faint stirring of riverside trees, the layers of shadow and slanting light, the air alive with the shimmering brightness of insects' wings and, above all, a fading sky so luminous and blue that it seemed the reflection of a better world. All this I absorbed, and with it an intensity of peace that I shall never forget.

The experience of that evening has always remained with me. Once or twice, by the sides of other rivers, it has almost been recreated. And whenever, lying in the grass on the edge of the Eden or the Wharfe, I feel the wonderful calm of a summer evening beginning to wash over me, I think of the Hodder and give thanks in a gesture of piety that also belongs to that evening 20 years past.

For, eventually, I left the river with the sinking sun and, finding myself in the steep woods below the prep school, I thought of my single Woodbine and smoked it under an elm tree, slowly and reverently. I was as happy as I ever have been and, doubtless with a touch of adolescent affectation, but with some genuine feeling of devotion mixed in with it, I intoned, between each lungful of smoke, the Latin words of the *Ave Maria*, repeating them three or four times. They seemed to hang in the air with the drifting smoke of my cigarette and I was uncertain whether they found their way up through the leaves or could only sink down, to be swallowed by the damp earth. They are words I have often used since, at the endings of other summer evenings by a river. Now they are a whispered reverence but always they bring back something of the serene rapture of that evening when they were first chanted by the water's edge. They are, I suppose, my response to the conviction that I have been unworthily rewarded with perfection, that I have reached paradise without the inconvenience of first lying down to die.

Teetering once more on the edge of blasphemy, and unsure anyway how to finish this inconsequential piece, I can think of no better conclusion than to repeat the words that have so often been muttered as mist begins to rise from the water and the squeaking bats flutter and swoop catching our prayers and helping them on the beginning of their journey to Heaven – muttered in response to some impulse of thanksgiving and supplication. And so I mutter them once again, this time into my word-processor, mutter them, as always, for myself and, this time, for all other fishermen as well. But on this occasion more particularly for all those who have ever fished the river I never fished properly, the river which made me a fisherman in spite of myself, and for those, too, who have preferred just to sit there and smoke, staring and marvelling at the beauty all along its banks:

Sancta Maria, mater Dei, ora

pro'nobis peccatoribus nunc et in hora mortis. Amen. (Holy Mary, mother of God, pray for us sinners now and at the hour of death.)

  🙦 *'Ah, if you think the fishing is good now, you should have been around when I was a boy' is a lament often voiced by game fishers of long experience.*

🙦 *But have things really changed all that much? Did those rivers really ever exist where at times there seemed to be more fish than water?*

🙦 *In some cases, and with salmon rivers in particular, they probably did and the diaries of those ancients fortunate enough to fish them proved this to be so. Certainly there were fewer fishermen fishing for more undisturbed fish.*

🙦 *G. P. R. Balfour-Kinnear was already a salmon fisher of considerable experience by the time he contributed this food-for-thought article in 1959. But was there just one single change in sixty years of fishing that spelled the beginning of the modern era?*

CHANGES IN SIXTY YEARS' FISHING
by G. P. R. BALFOUR-KINNEAR, *January 1959*

FISHING TACKLE HAS, like most mechanical gear, been much improved in recent years. Our fathers fished with heavy greenheart or lance-wood rods, many of which had hickory butts. These old rods, if meant for salmon fishing, were not made for weaklings – nineteen feet was a common length and some were as long as twenty-one feet with butts two inches thick. It is not surprising that salmon fishing was not so popular as it is today.

Cane built rods were first made fully 100 years ago, but they were so revolutionary, or so badly made, that they did not become univer-sally popular for many years. A modern salmon rod of 14 feet can throw all the line that is necessary. Within the last few years fibre glass and steel tube rods have been made available for those who like them.

Perhaps the next step will be a nylon tube rod.

In the old days the best lines were made of horse hair. The dressed plaited silk line was introduced about 60 years ago and that was a great improvement. It was not however until 1913 that Malloch of Perth patented the wonderful double taper 'Kingfisher' lines. To appreciate how helpful the taper is one has only to cast with a parallel line, and see how the casting distance is reduced, and how comparatively heavily the line lands on the water. Because of the double taper the line may be turned when one end wears, and is then as good as a new one.

General greased line fishing for salmon began about 1935 and to begin with many of us greased our lines with mutton fat which was just as effective as the modern greases. The introduction of this method of fishing made it possible to catch spring and summer salmon in calm places and in low water conditions when the sunk fly would not have been so productive. In 1956 the Americans invented the 'bubble' line. This line has a series of minute bubbles between the core and the outside casing, so that it floats without grease.

This line is a good innovation, because it not only saves the trouble of greasing, and having to wash greasy hands before changing a fly, but with it there is no grease to reach the cast and make the fly skate.

These lines have been introduced to Britain only in limited numbers.

Thread lines for spinning are a comparatively recent improvement. When I was a lad it was customary to use the fly line and rod, and to landline the bait, either collecting the line recovered in the hand or coiling it on the bank or in the water. It required much energy and a little skill to spin in those days. Silk thread lines were then invented and they were followed about 1925 by Japanese gut substitute which was made from seaweed and cost 1s. 6d. per 100 yards. All these lines were replaced about 1948 by nylon, although nylon was on the market in short lengths for some time before they were able to make it into complete line lengths.

Sixty years ago fly reels were made with longer line drums of smaller diameter. The modern reel has a comparatively short spindle but a much larger diameter line drum, so that line may be recovered quickly. The old trout reels were sometimes as small as 1½ in in diameter whereas the modern trout reel is seldom less than 4 in. Those early reels had external cranks round which the line might snag. In order to avoid this, and to take up less room, the handles of the modern reels are all fastened to the revolving plate. Incidentally early reel makers had not thought of making holes in the side of the line drum to let the water in to rot the backing!

The wooden 'Nottingham' type of reel, in which the line

drum runs free, was in use more than sixty years ago. It was followed by the 'Silex' which was made of metal and, being smaller in the drum, threw a lighter bait. Both of these reels were originally so large in line drum diameter that a considerable weight was required to make an adequate cast.

This type of reel was improved by Pfleuger some thirty years ago. The Pfleuger reel has a wide spindle of very small diameter and so light baits may be cast with it.

Malloch of Perth patented the 'Malloch' reel in 1883. This was the first fixed drum reel. The line drum turned 90 degrees on the rod handle, so that the line could run off over the end of the drum, while the drum was stationary. Malloch's reel was improved upon by Illingworth in 1905. The 'Illingworth' was the first proper fixed drum reel that did not twist the line as did the 'Malloch' reel.

Malloch got over the twist difficulty by occasionally reversing the line drum. The 'Illingworth' did not twist the line because it wound it on to the spool over the end of the drum and not by turning the drum as in the 'Malloch'. Although the 'Illingworth' did in fact twist the line to wind it on it untwisted it again when the cast was made, whereas the 'Malloch' twisted the line when the bait was cast but failed to untwist it when it was reeled up by turning the line drum instead of a flier. It is rather extraordinary that as long as 22 years elapsed before improvement was made on Malloch's idea.

The metal eyed hook, introduced I think about 55 years ago

(but perhaps more), was an improvement on the old gut loop. The flies hung better on the gut loops, but many a fish was lost owing to the loop being necked with casting. As the gut loops perished through time it was not then advisable to keep a large stock of flies. The actual fly patterns have changed very little except for the introduction of tube flies. The idea of using one or two trebles instead of a single hook is not a new idea. Trebles were in use 30 years ago.

Canvas phantoms and metal devons were fished with sixty years ago, and so were spoons. Recent years have seen the development of many new types of spinning baits, spoons and plugs. To my mind the greatest improvement is the hollow rigid bait that runs up the cast when a fish is being played, and so does not lever the hooks out. Plugs originated in America and they use them there far more extensively than we do both for salmon and trout. A plug still seems to be their favourite lure for bass.

As it is so easy to fish with any of the spinning baits, with the modern reels, many fishermen would like to have spinning stopped both for salmon and trout. Is there not something to be said for this, at least in the case of the brown trout?

Silk worm gut always varied greatly in strength according to how it was cured. It perishes with age and is not nearly so strong as nylon of the same thickness. Thick, heavy gut on account of the amount of soaking it requires, is more troublesome to knot. It is therefore surprising to me that some fishermen still use it.

The old fashioned cloth fabric waders, which wore so badly at the feet, have been replaced within the last few years by plastic covered waders, and those moulded in one piece of solid rubber. Both of these new types were introduced and made by Edinburgh firms. The rubber waders are so elastic that it is easy to walk in them; so much so that I once forgot that I had taken them off and walked into the river without them!

And what of our rivers? Alas! The picture here is not pleasing. Some salmon rivers are now depleted of fish owing to hydro electric schemes and many never hold salmon again. On account of increasing population (30 gallons a day per person) water abstraction is an alarming menace. I know of one river where an extra 6,000,000 gallons of water a day is being taken away. The level of the river is unchanged as it now receives in exchange 6,000,000 gallons of new sewage daily.

Chemicals are ruining our rivers. Fly life has been almost completely destroyed on many rivers owing presumably to the spraying of insecticides on the surrounding country. Modern sheep dip and strong detergents, which have only recently been universally used, are also extremely detrimental to fly and insect life. In the old days – and not so very old – one of the sights on the river Tweed was the hatch of March Browns. They are now extinct on lower Tweed. As proof that it is pollution

that is destroying the fly life, you will find the fly population increase as you go farther and farther up the rivers that are suffering.

Rents for fishing have soared. This is, of course, partly due to the low value of sterling, but also to the fact that there are now so many more fishermen. About 65 years ago my grandfather paid £25 for fishing for the season. That same fishing, which is not nearly so good now, lets for £275. The motor car has proved to be a two-edged tool. It enables us to get to out-of-the-way places only to find other people there who would probably not have walked or bicycled, as we might have done.

❧ *So it was the advent of the car that proved itself the noisy herald of what was to come. In the next piece, Tony George went even further back in time to the turn of the century to make a worthwhile comparison.*
❧ *Did he believe that the changes – always for the worse – happened almost overnight simply because rivers had, almost overnight, become more accessible? Even then, all the usual grumbles were being heard.*
In that age of vast social differences, poaching was rife, rents were escalating and catches were down.
❧ *Has anything changed?*

SALMON FISHING NINETY YEARS AGO
by TONY GEORGE, *December 1980*

IN A WAY that does not apply to other branches of the sport of angling, salmon-fishing assumes quite different identities and flavours from era to era according to the patterns of return-migration prevailing, and this factor correspondingly has a bearing on the sort of person adopting salmon-fishing as a sport.

An incisive and telling comparison could be made between the era of the 1920s and that of the 1970s, or even between the 1950s and the 1970s, but for our Christmas story this year let us consider a period quite unlike our own, and of a kind not experienced by any living salmon-angler, that finally expired 60 years ago and that was at its zenith almost a century ago.

By the 1890s, on a trend becoming more strongly established by the season over 30 years, the main salmon run migrated steadily later and later until a large part of it passed out of the netting season altogether. The spring and early-summer fishing deteriorated to such a degree that the grilse run provided the first-quality fishing on many east-coast rivers, but on the more famous of these the grilse were but an overture to the principal sport of the season: the autumn run of new and heavy fish straight from the sea.

The nature and geography of the autumn run was described by a writer in *The Fishing Gazette* in 1894: 'No north-coast, no west-coast, no island rivers, have in autumn a run of such large, bright, sound fish as takes place on the south-west coast and, without exception, in all those rivers of the east coast of Scotland of any magnitude from Tweed to Spey . . . Not one of the rivers having this splendid and sustained run of autumn salmon fishes really well until after the netting ends . . . The Tay fishes soonest or earliest . . . Next in point of earliness for a run of autumn salmon are the Spey and North Esk . . . But taking the run of the seasons as also of the rivers, anglers would do well not to count on the autum salmon fishing beginning in real earnest until about the middle of September, when usually splashes of rain come, and the weather gets cooler . . .'

To recapture more fully the flavour of the period I have incorporated details of events and descriptions relating to a single year: 1894. This year is selected not because it was in any way outstanding – on the contrary, more is it characteristic of the vicissitudes that afflict the sport – but primarily because I have isolated a considerable amount of information about it.

Perhaps the first and most significant point to make is that autumn salmon fishing towards the end of last century was a socialite sport in a way that it has never been since. There is a specific reason for this quite apart from, or rather tied to, the quality of the sport itself. Politics was then a profession for 'gentlemen', whether of the Tory or of the Liberal (Whig) persuasion, and when the long late-summer and autumn vacation began, the memberships of both Houses, together with their families, relations, friends and retainers, decamped almost *en bloc* north of the Border for the fishing and shooting. When, early this century, the main run changed from the autumn to the spring, salmon-fishing lost much of its social cachet, because the governing classes could not get away while the Parliament was in session,

and the sport became the more plebeian preserve of professional and business men that it largely is today.

This was the era in which it was customary for journals to publish notices in prominent positions such as the following: 'The lets on the river North Esk of the principal beats for the autumn salmon fishing this year [i.e. 1894] are: Morphie – Sir John Gladstone, Bart; Canterland – Lord Cavan; Inglismaldic Castle – Mr Thos Cordes; Hatton and Kirktonhill – The Hon Edward Drummond; Craigo – Mr E. M. Crossfield.'

All these tenants were prominent in political, military and social circles.

As a lead into the main part of the sporting season of 1894 there was the buoyant grilse run customary at the period. *The Fishing Gazette* of August 25 commented: 'The netting season closes today for the year in connection with quite four-fifths of the most important salmon fisheries north of the Tweed. Generally in spring it was unremunerative, but in midsummer it pulled up owing to a good supply of grilse and sea-trout . . .'

Some decent sport was had with the grilse, but this was just a prologue to the main event. Most of the tenants did not come up until August.

The beginning of the autumn fishing in 1894 was induced by an enormous August flood, when 2 ½ inches of rain fell on the north in 12 hours. But in the second week of September this ominous report appeared: 'The dry tract of weather having continued, most Scotch rivers last week and early this week were running in rather weak volume for good sport.' This reminds one of a second and vital difference between then and now: there was no 'greased line' in those days, and once the rivers had 'fallen in', that was largely that on most rivers and beats until the next rise occurred to bring some life to the sunk fly.

A third and important distinction is that many rivers not now recognised within memory as being true autumn rivers were then among the best and most famous of late fisheries. Three examples are the Spey, the Aberdeenshire Dee and the Don. A September issue of *The Fishing Gazette* reported: 'The Duke of Richmond and Gordon and his large Gordon Castle party have already begun to have first-class sport at Fochabers. For yield of fine back-end salmon to the rod the Gordon Castle Spey fishery for the

space of about six weeks (to 15 October) had no peer. For little over a month's fishing between 1,100 and 1,200 fish have been caught . . . Almost every autumn one or other of the anglers gets a salmon of 50 lb, or close on 50 lb, weight.'

The same described 'the 60-pounder landed above the bridge at Fochabers last week by the Duke of Richmond and Gordon's fishermen. Its length was 4 foot 4 ½ inches, girth 2 foot 4 ½ inches, and measured just above the tail 10 inches round . . . It was a fitting close to the net fishing, which came to an end on this day week.'

The weather continued dry, but because of its rapid flow even within a mile or two of the sea, a low water with plenty of new fish may suit the bottom beats of the Spey: 'Although the water is of a low size, good sport continues to be enjoyed on the lower reaches. On the Gordon Castle water the Earl of March killed a salmon of 44 lb, Mr F. B. Mildmay one of 42 lb and Lady Evelyn Gordon Lennox one of 38 lb.'

Most other waters were less fortunate that back-end. The dry spell became a drought and by the middle of October the Aberdeen correspondent was writing: 'Not within the memory of the oldest angler was the Dee ever so low all through the autumn season.'

When the weather finally broke, the tenants were left with less than a fortnight's fishing. The final report on the Don read: 'By good fishing I mean a bag of 17 salmon in one day. That was accomplished; also 13; and eight fish were not uncommon. The last fortnight of September and the first fortnight of October were blank; but the fish which came up latterly were really in splendid condition. The biggest taken was 39¾ lb, as bright as clean polished silver. Weights of 27 lb and 28 lb were frequent.'

The Aberdeenshire Dee (which then closed on October 31) also finished well. When the flood at last came: 'Several old netting men declare that such a wonderful run of fish was never before seen, even in the Dee.'

As always following a drought, disenchantment was widespread: 'Always my luck,' complained a rod on the Dee: 'I have given over lamenting about it long ago. Whenever you have a good water and too much sport, send for me, and if my presence doesn't work a change it will belie my experience of 20 years.'

Moaned the columnist, Mac: 'I am half in mind to take on for the trouting one of those charming river fisheries, and be done with autumn salmon fishing altogether. Every autumn is more or less a disappointment . . .'

So far the emphasis has been on the causes fundamentally divorcing the present from the past, particularly the runs and the people. In lesser but significant matters it is paradoxically striking how contemporary much of the comment sounds. Not only drought and associated acrimony testify to the sport's continuing state of incipient crisis, but high rents, bait-fishing, poaching, angling fish-salesmen, illegal netting and disease all figure prominently in the scene of the 1890s.

A vein of gossip (and they were much more gossipy than today's magazines) about the ever-increasing cost of salmon fishing runs through all the journals of the period. In *The Fishing Gazette* of August 18 'Deesider' (and not our current one, surely) reported that 'autumn waters are being rapidly picked up at greatly-enhanced prices. On the (Aberdeenshire) Dee there is hardly a cast to be had.'

Mac commented: 'I hear that the late Mr Irvine's trustees are wanting £400 for the Drum water for the back-end fishing alone. Tidy, isn't it?'

The MacKay complained: 'I know of one (Dee) fishery which, along with an extensive mixed shooting and a residence, was let for £60 a few years ago, and has now been let for £350 minus the shooting. The same proprietor now draws the tidy income of £350 from his angling waters, besides retaining a good slice of the river for the delectation of himself and friends during the autumn months. His father would have been· glad of an offer of £30 for the lot.'

Complaints were common about the alleged deterioration in sporting ethics. One correspondent considered there was no future for the Dee, what with: '. . . over-minnowing, over-gudgeoning, over-prawning and over-deviling'

(whatever that may be), continuing that genuine sportsmen 'are dead against the pot-hunting which is getting so common – parties selling all their fish. Add to this that the river is currently said to be severely poached . . .' *Plus ça change . . .*

Another correspondent observed: 'The marketing of salmon caught by the rod on several northern rivers is getting rifer and more the fashion amongst anglers every year. The sporting expense *must* be paid by the fish, you know.'

There was a great deal of comment on poaching, and particularly on snatching. Apparently it was as prevalent in the upper Tweed as it is now, if not more so. A correspondent fulminated: '. . . foul-hooking has disgusted me with salmon-angling. I have finally resolved never again to fish in the neighbourhood of snatchers . . .'

River reports were full of complaints. North Esk: 'As for the wholesale sniggering in the holes at the backs of the dykes which are packed with fish, it is sickening and beastly.' Autumn was the worst time: 'Large brown trout on the eve of spawning, grilse black and bagged, and salmon almost ripe for the redds, were openly and freely snatched in the river Bogie at Huntly by the locals during the floods in the latter part of October. This is no new game; on the contrary it is a fixed institution . . .'

Illegal netting seems to have been just as bad as it is today. The position on the Tweed was literally anarchic. By the 1890s the Tweed salmon run had become so late that the main part of it was arriving after the nets had finished on September 14. As a result, the netsmen were in open revolt. *The Fishing Gazette* of September 22 observed: 'Last week the salmon net fishing season on the Tweed closed. Ever since the opening in February the results have been unsatisfactory. Last year the Berwick Salmon Fisheries Company lost £2,500 and this year there will, it is believed, be a further loss. Hardly one station on the river will square accounts.'

The issue of October 6 continued: 'Serious disturbances occurred at Berwick late on Tuesday night, owing to the antipathy of the fishermen to the Tweed water bailiffs. As the latter were proceeding down the river in their steamer in search of illegal nets, about a hundred men ran along the pier and threw stones at the vessel. When the steamer reached the other side of the Tweed at Spittal, ten boats manned by fishermen put out to prevent the bailiffs obtaining nets. Amid great excitement and noise the fishermen succeeded in reaching the nets first and defied the bailiffs . . . The mob on Berwick pier was so unruly that the police had to charge the crowd.'

The Scotsman newspaper commented on the background to the extensive and persistent illegal Tweed netting: 'In 1886 the late Government had the alternative before them – either to face the responsibility for bloodshed or to allow the Queen's name to be insulted, and illegal fishing to be carried on under the eyes of her officers. *Solvitur ambulando!* They adopted the easy if not very dignified course of walking away. The gunboat was withdrawn, and the task of protecting their own property, as well as that of the Crown, was left to the Tweed Commissioners. The result has been as might have been foretold. The poachers, drawing encouragement from the hint given them on such high authority, multiplied their nets; each year a large number of unseasonable salmon have been caught; till now, as is notorious, they can be bought almost any autumn day in Berwick and the neighbourhood for 3d to 6d a pound.'

Nevertheless, resulting from the lateness of the run, we note in *The Fishing Gazette*'s report 'From the Borders' of December 1 that despite the poor (legal) nets catches and angling sport, there appeared to be a good stock in the river: 'On Friday the rod fishing on Tweed and her tributaries closed for the year 1894. Probably never in the memory of man has there been such a wretched season recorded. It has had not a single redeeming feature from February 1st to November 30th. The number of salmon and sea-trout now in the rivers appears to be very great and the general conditions for spawning are very good. No disease has yet shown itself, in spite of the crowded state of some of the reaches.' But the following week's report stated: 'I am sorry to say that the fungoid disease has again broken out in the river with some virulence.'

There seems always to be something chronically wrong with the Tweed, and in 50 years' time I expect it will be just the same.

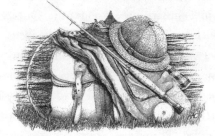

Chapter two

WHY DO WE FISH?

• *There are, they say, four milestones which all anglers pass in their fishing life.*

• *The first is just to catch a trout. Any trout will do, be it large or small as long as it is a trout. That fish is remembered for all time. Mine was a trout I came to call Ebenezer and he lived under a bridge in a little Welsh hill-stream. It seems a hundred years ago that I first caught Ebenezer after many attempts on a worm.*

• *Why call a trout Ebenezer? When laid on the fresh Spring grass, he looked beautiful, spots as big as blood splashes and black fins all smallwater fishers dream about. Then I was a three-times-a-Sunday chapel man and I remembered Ebenezer as an aged sage from the Old Testament. My fish was as old as the hills and as much as I wanted to take him home as a trophy, I couldn't bring myself to end the days of this proud ancient.*

• *The next March I caught and returned him once again. It was going to be a much looked-forward-to St David's Day ritual. The next year he was gone but old Ebenezer is still very much alive forty years on and more.*

• *The second marker is to catch the most. That's not too difficult with gaining experience and the knowledge of how to tweak Lady Luck's arm at the right time. For all but an unfortunate few this stage is passed through quickly.*

• *The next and more difficult milestone to pass is the catching of the largest trout. When the truth finally dawns that this can never possibly be achieved, for who is to say what is the biggest fish, we then pass on to the ultimate fly fishing experience of catching the most cagey trout that swims. This trout has a knowledge of fly dressing possessed by no mortal man. He bolts at the flicker of a rod or the lightest footfall. Sanity prevails when he is outwitted by a beginner making his first clumsy casts with the wrong fly.*

&. There is in fact a fifth stage and this is achieved without any effort and with almost a sigh of relief when it finally dawns that fishing isn't really about catching lots of fish, or the biggest or the most difficult. It's all about being in tune with good old Ma Nature and being in the company of like-minded anglers.
&. Brian Clarke summed up the whole thing about why we even fish at all superbly well.

A PHILOSOPHY FOR CATCHING TROUT
by BRIAN CLARKE, September 1973

FEW ANGLERS have the ability to become really first-class: the requirements, ranging from a great deal of opportunity to considerable degrees of intelligence, inventiveness and natural intuition, are too rarely found in an individual. A second, rather larger group of anglers, has the ability to become 'good', with perhaps intuition, that sub-conscious marriage of experience and sixth-sense, prescribing the gulf between the two.

By and large, and a long way behind, that leaves the rest of us: the great unwashed; the average, ordinary anglers who are separated from the water and our superiors by good yet immutable reasons of family, home, business, distance, or sheer expense – indeed, the ordinary kinds of bloke who, like myself, have a limited opportunity for fishing, inhibiting the expression of an unlimited interest.

For the likes of us, there is only a slender chance of becoming 'good' anglers, much less first-class anglers. Yet within the constraints of limited time for experimentation, observation and the rest, there is nothing at all to stop us becoming better anglers, and that can be our aim. Not even that process, however, can begin without commitment, and effort, and that is what these articles have been about. In writing them, I have attempted to show how, sometimes clumsily, sometimes awkwardly, and often self-consciously (particularly when surrounded by better anglers, or other anglers who had not begun to make the attempt), I tried to improve my own performance on a basis of thought, in spite of the problems and my own technical shortcomings.

Perhaps the hardest thing, as will already have occurred to readers of this series, was to take the first, most painful step of all: to admit that one must blame oneself more, and the fish and the weather and one's equipment less, when catches are consistently low.

As earlier articles have indicated, I forced myself to this conclusion only slowly: it took half-a-dozen seasons, at perhaps a dozen outings each, to make myself realise that I was getting nowhere. My whole approach had sunk into a mindless, mechanical rut of mediocrity, and my returns – or, rather, my lack of returns – were precisely what I deserved. My leaders were, as on the day I had begun, still 9 foot long, 7 lb breaking strain, with two droppers; my fly-box was still full of Jersey Herds, Peter Rosses and what's-its-names; my retrieve was a clockwork, 8 inch pull after 8 inch pull, day in and season out; and when occasionally I couldn't retrieve, or found it resisted, I had a trout on, for reasons I neither cared nor attempted to fathom. Once I had faced the absurdity of this situation, and had realised what a waste it was of the little time I did have for fishing, I set out to establish a sensible reason for tying on one fly instead of another, and for retrieving it in one way in preference to another. This, in turn, led me to think for the first time about the reasons why trout were caught on flies at all; thence to a brief look at some of the creatures trout ate when hungry; and subsequently to a narrowing of the entomological field to three basic forms of food for imitation: midge pupae, sedge pupae, and olive nymphs. The reasons for settling upon these particular creatures were set out at the beginning of the series, where I also told how I set aside the whole of the 1972 season for an experiment in fishing these food forms, in preference to lures and their kind.

Attempting so much was, of course, a tall order; and my approach, with so little time to put into practice all I read, observed and thought about, was necessarily superficial. Nevertheless, it was a calculated experiment: and the acid test of any experiment is the results it produces. So what, when all is said and done, came out of my efforts to reduce the overwhelming element of chance in my fishing?

Well, more fish, for a start. My average over a season of 14 outings, notwithstanding a fair share of blanks, went up staggeringly, from 0.7 to a fish per outing, to over three trout per outing: and all were taken from day-ticket lakes and reservoirs, publicly available.

I mention fish first, because that is an objective, tangible measure of results. Far and away the most fulfilling aspect of the experiment, however, was that it revealed new dimensions to fly-fishing which hitherto I had not imagined. The sheer scale of what is to be learned and understood suddenly dawned upon my blinkered mind; and as a result, the poverty of my own attempts was put firmly in perspective. The more one learns, I began to see, the clearer it becomes how little one knew before, knows now, or even can hope to know in the future: the higher up the mountain one goes, as it were, the more distant the horizon becomes. That is one of the reasons why, I am sure, the few very expert fly-fishermen I have met have all been comparatively modest, very helpful men.

In addition to this – in spite of it, I suppose I should say – I became a great deal more confident about catching fish than I had been

before. While it is not possible to know everything, it is possible to learn enough to take fish with fair regularity, for reasons we can understand. I suppose if I were asked to express this understanding in specific terms, I would say that the difference between mindless chuck-and-chance, as opposed to informed chuck-and-chance (with the fish always having the last say, if not, as in my own case, the last laugh), was shown towards the end of the season, when someone nearby caught a fish. As the light began to dawn for me I ceased, within a few minutes of the capture, to sidle along the bank and ask, with the air of one seeking a modest loan, the name of the successful lure. Either I already had a fair idea of the most successful recipe, or I was determined to concentrate on some experiment, or I asked a completely different question: 'May I spoon your fish?' There is a universe between the two attitudes, and it has nothing whatever to do with complacency.

On looking back, therefore, as a final article in a very generalised series must, there is little about the basic form of experiment that I have recommended that I would change. Notwithstanding the puzzlements of trout behaviour, and the realisation towards the end of the season that all was not as tidily ordered as I had imagined at the outset, these were things that I learned as a result of the experiment, and not that I knew before it: only my calculated perseverance, as it were, made clear the exceptions to the rule.

So for me, the experiment will continue. Indeed, I am so convinced I am on the right lines that it will replace entirely my former lethargic approach – although I intend, for reasons of further experiment, to extend the range of imitative patterns I use.

In recommending to others the type of approach I have taken myself – beginning with the trout, and working backwards – I have gradually become conscious that I was advocating not so much a way of catching fish, but a philosophy for fishing. This particular philosophy, however, has a sharp edge to it: it is geared to catching more trout, of course; but it is also geared to obtaining more pleasure from the way they are taken.

I believe both these are possible by attempting a thinking view of our sport, rather than an unthinking view. And to take a thinking view, the first step is to attempt an understanding of what kind of creature the trout is, how it lives, and in particular, what it feeds upon. There is no hidebound purism in this: as I have already said, it is a means to an end – a combination of more fish and greater pleasure. And anyway I have already expressed my own willingness to use a lure, if that is the only thing which will break a blank; and I have readily admitted my own incompetence as I take the first early, self-conscious steps myself, with little over one season's experience behind me as I write. Additionally, it has already become clear, through both bankside encounters and letters received as a result of this series, that there are vast numbers of ordinary anglers, quite apart from me, who are coming to recognise the need to put more into their sport, if they are to get more out in return.

For the angler, it is fair to say,

there can be no finer investment than putting thought into fishing. He will get more fun, interest, diversion and sheer excitement than any blinkered, repetitive view of his game will allow.

And if we do not go fishing for fun, for interest, for diversion or excitement, why on earth do we bother at all? For the corpse of a fading trout? Not one of us, I'm sure, believes that to be so.

❧ *Any salmon, particularly one fortunate enough to have completed the miracle journey back to his natal streams a couple of times, could be excused for rolling over on its side and laughing fit to burst every scale on discovering just how centuries of sleepless nights have been spent by anglers eager to outwit him. Is the river too high, too low, are we too early or too late, is the fly too large or too small, is it fishing too high in the water or too low or is it moving too slowly or too fast and, perish the thought, are the salmon even in the pool at all?*

❧ *And why, if a salmon doesn't eat when in fresh water, does it take a fly at all? Add all those variables together, multiply them a dozen times and that's what makes salmon fishing the terrible beauty it is.*

❧ *Like all dedicated salmon fishers, Crawford Little has suffered, and has thought through all these and more problems to arrive at a logical answer that works – sometimes.*

❧ *A basic truth of salmon fishing is that if you've got water you're in with a chance of a fish, but water is something we either have in enough quantity to get Noah reaching for his ark plans, or it's in such short supply that the drought-stricken angler wouldn't be too surprised if a herd of thirst-crazed gnu thundered down to the riverside in a cloud of dust.*

❧ *Let Crawford investigate the water gauge and its influence on a salmon fisher's expectations and chances of success.*

THE HEIGHT OF SUCCESS

by CRAWFORD LITTLE, *February 1991*

IT HAS been said that fishing the salmon fly is comparable to buying a ticket in a lottery. We might argue that the successful salmon fisherman can make his own luck. Certainly, we should all make the effort to choose good tackle suited to our particular needs, and learn how to use it to something approaching full potential.

We should make sure that when a salmon takes, it will not be on a cheap or unsound hook or frayed and weakened leader. Our reels will be lovingly polished and oiled in anticipation of that electrifying moment when they chatter, then scream. We use the best knots, ensuring that their coils are moistened with saliva and snugged down carefully. And we fish with a determination to tempt a salmon at each and every cast.

Yes, we do all these things. But still there is that strong element of uncertainty. We lay plans and make arrangements for our fishing trip, and then the anxieties start. At no other time do we take such an interest in the long-range weather forecast. As the day or week approaches, we keep tapping the barometer. If we hear of a fisherman newly returned from the river or area that is the centre of our thoughts, we want to know how he has fared. We are not just keen to hear what he has caught but, above all, the height and state of the river. Whose heart does not fall if, on the week prior to his visit, he hears that the river is too high, or too low, and there is little, if any, hope of change? And how many Monday mornings have been ruined by a gillie's announcement that, without rain, or frost or whatever, we might as well stay at home?

What makes it all the more heartbreaking are the vagaries of the British weather. We expect high waters in the opening and closing months of the season, but may fail to get them, as those who fished Tweed in the closing weeks of the 1990 season will testify. There again, we might get too much. As I write, I am looking ahead to the first two days of February, a Friday and Saturday, when I shall be casting a fly near Coldstream. My tackle has had its winter overhaul. My army of tube-flies, Broras and Waddingtons has been brought back to full strength, and new supplies of strong nylon bought in. But who can say that my prayers for a falling, clearing water will be answered? Nobody but the Almighty can make that sort of luck for themselves. My only hope is that, as we have had so much rain over Christmas and New Year, interspersed with days of snow-laden blizzards, there cannot be much more to come. The Nith is flowing bank-high. The loch hosting 'my' duck day-roost is so deep that the bankside vegetation and islands are covered, and the evening flight ponds have turned from shallow dabbling areas into deep-water pits. The duck have deserted me. Let me pray that whatever luck I might enjoy with salmon will not do the same.

Thinking of salmon and water height, and having mentioned duck, reminds me of a story from Chesapeake Bay, on the east coast of North America. An old bayman was asked what was the best size of pond for black ducks. 'Wal,' he said, 'it shouldn't be too big. Then again, it shouldn't be too small.' He was then asked how deep the pond should be. 'Wal,' he said, thinking long and hard, 'it shouldn't be too deep. Then again, it shouldn't be too shallow.'

Much the same sort of country-style logic applies in trying to define what makes a good height of water for salmon fishing. It certainly should not be too low, but then again it should not be too high. It definitely should not be too coloured but, there again, a touch of colour may be no bad thing. There are so many ifs, buts, ors, ands and maybes, but we know what it is when we see it. Following on the heels of a spate, the water falls and clears to that point when experienced fishermen start to itch with expectation.

Sometimes, the perfect water height comes like a brief, piercing shaft of sunlight in an otherwise black sky. For example, in looking ahead to the opening of this Tweed season, I can look back to one in the mid-80s, when January had been a real barnstormer of gales and snow. The first day of February fished well, but there were ominous signs of a coming thaw. Many folk simply headed for home the following day as the river roared down in mighty flood. And so it remained, until frosts on the following Sunday closed the taps on the thaw, allowing serious fishing to start again. On the Monday evening, Tweedside eyes were smiling again.

Then there are times when the perfect water height can continue day after day, when rods can enjoy sure, steady sport. This is what is at least meant to happen on the Spey and Dee as the snows melt on the high mountain ranges in spring. Of course, it does not always work out as well as we might hope but, in our dreams and memory banks, we can picture weeks in late May with the strath coated in yellow blossom and entire weeks spent with a floating line and size 6 Munro Killer.

Loch-fishing for salmon and grilse in the West Highlands and Hebrides creates its own set of concerns and anxieties. River-fishermen will be praying for rain to bring in fresh runs of fish. And, obviously, this is also a requirement for the loch. But too much summer rain can bring loch-fishing to a standstill. Thinking of the manner in which lochs act as a sump within a river system, I suspect that their acidity is closely balanced. This can affect even great expanses of water. One day, when drifting the bays and islands of Loch Lomond with my father and the late Bill McEwan, the fishing suddenly went dead on us. Where we had lately been raising salmon and sea-trout, we could not tempt even an incautious finnock to swirl at the dap.

'The water has coloured,' said Bill.

'Don't talk nonsense,' I said. 'It's not even raining.'

'Use your eyes, boy!' he laughed. 'It's raining in the hills, and just look at the water.'

He was quite right. The loch had taken on a bronzed, peaty tint and its level was creeping up the rocks and boulders of the bonny banks. So we all laughed, and fished with our minds only half on the job as we discussed the inhabitants of the loch, both wild and tamed. Then it rained the wild rain of the west, and only my father laughed at two packets of sodden cigarettes.

Once river or loch water has coloured, it needs time to recover.

On small, rock-girt spate streams this may take only a couple of hours. I have seen such a stream, in spate at supper-time, fall and clear to a summer low by the following breakfast. That was unlucky for us. In a week's fish the only decent water had passed during the witching hours. If we had risen to a falling spate, we might have enjoyed the sort of bonanza that throws aside all thoughts of lunch or supper.

Other rivers, those with much larger catchment areas that flow through rich agricultural land, can produce the opposite extreme. Tweed is such a flow, as are the rivers of the Solway where I live. I can stop at the bridge over the Nith on my way to the village shop on a Monday morning and *know* that the fly will not fish until Thursday, or Wednesday at the earliest. And then, of course, it will be raining on the Wednesday morning and the river will be back to bank-high and running the colour of potter's clay. That is enough to keep even the wormers at home!

Living on the banks of such a river does, of course, allow you to be philosophical in your approach to salmon fishing. Like the farmer, you must learn to accept, albeit grudgingly, what the weather pro-duces and how that affects the fishing conditions. I therefore had every sympathy for the owner of a boat on the neighbouring Annan, who had planned a press weekend when he could show some scribes and one scribbler what his own beat, and the entire river, was capable of producing.

Certainly, the Annan is not as well-known as it might be. It tends to labour in the twin shadows of the Nith and Tweed so far as its autumn salmon fishing is con-cerned. While it may not earn itself a place in the First Division of Scottish salmon rivers, it is certain-ly well-placed in the Second, and offers some outstanding value-for-money beats and association water.

The Annan follows the general pattern of Solway rivers in that, despite the season opening on Feb-ruary 25, nothing much is caught in the opening months. Sea trout are traditionally expected to be prolific in June, July and August but in recent seasons their numbers have been reduced, typical of so many rivers. Nevertheless, on the Kirkwood beat where the press visit was centred, two visitors who were prepared to fish hard through their July week in 1988 caught 22 sea-trout.

Annan efforts do not, however, really get underway until August produces the early harbingers of the autumn runs, with sport reaching a peak in October. The season closes on November 15. This pattern is clearly revealed by an inspection of the Kirkwood beat's monthly catches for 1988: August 10, September 12, October 24, and November 14. And with five salmon taken in February, that amounted to a season's total of 65 salmon. However, returning to my point about the essential factor of water height, the effects of a prolonged drought were revealed in 1989, when the annual catch fell to just 32 fish.

Such catches will be of little interest to those fixated by great beats on classic rivers. They are perhaps, of greater interest to those who think mainly in terms of a family holiday, with some fishing on the side, or those who do not want to grovel in front of the bank manager before taking a beat. Full details of the beat and associated self-catering accommodation are available from Kirkwood, Lockerbie, Dumfriesshire, DG11 1DH, or telephone 05765 200.

And what about that press visit? Well, despite everybody enjoying themselves as only the press know how . . . yes, you've guessed it. It looked as if the spate was all set to fine down perfectly, but then came another downpour of rain, the colour returned, the river rose and the fish went down.

When salmon are on, they really are on so hard that you would wonder what all the fuss was about. Catches of half a dozen fish in almost as many casts do happen, but what to do on those far more common outings when off is a better word to use?

Few salmon fishing situations are new. It is usually merely a question of knowing the slight differences in fly that tends to put a hard-earned and most satisfying fish on the bank. Is there ever such a thing as an uncatchable salmon?

ANY FOOL CAN CATCH A SALMON

by CRAWFORD LITTLE, *January 1987*

ANY FOOL can catch a salmon. Any fool, that is, who happens to find himself in the right place at the right time. Give a 15 foot carbon rod with a floating line and a size 8 Stoat's Tail to a chimpanzee, put him on the banks of a famous beat on a classic river at the height of the summer salmon and grilse runs and, eventually, he will catch a fish. Well, maybe not, but I have heard of absolute beginners who, after being shown the rudiments of casting, have been into a Spey or Dee fish within minutes of wetting their lines.

The taking habits of salmon are said to be unpredictable. This is true to an extent, but there are times when they can be easily caught. The height of the water, its temperature and that of the air are fundamental, but nothing like so important as the presence of fresh fish. A fresh-run fish, new off the tide and still bearing sea-lice, is the easiest of all salmon to catch; just so long as it happens to be pausing in its upstream journey at the time it encounters the fisherman's lure. I feel sure the essential feature is

that a running salmon is pausing, rather than that it is fresh-run. With a rise in the water height bringing on ideal running conditions, stale, potted and hitherto un-catchable salmon become takeable.

This concept of the pausing salmon interests me. The pause may be for only a few seconds, for an hour, for a day, or for as much as several months. At the opening of the season, springers seem aware that there is no great rush. Many months lie ahead before they spawn, and they nose their way cautiously into the lower pools of the river, pausing frequently. Autumn runners are quite different. It is as if they realise that, heavy with spawn and milt, they have no time to waste, and they run hard for the upper reaches, loathe to pause.

The general pattern, however, is that with the smallest rise in the water, salmon become restless, and for a brief period, sometimes as little as half-an-hour, a well-presented fly can provoke a satisfying response. With increasing water height, fish begin to move. They may have been waiting weeks or months for this opportunity, suffering in reduced flows and soaring temperatures, their vital oxygen leached away. They are ready to flex their muscles; and away they go.

At the height of a spate, salmon are running hard through the slower stretches and easing their way along the cheeks of the heavier flows. It is hard work. Occasionally they pause in a relatively sheltered backwater. The local, armed with his worming tackle and an intimate knowledge of the river, may catch one. Other fishermen will be keeping a close eye on the water-level, praying that it will fall before an all-too-short holiday comes to a close. Eventually, they will be able to make a start, probably with spinning rods. It may be the next week's tenants who will enjoy the cream of the fly-fishing as, with the water clearing and falling ever closer to normal height, the salmon pause more frequently, looking for new lies in anticipation of the river falling below running level. The bonanza will be when most of the fish are pausing. Then, as they become established in their new lies, catches will fall away.

As a writer, I find it tempting to concentrate on those times when the fishing is easy. We can all do it,

preaching that the pattern and size of fly, and the depth and speed at which it is fishing, are relatively unimportant. If you stacked together all the 'relatively unimportants' that you have said of salmon fishing, you could be excused for thinking that practically anybody and anything can catch a salmon. 'The ability to cast a long line is not important; I would happily fish with one pattern of fly; cast it out and let it fish round by itself; mending line is unimportant; all this fuss and nonsense about whether to use an intermediate or a floating line; one hook's as good as another . . .'

Well, if you believe all that, you're probably the chap I saw earlier in the season on the Spey, standing next to a chimpanzee with a net in his hands and an expectant look on his face.

All these cheeky references to the Spey! Lest I cause offence to the *aficionados* of that mighty river, I hasten to add that on the many happy days I have spent on its banks, I have found it sometimes to be one of the most demanding of rivers, needing hair-raising wading and every last ounce of effort and casting skill I am able to muster. Equally, at times conditions are just right and, as I have said, any fool can catch a salmon, particularly with a spinning rod, fixed-spool reel and a 2-inch, black-and-gold Devon minnow.

In ideal conditions, everybody is in with the chance of a fish, but the more skilful and thoughtful angler normally catches most. The difference between skilful anglers and mediocre anglers becomes far more pronounced as conditions deteriorate. Only the more accomplished fishermen then have much of a chance of grassing a fish.

I would not describe myself as particularly skilful at salmon fishing, although I sometimes find that I can match the antics of those who say they are. However, I would say that I am a thoughtful angler. I spend an inexcusable amount of time in considering ways to achieve the downfall of a fish. By thinking the problems through and coming up with what are, to me at least, plausible solutions, I am able to fish with confidence. Also, having sole access to salmon fishing quite literally on my doorstep, I am able to put many of my theories to practical experiment. Most of the theories are soon discarded, but occasionally I surprise myself with one or two that work.

Of even greater importance is the fact that I live north of the Border and have a job that keeps me regularly in touch with some very fine fishermen with sufficient free time to accompany them and learn something of their skills. I am enormously lucky to be invited to fish a number of fine rivers by those who are prepared to tolerate my eccentricities for a few days. I might do better to keep to one beat, where familiarity with the water in all its moods would lead to greater success. However, I have that at home, and by visiting many waters, I find that I am always learning something new, which stands me in good stead on other waters. For example, if I had not visited the rivers of the north-east of Scotland, I would know little of the techniques of hand-lining and backing-up a pool, but these methods have taken fish for me on lowland rivers as well.

Whatever the reasons, my own philosophy of salmon fishing with the fly, in any conditions, is that the fundamentals that must be right are the choice of fly and the speed, angle and depth at which it is fished. Let me describe the taking of a fish or two on a recent trip, which will illustrate these points.

Nick and Di McAndrew (Di, incidentally, is without doubt the finest lady angler and caster I have ever known) telephoned to ask if I would like to spend a few days with them on the Beauly. Di and Nick are the finest of fishing hosts, so I leapt at the chance.

On arrival, I was surprised to learn that the total catch for the previous week, tenants changing mid-week on the Beauly, had been only two fish. Fishing with Nick and Di was Jim Hunter, a tremendously keen fisherman. With that trio on the river, I knew that conditions must be bad if they weren't achieving much success. However, I was fired with enthusiasm. In a perverse way, I enjoy the challenge of difficult conditions. The capture of a salmon when it is least expected takes on a far greater significance than a big bag of fish taken on the floating line in ideal conditions.

Fish that had long since lost the sheen of the sea were showing regularly in that apparently purposeless way of resident fish. I thought of the fresh-run grilse I had plucked from the Cumbrian Eden the previous week, after the main run had become stale. It had taken a tiny Waddington, hand-lined gently through dead water in the dub of a great long pool. But no clues were to be drawn from that. The Beauly might be low, but there was plenty of force in the pools and streams where the fish showed.

It was quite late in the season and the temperature, in the mid-40s, seemed to suggest quite a large fly fished on a sinking line. Willie, the gillie, thought that it should be a dark pattern. I tried this for a few hours, then sat down for a head-scratching session.

I have long thought that the magical figure of 48 degrees Fahr, suggested at the point at which we should change from sunk to floating line, or *vice versa*, should serve as nothing more than a general guide. If the temperature is hovering at the start of the season, going only just over the datum point, then I may stay with the sinking line. At the end of the season, as the temperature falls slowly below

48 degrees, I may stay with a fly fished just below the surface, although the fly may be quite large, as big as a size 4. I changed to an intermediate line.

As I looked for a smaller fly to replace my 2-inch Willie Gunn, the sunlight danced on the body of a Bourrach. Streamy water, the surface boiling and whirling from the effect of a boulder-strewn river bed; plus the bright sunlight? That Bourrach from Speyside that I had tied on a long-shanked Wilson double looked marvellous with its oval-ribbed, silver tinsel body, blue hackle and tail, silver wire and yellow floss butt, and sparse, long wing of yellow bucktail.

As I tied it to the cast, I looked downstream to where Di was fishing on down the pool ahead of me. She had won the ladies' salmon-casting event at the Game Fair more than once, and was putting out an awesome length of line. Just then, a fish showed slightly upstream of her. There was nothing new in that; he had shown so many times in the last few hours that we were practically old friends. But the manner of his jump had changed. It seemed more purposeful, as if he were responding to the ever-present urge to run. I hurried down to

him. I was soon at my maximum range and still having to cast quite square in order to cover him, but I was reassured. I had been told that Beauly fish often show a preference for a fly presented in this way. He took, and a few minutes later I hustled him into Di's waiting net.

Back at the fishing hut for lunch, we discovered that Nick had also scored. The pattern of fly was different, but the size was similar and, again, the fish had come to a squarish cast.

As the light faded, I hooked another fish on the Bourrach, a bigger one this time, hand-lining the fly in the deep water below a steep bank. Once again, Di did the necessary with the net. It was an obvious place to try in the dusk for a running fish, and in saying 'running' I include fish that may be doing little more than cruising to the head of the pool and back again.

I hope that what I have written will be seen as more than a description of the pleasure I gain from fishing in fine company on splendid rivers. Certainly, as I headed south I was keen to turn a brief encounter into a more lasting relationship, but I hope that my words show also that when the mood of the fish is apparently to ignore our flies, we must seek a stronger provocation to stimulate a response. The change in stimulus may be quite subtle, but it can radically affect our thinking on the depth, speed and angle at which we present our chosen fly. This opens the door on a multitude of fishing techniques: traditional sunk and floating lines; the use of intermediate lines as a development of Alexander Grant's oiled-line technique; controlled drag; the use of droppers; hand-lining and backing-up; the dry-fly; and even the upstream wet-fly. The list is endless. If the editor is prepared to continue to tolerate my eccentricities, as my kind fishing hosts have done, these are some of the subjects that I would like to consider in more depth in future articles.

 Fifteen years ago, I discovered the salmon mother lode. Salmon anglers heading further north to pastures greener had passed over the little bridge for years in their thousands.

 A chance visit to the estate office brought the reply that they wouldn't charge me for fishing. They didn't know how much to charge anyway but if I caught a fish, then a couple of pounds would do.

 With two sparkling salmon and half a dozen sea-trout in the bag I enquired if I could just possibly have a full week the following year. Incredulously, I heard myself being informed that I could have any week I wanted as no one else wanted the fishing.

 'Would £30 be too much?' For the next dozen years, the fishing was even better although the cost did totter upwards. Thirty salmon on the fly, and sea-trout up to double figures was the norm, and then in the space of a couple of years it died and has yet to show signs of recovery. Was it disease, over-netting or just part of a larger lifetime cycle than man's?

 One tempting alternative to finding reliable salmon fishing is to buy into a time-share, and in the affluent eighties many eager anglers with deepish

pockets took the attractive lure. For some, things turned out well. For others, all that glistered turned out to be anything but glittering gold.
❧ The problems associated with time-shared fishing are not new. G. P. R. Balfour-Kinnear spelled out the difficulties in 1960 and twenty years later John Byfield added his own telling comments.

THE SNAGS IN SHARED SALMON FISHING

by G. P. R. BALFOUR-KINNEAR, *June 1960*

I WAS recently asked for my advice as to the advisability of buying a share in a salmon fishing. It sounds a straightforward proposition, but is it so in reality?

As some fishermen may be thinking of becoming joint owners I would like to point out what, in my opinion, the snags might be so that they may do what is necessary to protect their interests. These difficulties do not, of course, arise when buying the whole fishing rights, as is usually done, but only when buying a share in them.

Because there are more people wanting to buy rod salmon fishing, than there are fishings for sale, these are often sold for big prices. If therefore, you are offered say a half share in a two-mile beat, on one side of the river, for say, £1,500, the offer looks attractive. Is it really as good as it sounds?

You could get five per cent tax free interest on the £1,500 so you are paying a rent of £75. You will, on some rivers, have to pay river tax in addition and also your proportion of the wages of a watchman who may be shared with neighbouring beats. If that adds up to say £115 then both sides of the two mile stretch must be worth at least four times as much, i.e. a rent of £460. As the value of each side is enhanced if the other side is also available, this rent could be fairly stated as, say, £660. That may, or may not be too much for the beat in question. If it is too much then the offer of a share at £1,500, which looked so very attractive, is not a bargain after all.

You may even be left to carry the baby, as you will see.

If there is no binding agreement with your partner, and also with the owner of the other side of the river, as to the number of rods – which is not only binding on them, but also on their successors and assignees – you are in a bad position.

If your partner (or his successor) sells his share to a syndicate there is, so far as I can see, nothing to prevent the members of that syndicate from fishing the whole of the side of the river in which you are interested, because you could have done likewise. The owner on the other side, now finding that his fishing has been spoiled because of all these rods is likely to sell his side to the syndicate.

You are then not even as well off as the members of the syndicate because they can fish the whole water, whereas you are limited to sharing only your own side with them.

The purchaser, in both instances, instead of being a syndicate, might have been an hotel. In either event you are left paying a rent of £75 and also a quarter of the taxes, and a quarter of the cost of keeping, yet you are no better off than if you were a casual guest staying in the hotel, or, as I have said, a member of the syndicate limited to one side of the river.

Be sure, therefore, to see that your interests are protected, if you are only buying a share, and not the whole exclusive rights of any fishing.

THE GREAT DIVIDE
by JOHN BYFIELD, *December 1990*

IN THE beginning were UDN, Greenland nets and acid rain. Then came timeshare, which in my opinion is the worst of the lot – for while the others leave you with *something*, timeshare leaves you with nowt if you cannot afford to join.

So what can one make of an issue which has already had such a profound effect in depriving salmon-fishers of the right, tacitly accepted for generations, to fish rivers they regard as their own?

Clearly, timeshare is a privilege enjoyed by those wealthy enough to release sufficient capital. In this respect it is no different from the ability to pay £40,000 for a personalised number-plate for your car; if you have that sort of money, value-judgments are non-existent.

One can imagine the quandary of a long-standing tenant, whose only option is to purchase a time-share if he wishes to continue fishing. Quite apart from the difficulty in finding the necessary money, most anglers on the wrong side of 60 have a very real problem in deciding whether they want to become tied into a lease with a minimum term of 25 years.

Certainly, a change to timeshare on any fishery will give new-comers the opportunity to jump any existing waiting list, since money is suddenly the only criterion. In this connection, it will be interesting to see, over the next few years, whether this results in friction or other unpleasantness, unheard of among tenants familiar with long-established custom.

So how has this timeshare business come about? With the clear precedent of timeshare villas on the Costa del Sol, owners of salmon fishings have seen an opportunity to commercialise their assets. 'Owners' of the more prestigious fisheries may well, of course, be financial institutions (insurance companies, pension fund organisers) acting on behalf of share-holders interested in only one thing – profit. Insofar as it is all

perfectly legal, and an example of the operation of 'market forces' selling a commodity in the most advantageous way for its owner/s, there is no obvious way in which timeshare may be thwarted.

The current valuation of salmon fishing for outright sale is about £8,000 per fish, whereas the value per fish of a timeshare can be as much as £20,000. When one considers that timeshares are often (and increasingly) sold for fixed-term leases of between 25 and 99 years, it is obvious that a timeshare venture by a riparian owner means that he can benefit from an enhanced sale price – and yet look forward to the fishery eventually reverting to his ownership (or that of dependants).

It is when one comes to consider the way in which sale prices can be hoisted that blatant commercialism takes over. For there is good reason to suppose that time-share sales are often delayed deliberately for a period of, perhaps, three years. During this time, it is alleged, every legal means is used to boost the catches by which the final price is determined. Extra sub-division of beats and/or multi-plication of rods are two ways of achieving the required short-term result. It has even been alleged that the locals have been encouraged to fish to a degree never permitted in the past, simply to swell the three-year average return.

So what conclusions can be drawn about timeshare salmon fishing? I would certainly not be the first person to observe that the last thing we would choose to do would be to tie ourselves and a lot of spondulics to 50 or so years' commitment to fish a particular week on some famous river, come hell, high water, drought or – occasionally – perfect conditions. Given the choice, we would use the same money to enable us to fish a variety of different rivers, paying an annual rent in each case; but then, each person to his or her own tastes.

Second, it clearly discriminates against the majority of anglers who cannot commit £100,000, or even £30,000, to 50 years of timeshare. Many of us like to save upwards of £500 and treat ourselves to a week on a famous river – not necessarily better than the ones we usually fish. Such a sum is more in keeping with what we might otherwise spend on a foreign holiday. Those with the much larger sum of money to buy a timeshare may well be justified in regarding it as an investment in the long term. But salmon fishing is a fickle business. Who is to say that, in far fewer than 50 years, their costly autumn timeshare may be less valuable if the spring fish multiply at the expense of the autumn?

Third, some anglers have lost their fishing, and a very traumatic experience such must be if you live locally. Even for non-locals, timeshare fishing is effectively removed from circulation for at least the term of the lease, or until a timeshare owner wishes to sell (for whatever reason). Under the previous arrangement, you could put your name on a waiting list, or hope that a tenancy might become available for an odd season; both being possibilities which occasionally produced the goods.

The thought occurs to me that, in cases where the timeshare is not bought in perpetuity (i.e. free-hold), what the selling riparian owner has secured is, for example, 50 years' rent in advance. I have been putting a few numbers to this concept, and the results are thought-provoking.

If we stick with my previous example of a 50-year timeshare and associate it with a price of £50,000 (purely to keep the numbers simple), that represents an *average* equivalent rent of £1,000 per year. Due to inflation, such a rent might be typical of a value in mid-term of the 50-year period.

Looked at, first, from the view of the riparian owner, he has suddenly acquired £50,000 which, at an interest rate of only eight per cent, would grow to £2.345 million if left untouched for 50 years. By contrast, an annual rent income of £1,000 would grow to only £619,762 after the accumulation of compound interest of eight per cent for 50 years. Verdict: by this test, a definite windfall for the original seller.

What about the purchasing angler? At first sight, it might be thought that, since an *average* 'rent' of £1,000 implies a starting value somewhat below the average, such a 1990 figure might be £500. In fact, if you apply an annual inflation rate of even five per cent over 50 years to such an initial value, this notional rent has grown to £5,461 in the final year of 2040; by which time a total of £104,674 would have been paid in rent. It is necessary to adjust the 1990 rent down to £239 in order to make the total 50-year payment agree with our timeshare price of £50,000 (at an inflation rate of five per cent).

Now, a rent of £239 per annum does not carry great promise of prime salmon fishing at 1990 prices (notwithstanding the fact that there *are* worthwhile salmon fishing opportunities to be had for that amount of money), and you could easily spend four times that figure for a week's salmon angling on a famous stretch. With £50,000 in your piggy bank, you could pay the £1,000 in rent and still (in 1990) have your remaining £49,000 grow to £53,000 at ten per cent interest by the time your next rent demand came through the post.

There is, of course, the argument that even a leasehold timeshare can be resold, possibly at a higher price — even allowing for the elapsed part of the lease. In that sense, it can be regarded as an investment, subject to the ups and downs of similarly risky ventures. But the benefits are not nearly so certain as those accrued by the riparian owner, especially when he has only temporarily relinquished possession of his asset.

As I wrote earlier, timeshare would not be for me, even if money were pouring out of my ears, and it is arguable that its principal attraction is to those people who wish to use their wealth to secure the chance to fish beats such as Carron and Laggan, on the Spey. But then, fisheries of that class have always been the preserve of the rich, and anyone who imagines they could fish the Norwegian Åaro by joining a local angling association is living in cloud cuckoo land.

The real threat is that the spread of timeshare results in significant amounts of salmon fishing being rendered unavailable, except to those able and willing to pay for it on an annual basis. This raises a basic question about those fisheries not yet affected by timeshare: what features are vulnerable to timeshare marketing? The primary attribute is clearly that of excellence, be it sheer numbers of fish, very beautiful surroundings, good and easy access, comfortable fishing conditions, good fly water, or a combination of these. All are attributes by which good salmon fishing has always been valued.

So, if the fishing you enjoy yields one fish for every six or ten days, has factories on the banks, a car-park one mile from the water, no hut, and can only be spun or wormed, sleep easily in your bed! More seriously – and it *is* a serious matter – timeshare is most attractive to those riparian owners who have fisheries patronised, traditionally, by weekly tenants and with available accommodation in lodges near to the fishing. This is clearly much more typical of game-fishing in Scotland where many anglers, foreign as well as UK nationals, take their holidays a week at a time.

By contrast, many salmon fishings in the south (e.g. the Hampshire Avon or the Wye) are let throughout the season on a one-day-a-week basis to anglers who live and work within, say, 50 miles of their fishing. The idea of anyone taking a 50-year timeshare on a single week's fishing each year on the Avon in its present depressed state would surely appeal only to a dedicated masochist. No, I can foresee such fishings continuing to operate only on the basis of one day a week throughout the season. But having said that, what riparian owner would refuse 50 years' rent in advance if he could get it? The fact is that most anglers would not consider for one moment entering into such a long-term arrangement when we have seen the spring fishing – so vital to the Avon, Wye and many other southern rivers – virtually disappear over the past 30 years.

Finally, is there anything on the plus side, in favour of timeshare? We have already seen that it has the potential of giving the riparian owner access to much larger sums of money than he would receive from rents paid annually. While much of this will be spent away from the river, in other instances this extra money will enable fishings to be improved; for example, by buying off netting rights (with benefit to the whole river). But the fact remains that such expenditure will occur only if the freehold owner considers that direct benefit will fall upon the specific fishery and enhance its future value.

Some of the revenue will also be spent on improving facilities on the fishery, such as building croys, river-bank management, and so on. On a timeshare fishery, each and every one of these improvements

would have to show an eventual financial cost-benefit even if the long-term objective were preservation of the asset ultimately reverting to the riparian owner. Short-term benefit or demands may also be associated with maintenance charges (scheduled or otherwise) which could fall upon the timeshare owners as an unwelcome additional outlay, even if such expense served to maintain the resale value of the timeshare in mid-term.

All in all, in my opinion timeshare in salmon fishing is not very attractive to contemplate when such a relatively scarce commodity is marketed in this way. For you cannot create new salmon rivers in the same way as more villas are built to satisfy demand. My own hope, while accepting a certain amount of timeshare as inevitable, is that its spread will be limited to a few, very expensive, fishings. Most depressingly, conversion to timeshare could wreak its worst damage in destroying the many assocations, which do such good work in providing salmon fishing opportunities for those otherwise least able to afford it.

⁚ *If nothing stirs to a well-presented offering after the first day, then that's not too bad and enthusiasm levels remain on a high. But if, after three more days of fruitless casting, the salmon still fail to react, then there's a very real danger of fishing becoming more a metronomic going through the motions just because you are there.*

⁚ *While there's little doubt that luck has a role to play in salmon fishing, the competent angler relies more heavily on a systematic approach that incorporates concentration and confidence.*

⁚ *Salmon fishers are famous for a fund of excuses to explain their lack of success. Some may be justified but others are not. Crawford Little has heard them all and explains the often subtle differences between the genuine excuses and the fanciful.*

SALMON: A FORMULA FOR SUCCESS
by CRAWFORD LITTLE, *August 1990*

I HAD JUST sat down for a rummage through my fly-box. I was quite sure there were salmon in the pool but, so far, I had failed to tempt any of their number. It was then that the small boy came wandering along the riverbank.

'Any luck, Mister?' he asked, as he stopped in front of me. I looked at him and attempted a smile. Like a thousand salmon fishermen before me, I tried to think of a smart reply. What was the point?

'No,' I said. 'No luck today – at least, not yet.'

The youngster smiled back and gave me a knowing look.

'Och well, dinnae worry, Mister,' and off he went.

Small boys are not the only ones to enquire about your luck, or the lack of it. In fact, the question 'Any luck?' has become an almost universal greeting at chance meetings of fishermen on river or loch. And this sort of talk must get through to some salmon fishermen, because more than a few of them will tell you that luck is all you need to catch a salmon.

It is so much easier to say that 'Old so-and-so is a lucky devil who always catches more than his fair share of salmon,' than to admit that the man in question may be a far more skilled and experienced exponent of our craft.

THE BEST OF TROUT AND SALMON

Perhaps luck does play its part, from time to time, in catching a salmon, but if you want to know what I think, then it is that there are some fishermen who, quite simply, are able to make their own luck.

Thankfully, because I have been able to fish with a fair number of truly outstanding tempters of salmon over the years, I now reckon that I am able to make a fair stab at suggesting why some folk do, indeed, catch more salmon than others. In fact, a fairly clear pattern emerges, and success with salmon can virtually be defined as a formula. In defining this formula, let me start with a look at the ladies.

It is, perhaps, a part of my Scots heritage that leads me to talk of 'fishermen' rather than anglers, and yet to use the term seems to deny the possibility of the female gender. So let me put the record straight, here and now, by stating that many successful salmon fishermen are women!

Men out there, take note. This is no sort of chivalry, or other window-dressing for *Trout and Salmon*'s female readers. Nothing annoys me more than those 'clever little women' articles that occa-

sionally crawl into the pages of our sporting magazines. The facts speak for themselves: and there is no denying that, among those women who regularly fish for salmon, their average level of performance tends to be higher than that of the average man.

Some of us might seek to write off Georgina Ballantine's record British salmon on the grounds that she was just 'lucky'. She was harling, after all, with the boatman overseeing the entire operation. However, it is a great deal harder to explain away the largest British salmon ever taken on a fly. This fish was caught in 1924 by Mrs Robertson from the Wood o' Shaws pool on the Mount Blairy Water of the Deveron, and was not weighed for 24 hours after its capture. Yet, despite inevitable weight loss, it was still able to pull the scale down to 61 lb. What about Miss Doreen Davy's record British spring fish of 59½ lb, taken from the Wye in 1923?

What can those who seek to become successful salmon fishermen learn from this? The fact of the matter seems to be that, just like those top chefs who emerge from what is − dare I say? − a traditionally female world, those women who become at all serious about salmon fishing are *determined* to succeed. If they are going to do it at all, then they are hell-bent on doing it well. So here is the first component in the formula for success with salmon: a very real determination to succeed.

It has just struck me that, before we go any further in looking at success, I should perhaps define what – exactly – I mean by the word. After all, your own ideas may be different from my own. For one thing, I pay scant attention to the hotel bore who will tell anybody and everybody of how he managed to pluck a single, stale fish from a low summer river, when all the other guests were drawing a blank.

Nor do I take the faintest notice of catches taken on the prawn or float-fished shrimp. For those of us who know how it's done, it is something of an understatement to suggest that there seems to be little merit in clearing the salmon from a beat with a combination of prawns, shrimps and worms under low-water conditions. I have read and heard it suggested that such techniques should be allowed on the last day of a fishing tenancy, if the guests have drawn a blank due to low water. What next? Phials of Cymag, and a net to tow behind the boat of those who have paid their money but not caught their limit on a trout fishery? But again, I digress.

Equally, while I leap to criticise those whose attitude seems to be 'fish by any means' where salmon are concerned, and acknowledge that there is indeed more to fishing than catching fish, it seems inevitable that the numbers of fish caught must be taken as the yardstick for success. But, for me, it is success with the fly that comes first and foremost. Success with the spinner in cold water conditions is a pale runner-up and nowadays, to be honest, my interest extends no further. For me, it is when the water is falling and clearing on the heels of a spate, with the pools running in perfect ply to swim the fly, that the truly successful fisherman is revealed. But you may say that any fool can catch a salmon under such conditions, so let me take the definition a little further.

The late John Ashley-Cooper was certainly the greatest known fisherman of his generation, and the latter half of this century. Beside him, in terms of salmon-fishing success, others pale into insignificance. But he did not gain his reputation by catching an odd salmon here and there, while others caught nothing. What he did was catch two or three when everybody else was catching single salmon. When others had two or three, he would have five or six.

I know there are some folk who like to knock Major Ashley-Cooper's degree of success. They will say that he was only so good because he enjoyed regular access to some of the finest fishing in Britain, Norway and Iceland. And this also leads some to question whether success should be too readily attributed to those whose connections (or bank balances) are such as to ensure that they are regularly in the right place at the right time. Their questions on both points would be clearly answered if they were a fly on the wall when a party gathered at the end of a week on a splendid beat for a dose of self-congratulation at having caught, say, eight fish between four rods. Because, after the party had left, they might hear the old gillie muttering to one of his cronies that, if the Major had been there, he would have had a dozen fish himself!

Then there is the intriguing and, let's face it, at times frustrating fact that, given a party of equally able fishermen on the same water, one day will favour one man, and the next another. Imagine a good beat being fished by three rods and perhaps producing six salmon a day. One day, one rod will have five fish, another rod will have one, and the last man will draw a blank. The next day, it may be the previously successful man's turn to suffer, while the other two take three apiece. It does not necessarily depend on who is fishing which pool, from the boat, with the gillie, or whatever. But stop and consider what implications might have been drawn if, as sometimes happens, the rods had been fishing as day guests. The man who had five fish on the first day would have been lauded as a great and successful fisherman but, if he had fished only the following day, and drawn a blank, he would have been given the 'thumbs down'.

The successful salmon fisherman will be a competent caster and controller of the salmon fly. This is achieved by building on firm foundations, which start with the choice of the right kit from the tackle shop. The experienced fisher knows what he needs. The novice, who is determined to succeed, may need some guidance. I have written before, at considerable length, about choosing tackle. A rod, reel and lines should be chosen to suit the individual, and those rivers that he chooses to fish. It is not simply a case of stating 'This is the best rod', and leaving it at that. And it is certainly not a case of choosing the most expensive rod you can afford. There are a number of 'good buys' to be found in the middle price range.

Besides the basic outfit, the successful fisherman needs little more than a reasonable selection of tried and trusted fly patterns in a range of sizes, some nylon for leaders, and a pair of waders. Here I would say nothing more than to mention that the fisherman who is determined to succeed, and therefore expects to find a salmon attached to the end of his line from time to time, will be careful as to the nylon he uses, and will not skimp on cheap, poor-quality hooks.

Again, this does not necessarily mean that the most expensive are necessarily the best, and once more I can think of some excellent hooks for flies in the middle price-range. Once again, we are seeing the results of Far Eastern technology making inroads. And in making the link between nylon and hook, no care and attention should be spared in tying the best knots, lubricating them with saliva, and then ensuring that the turns bed down neatly. Nearly good enough, in this and other respects, is not good enough. Who leaves a wind-knot in their leader if they are fishing seriously?

Having chosen the right tackle, successful fishermen invariably show that they know how to use it. As I have already said, they will be competent casters and controllers of the fly. But this seldom happens by accident. Some of them will have been taught by competent fathers or uncles but, more often in the modern age, they will have received some instruction from a professional.

I can hear you groaning but no, this is not a blatant plug for my own tuition days or fishing courses. Please look upon it, instead, as an expression of utter disbelief and total amazement at the hundreds and thousands of folk who seem quite happy to spend small fortunes on tackle, travel, accommodation and fishing rents, but will not invest a few days and a relatively small amount of cash in order to be able to realise something approaching their full potential! I suppose this sort of thing is encouraged by the 'mediocrity merchants' who widely publicise the fact that they have caught some salmon, but never cast farther than 15 yards. However, as I said earlier, we should study success only when it is consistent. Let me leave it at that.

Those who fished with John Ashley-Cooper will agree that he had no secret potions to smear on his fly, nor incantations to chant, but few waded as deeply and as competently, nor threw such a long line. He stated that this was absolutely fundamental to his success on both the mighty rivers of Norway and on our own large rivers, such as the Ness, Spey, Tay and Tweed. The combination of deep wading and long casting allowed him effectively to cover salmon that were beyond the range of fishing mortals.

There again, casting ability and range is not the be-all and end-all

of salmon fishing. Far from it. Indeed, I can think of a number of folk who can throw an incredible length of line, but who are relative failures in terms of catching fish. They have failed to recognise that casting is nothing more than a means to an end. A salmon does not take our fly in appreciation that we have just Spey-cast 30 yards of line, straight as an arrow. It takes the fly because it is of a reasonable size and dressing, presented at the right time in the right place and at an appropriate speed, angle and depth.

The thoughts of a successful salmon fisherman should have been with the fly throughout its swim across the river. He may have hovered it here and accelerated it there. It is not overstating the case to suggest, certainly on many rivers, that if some fishermen would think more about the way that their fly were fishing, and take an active role in ensuring that it swam attractively, rather than behave as passive observers, they would catch far more fish – perhaps two or three times as many on waters where the current doesn't do it all for you. And yet, how many fishermen do you see who seem to view the swim of the fly as nothing more than a punctuation mark between what they can only imagine is the far more important job of casting? This control of the fly, partnered where and when necessary with the ability to throw a really long line, can often be shown as the dividing line between success and failure.

Nor will the successful salmon fisherman allow himself to become stereotyped in his approach. I think that, for far too long, the solutions to salmon-fishing problems have been painted in black and white, with the shades of grey swept under the carpet because they do not fit such-and-such a theory. Take, just as one example, the old rule about a small fly fished off a floating line once the water temperature exceeds 48 deg F. Certainly, it holds good for a lot of places and at lots of times. But does it really explain why a hundred or more fishermen will be presenting a size 8 Munro Killer off a floating line over the pools of one stretch of fishing, hour after hour, day after day and week after week, when little or nothing is being caught?

Such an approach is justified by pointing to the fact that such fish as were caught were taken on this outfit. Of course they were! They

were offered nothing else. Remember that old gillie, muttering as to how it should have been a dozen or more when it was only six?

I do not think that many *successful* salmon fishermen would stick with the same line, fly and style from Monday morning to Saturday evening – unless, of course, this combination were producing the goods.

There again, the successful salmon fisherman does not jump blindly from one technique to the next. One such person of my acquaintance, for example, concentrates his efforts on discovering what he describes as 'the depth at which the fish are feeding' although, contrarily, he readily accepts that, where salmon are concerned, they are not – of course – feeding at all. But he adopts a systematic approach in working his way through the options, from floaters to fast-sinkers.

In a similar vein, I think back to the methodical approach that I was taught during my early encounters with the Spey in the opening months of the season, when the spring runs were still very reliable. This was at a time when the great majority of fishermen approached the river with a combination of fly and spinner. Let us not forget that, prior to the introduction of long, powerful carbon rods, handling a sinking line was a real slog. Casting range, and therefore technique and water coverage, was limited.

Success was sought with the methodical approach. We would start by fishing down our allocated pools with the fly, taking two long paces between each cast. Then we would walk back up to the top of the pool, change to a slightly smaller fly, and then fish it down again. Next time would be with a wooden Devon and then, finally, and particularly where the stream justified it, a silver or zebra Toby. Having done all that, you were reasonably sure that the options had been exhausted.

In modern times, with a far greater allegiance to the fly-rod, more folk would give the fly a better chance to prove itself. My own approach might be to start with a big Willie Gunn, then perhaps a rather smaller Gordon's Fancy, followed by a Collie Dog or, perhaps, a Tadpole. Then, if I were in the mood for it, I might spend a little time with the minnow, multiplier and long carbon spinning rod. Incidentally, but perhaps not alto-gether irrelevantly, have you discovered the difference between fishing with a fixed-spool reel on an eight- or nine-foot rod and a multiplier on a smoothly sensitive, but powerful, 11- or 12-footer on big flows?

The modern generation of long carbon spinning rods is all that stands between myself and the fly-only inclination. Put it down to my feeling that variety is the spice of life, and the fact that I sometimes fish rivers where the spinning rod has that little bit of extra 'edge' in terms of distance, depth, dominance and diversity. This diversity can help us to concentrate, be it with a range of flies and lines, or the option of the spinner. A change is as good as a rest.

Competence in salmon fishing, coupled to an ever-growing experience of success, leads to confidence and concentration. You must be reasonably competent to feel confident. If you do not feel confident, you will not concentrate. And if you are not concentrating on what you are doing and trying to achieve, you will not achieve anything like your true potential for success.

Confidence and concentration

are tied up with more things than just the fisherman's level of competence, however. Or, put another way, we can see competence extending into such diverse areas as getting the detective work right in ensuring that you are in what will probably be the right place at (probably) the right time.

And now we have finally arrived at some sort of formula for success in salmon fishing. A real determination to succeed will ensure that the budding tempter of salmon puts in the time, effort and money to choose the right tackle and ensure that he can use it to something like its full potential. Having attained a certain degree of competence, this will give him the confidence and concentration to catch fish – or, as others see it, to make his own luck (or, lest you have forgotten, *her* own luck!)

After that, with every fish that is caught, and as experience of success grows, confidence gives us the heart to fish with expectation and dogged determination so the confidence and concentration becomes more deeply rooted. Equally, with every blank day or week, the risk arises that this confidence will be destroyed. How these successes and failures balance out over the first few seasons of a fisherman's career will dictate the style of bed in which he (or she) will lie. So here's to tight lines, screaming reels, and feather pillows!

IN PURSUIT OF PERFECTION
by CRAWFORD LITTLE, *February 1990*

IF THERE is one thing that we salmon fishermen are not short of, it is excuses for when we fail to score. Our accusations and expletives are endless. We might say that those damned netsmen or seals have killed all the salmon before they could get into the river; we might blame the angle of the setting sun or the fact that our Stoat's Tail had seven turns of ribbing instead of six.

But what of these things? Should they be taken seriously as explanations for not catching fish, or are they simply excuses? The answer, in the best traditions of our indefinite sport is that sometimes they are, sometimes they aren't, and often the truth lies somewhere in between.

Take even the most basic of conditions which is, surely, that there must be salmon in the river. This seems so obvious as to hardly merit a mention, except for the fact that time and again we see holiday fishermen flogging a river at totally the wrong time of year. For example, you cannot expect to catch a springer in a river where the early runs do not exist, but it does not seem to stop some folk from trying!

The question of the presence of fish can, however, be taken a stage further. For one thing, the salmon that has only been in the river for one or two days is the likeliest taker of all, and the one that has been in for two or three weeks is far more likely to take than one that has been up for three or four months. But there is even more to it than that because, although some people may simply not believe it, it is quite possible to have too many fish, certainly in an individual pool, to create ideal or even likely conditions for finding a taking fish.

Experienced anglers learn to differentiate between the jumping habits of salmon. There is a world of difference between the slow surface roll of a potential taker that may barely break the surface, and the splashy leap of an angry resident. The spectacular but purposeless roll of the resident suggests that it may simply be frustrated at the presence of too many other fish, all trying to shoulder their way into the best taking places. Such sights were extremely common in the fish-rich days of the sixties, but became rare in the years following the decimation of stocks by UDN. Now that fish-stocks are improving, the sight of large numbers of leaping resident salmon is once again becoming quite common.

I have seen shoals of grilse cruising endlessly in some pools on the middle Dee. You watch them swim up, across and down. You see salmon crashing out of the main holding lies in midstream. The pool is fairly hotching with fish from neck to tail and you think you just cannot miss. But in such a pool at such a time 100 flies may be cast 10,000 times without success. That, indeed, is how many holiday fishermen would set about raising their blood pressure. They lash the water into a foam over the salmon when, as often as not, they would be far better to wait until dusk and fish either right up in the headstreams or any tiny pool, nook or cranny upstream of the salmon that might hold a runner for a few brief moments or minutes.

An obvious place for salmon to be concentrated is in a falls pool. As they wait for high water to ease their ascent, the salmon may increase in number until they are literally stacked in tiers. They become a great source of attraction for tourists and, perhaps, the local poaching gang. But my goodness, you can waste long hours on them if you happen to be a fisherman! Of course, such fish may be growing stale as well as concentrated.

This, I think, is one of the great time-wasters of salmon fishing – to concentrate solely on covering those fish that you have seen. Perhaps it comes as a hangover from earlier trout-fishing experiences. In fact, my makeshift rule is that you really should take a lesson from the trout-fisher and if a salmon comes up like a nymphing trout or one sipping down a surface-borne fly, it is well worth a cast but, if it is leaping high and clear, then you might just as well ignore it, except for the fact that it may be revealing the position of a holding lie that will be worth a cast when the next spate is falling away and a fresh batch of salmon are taking up the tenancies.

Compare the frustrations of casting a fly over such overstocked pools with what so often happens in the opening months of the season. We seldom see springers, for they do not run in vast numbers and, therefore, can slip quietly into the choicest lies after they have nosed their way into the lower stretches of the river. But the experience of seasons and generations tells us that they should be there so we persevere and, perhaps on the third or fourth day of our visit, the line steadily tightens into the thrilling draw of the first fish of the season.

I am now convinced that springers are not so much hard to tempt into taking as just simply hard to find. Perseverance and covering as much water as possible during the brief 'best taking time' of an hour either side of noon is the thing that earns rewards for the early-season salmon fisherman. But later in the season, if the salmon river has so many fish that we might almost be tempted to describe it as overstocked, a significant proportion of our fish will come from odd little nooks and crannies where a pausing fish may find a respite from the housing problems of overcrowded pools. So, how many fish for our perfect conditions? Well, certainly not too few but, there again, not too many.

The presence of fish is closely tied up with water height. For example, on a river where you expect good runs of summer salmon and grilse, things will be disappointing if there is insufficient rain to raise the level of water in the river in order to allow fish to run. In a drought season, the salmon will be held back in the estuary and, while fishermen with nothing better to do may while away their time trying all sorts of weird and wonderful tackle and techniques, they should not expect much, if anything, by way of fish on the bank.

Equally, however, you can get too much water. I do not mean simply that the river may be running in full spate, although Heaven knows, particularly on lowland rivers that turn the colour of pot-

ters' clay for days, this can be a disaster to all but the worming brigade. No, I am thinking more of those times when a series of spates come in rapid succession and the river is going up and down like a yo-yo. Just when it looks as if the best pools will be coming into play, down comes more rain, and the water height soars again.

When we lived on the banks of the little river Cairn, which can yield excellent back-end sport, I remember the start of one October where conditions looked set for a few bumper weeks before the season's close. A big spate was falling away and had cleared. Salmon were in the river. There then came a succession of dry days and wet nights. Up and down went the water levels and the fish just never seemed to settle into a taking mood.

Spate-river fishermen become obsessed with water levels. We talk of fish coming on to take on a steadily falling river. This is right enough, but it is really only a pointer to the fact that fishing will normally be at its best with the water at a certain height. An experience that extends to the east coast shows that best of all is where the river holds steady at that taking height. The Spey is an obvious example when its level is being held by a steady snow-melt at about May time. This produces excellent fishing conditions over an extended period. We see exactly the same on the Dee. But if heavy rain intervenes, while we may take fish on the first few inches of the rise, our chances then are not so good until the river has gone through the process of rise and fall back to a good, steady fishing height.

Besides the presence of fish and favourable water height and colour, there are one or two other factors which we can justifiably take into account. Water temperature, for example, has a bearing on the behaviour of salmon. At low water temperatures, salmon do tend to be that little bit sluggish, although this is far more noticeable in spring than autumn. Indeed, many autumn salmon fishers are found praying for a *drop* in water temperature. And certainly, although it may not happen often, experience shows that salmon are reluctant to take at those times when the air temperature is less than that of the water. The worst thing of all must be when there is 'grue', a soup of ice particles in

suspension in the water. Where the river is frozen over, however, things may not be all that bad. The real question is whether the ice can be broken. Many a successful day's early-season salmon fishing on Highland rivers has started with a session of ice-breaking. Indeed, there are a number of knowledgeable fishermen who argue that a session of ice-breaking, followed by a brief pause to allow the freed waters to carry the bergs and sheets downstream, can actually produce excellent taking conditions. They will argue that the fish resting below the ice are stirred up as it is broken. They are put on the alert and may respond to a well-presented fly – perhaps a two- or three-inch Willie Gunn or Black and Yellow fished off a sinking line.

I remember the first time this happened to me, although it is a good few years ago. We came down to the Highland river to find that it had almost completely frozen over during the night. Only the stronger, central stream was still clear. I honestly thought that the gillie was wasting my own and his time by suggesting that we should clear the ice, but the sparkling clean, silver fish that took not long afterwards soon changed my mind. I had another fish from that pool just 15 minutes later. Obviously, with such good initial learning experiences, I have never looked back and am always ready for a bit of ice-busting!

I suppose that this offers much the same advice as that for stirring up the comatose fish of high summer. You are supposed to send your dog in to swim across the pool. Now, while my labradors have always appreciated the unexpected change to take a cool dip, because normally I am telling them to 'get the hell out of it', this process has yet to earn me a fish, although I know others who swear by it.

Having looked at the two extremes of water temperatures, from low winter to high summer, I am far less upset by the lower than the upper end of the scale. As summer water temperatures soar, the oxygen is driven out of the water and, particularly in pools where they are concentrated, the salmon can literally suffocate. Such a thing happened on the Thurso when an enormous number of salmon that had been held in the estuary by drought conditions ran the river on a small rise in water height.

They became trapped in the lower pools and, in the falling water and rising temperature, died in their hundreds.

Wind, or the lack of it, should be seen as a point of debate so far as it concerns the production of ideal fishing conditions. So much depends upon where you are fishing. On those slow, canal-like stretches of some rivers in Scotland and Ireland you really do need at least a breeze to ruffle the surface; and I am one of those who like a good stiff blow to put a wave on the water before I feel I can get down to a serious session of backing-up. On the other hand, ask a Spey or Dee fisherman which wind he favours and his response will probably be 'none at all'. It seems to be a clear case of horses for courses. What all fishermen hate, however, like the sailor looking over his shoulder for squalls, is a fusty, brutal wind. The overhead caster will be worrying lest his cast sees him off with a 'flee in his ear'. Spey-casters will cope better, but their casting skills seldom make up for the fact that salmon rarely take well in such conditions.

Then there is the question of light. We are best, whenever possible, to avoid fishing a pool where the sun is shining directly down-stream. If the sun is low but shining from the side of the pool, tradition has it that we should fish a silver-bodied fly. The modernist, in failing light, might suggest you try a Whitewing.

Certainly, I do not like a harsh and clear blue sky. I am far happier when there is at least 50 per cent cloud-cover. And even more important, particularly after a day of bright sun, is to ensure that you are fishing through the last hour of dusk. Whether it is light, time of day or a combination of both matters little to me. That last hour so often produces the fish of the day. How many more salmon would be caught if all salmon fishermen would persevere just that little bit longer before taking down their rods and heading for home?

On that point of perseverance, let me mention, incidentally, that I, like so many fishermen, get a little prickly when people say: 'Oh, I would never have the patience to be a fisherman'. They must think of us sitting under umbrellas and staring at a float. Salmon fishing has little to do with patience, but a great deal to do with perseverance. There is more than a little truth in the saying that the best fly for the day is the one in the water. Nobody, so far as I am aware, has caught a salmon on a fly that was stuck in the handle of a rod resting against a fishing hut while the fisherman wrapped himself around a comforting dram. Remember that salmon are caught in all sorts of atrocious conditions.

Among my many fishing friends, colleagues, guests and acquaintances, I have encountered all sorts of fishermen. There are those who will while away the time when conditions are bad, but who you cannot see for dust and a blur of waving rods when conditions come right. These are usually those who have access to a river for an extended period. Then there are those who may only be able to fish a good beat for one week in the year and keep going hard from dusk to dawn. Such men have literally been known to fall asleep while fishing the river. Both these types will take a good proportion of the catch.

But there is, of course, another type. You see them often. They are down at the river fairly early, but take until 9.30 to set up their tackle. They walk down the river slowly, have a few casts, then stop for coffee. On their return, at

11 a.m., they pause to study some wild flower, but there is still time to work out a decent length of line before stopping for lunch. And so it goes on. At 6 o'clock in the evening, they will be found ordering a drink in the hotel bar. You will note that they have had time to bathe and change. 'I don't know. I've been on the river all day and I haven't touched a fish. I've been coming ten years now, and I still haven't caught a thing.' He pauses and looks out of the window. 'Old so-and-so says it's worth a cast in the evening, but it's been a long day and I really am rather tired,' and the barman, with an eye to bar profits, readily agrees.

Now please don't think that I am seeking to criticise such folk. Far from it. Such people enjoy their sport enormously and are the very back-bone of fishing. If, however, we were to do a time-and-motion study of them (perish the thought!) we might well find that their 'long day' actually contained about two or three hours of potentially productive fishing. In other words, about 15 hours a week. Now you can catch a lot of fish in 15 hours of fishing, but only if you time your efforts to coincide with, and are able to recognise, the best set of conditions that the week has to offer.

So I would say that we should not be prepared to look upon fishing conditions as nothing more than excuses for not catching fish. We will do far better to understand what is most likely to ensure that our chances are good, and then waste no time in setting about catching fish.

Ten years ago, I was one of those characters who might fall asleep while wading in a strong stream at the end of an all-out dawn to dusk assault on the river. In another 30 years, I may be prepared to fish only in what I believe are ideal, perfect conditions. Perhaps I am only fooling myself now, however, when I tell myself that I have achieved a proper balance, I can no longer bring myself to wet a line if conditions are atrocious. Gone are the days when I could say to hell with the fact that I am in the wrong place at the wrong time, on a high, coloured water, with the air and water temperatures all wrong and so on and so forth! At the other end of the scale, when conditions are as near perfect as I dare hope for, and there are fresh fish in the river, nobody and nothing will drag me away!

Scientists have long told us that salmon don't feed in fresh water. So why do they pouch a Medusa's head of writhing worms into a rapidly-shrinking stomach, sometimes launch themselves across a pool at prawn or shrimp or, when introduced into stillwater, feed on midges and small fry?
This has to be salmon fishing's greatest riddle and long may it be unanswered.
Forty years ago G. P. R. Balfour-Kinnear stepped back and looked at the puzzle with a clinical eye. Five years later he took a wider view to include sea-trout and reached a typically logical conclusion.

WHY DO SALMON TAKE?
by G. P. R. BALFOUR-KINNEAR, *June 1956*

SALMON VERY rarely feed in fresh water. Those who have studied the matter have come to this conclusion because if a salmon is caught in fresh water its stomach is invariably empty. Further, after prolonged absence from the sea, its alimentary canal becomes atrophied from want of use. These are established facts and are not in dispute.

It is also known that in preparation for its river fast a salmon generally stops its sea feeding sometime before it leaves the sea. This is presumably to see whether or not it is ready to do without its food. Should it find that it prefers to continue to feed it can do so until it is really prepared to do without and then enter the river.

We know, however, that salmon will on occasion take a fly, a spinning bait, a plug, a prawn or even a bunch of worms. Some contend that they only take something that has annoyed them, in order to destroy it. That theory is not tenable because they will not only take a bunch of worms, which would be unlikely to annoy them, but will actually swallow it.

As a salmon's stomach is invariably empty, when it is caught in fresh water, I suggest that it never eats until whatever it may have eaten previously has been absorbed. And since a salmon does not get rid of the contents of its stomach by vomiting while being played, that seems to be the only satisfactory explanation.

As we know that salmon sometimes take our lures it would surely be ridiculous to suppose that they only take them and disregard any other 'food' that Nature offers. They must occasionally eat small fish, freshwater shrimps, creepers, nymphs, worms and other natural food. I have only once in a long experience seen salmon taking natural flies. That was many years ago, when there were proper fly hatches on the Tweed, and the salmon gorged themselves on a hatch of March Brown. The fish rose continuously like a shoal of trout.

I am sure that had La Branche been there with a dry fly he would have done better than he did at Cairuton, where he failed to catch one and decided that Scottish salmon were always uncatchable on an undragged floating fly.

Having established that salmon do eat occasionally, the important point to determine is what they are likely to want to eat. Experience has taught us that their ideas, as to what they should and should not eat, change with the seasons and also with water and weather conditions.

In early spring, when the river is running high and the water is cold, the fish are inclined to be sluggish and lazy. They will not, in these conditions, trouble to come to a small fly or even to a little minnow. They then want something substantial such as a 3½ inch sprat, and if a fly is used it will have to be a big 5/0 or even 7/0 to be sufficiently worth while for them to exert themselves to pursue.

As the spring progresses, the successful baits and flies gradually become smaller until we get to summer conditions when the short dressed low water flies come into their own. Then as autumn approaches these little flies lose their fascination until only medium sized sunk flies are effective. The size of spinning baits must likewise be reduced as the season advances until the small natural minnow becomes the best killer in the summer, only to be changed, yet again, to a sprat in the autumn.

Let us now consider water conditions. If the river is coloured, owing to rain washings, the visibility when looking through it is obviously not as good as when it is clear. It therefore stands to reason that in a strongly coloured water, small objects may pass unnoticed or may escape if chased, so a salmon will probably ignore a small lure in flood water. To obviate this we use a larger fly or bait, increasing the size in proportion to the discoloration of the water.

The temperature also affects the size of the lure required and the speed at which it should be fished. If it is cold it is generally advisable to use a larger fly and a bigger bait and to move them slowly, whereas in hot weather a small fly or bait fished at speed will usually give the best results.

Now what of colour? This is of great importance. We have proved that salmon do eat sometimes, but only occasionally. That means that a salmon must be disregarding, almost continually, practically all the food that the river is bringing down, letting it pass untouched. It must also have many opportunities of catching parr, minnows and small trout of which it does not avail itself except on very rare occasions.

A moment's consideration will show that if a salmon is not taking the majority of the food items that Nature offers, the fisherman must show it something different in order to attract its attention and catch it – in other words something that is not quite natural. The difficulty is to decide just how unnatural the fly or the bait should be.

It is well to remember that nei-ther the fisherman's fly nor his bait behave naturally; and that in itself is often a sufficient reason to make a fish take. One sometimes hears of beginner's luck when a complete novice catches a couple of fish on a beat where the fish are stale and the expert fails. The reason for this is probably that the mad movements of the beginner's fly were new to the fish.

If you keep in mind that your lure is behaving unnaturally, however you may fish with it, you will readily understand why it is prudent to see that it is not also too unnatural in its appearance. If it is, then it is obviously a fake and will probably frighten the fish and certainly will not produce great results.

Unless the water is coloured, I personally try to have my flies and baits as near to the natural as possible. I seldom fish with a fly without first swimming it in the water beside me to see if it looks natural and as if it should be there. If it looks out of place I try another one until I get one that seems to blend with its surroundings.

In the case of a bait the procedure should be the same. It is what the bait looks like when it is spinning that matters. Unless the water is heavily coloured a sombre

bait will generally beat a more colourful one, and a flashy bait should
never be used except in muddy
water. A shining bait, such as a
spoon, should not be used on a
bright day unless the water is
coloured.

A golden sprat is not as unnatural as it may look, because where
there is yellow sand and seaweed

the sea fish assume the same colour
as camouflage, and even small cod
and pollock may at times be nearly
the colour of goldfish.

In conclusion, if you are ever in
doubt, choose the smaller of the
flies or baits you are considering,
and those which are nearest to the
natural. They will be quite unnatural enough when you fish them.

TWENTY QUESTIONS
by G. P. R. BALFOUR-KINNEAR, *March 1961*

EVER SINCE the fishing rod
was invented thousands of
fishermen have been
studying the habits and reactions of
our game fish and noting what
they will do, or not do, in any
given circumstances. As a result,
much useful information has been
gathered and recorded in innumerable books some of which most of
us have read.

There are, however, many
strange facts about the behaviour
of our game fish which have not
yet been explained. I shall draw
your attention to some of these pe-
culiarities by asking questions in
the hope that some fishermen may
be able to give, or at least suggest,
a reason for them.

The idiosyncrasies of fish that I

am going to mention are all indis-
putable facts which I have, personally, proved to be true. So far as it
is possible I shall deal separately with
salmon, sea trout and brown trout.

SALMON

1. Why is it that on one day
salmon are scared right out of a
pool by the mere sight of a prawn,
or even by the smallest shrimp,
when, on the following day
(while, so far as we can see, conditions are similar) every fish that
sees a prawn will take it greedily?

2. Why will salmon take a spinning bait readily every day for a
week or more and then, when there
has not been any change in the
water or the weather, refuse it for
several days but take a fly instead?

And the converse may equally well, and often does, apply. Why?

3. Why, sometimes, will every salmon refuse to take a sunk fly when fish are being caught on the greased one? One can understand a preference but not a unanimous one.

4. Is there any explanation as to why salmon may take a large spinning bait, only boil at a small No. 6 greased line fly, but take a tiny No. 10 all on the same day?

5. In May a natural minnow will catch salmon in all the rivers that I know except in the Spey where the fish prefer an artificial. Why is that? Is it because there are practically no minnows in the Spey, whereas most other rivers have them?

6. What is the actual effect of a red sunset glow on the fish? Why does it seem to disturb them, making them head and tail on the surface as though they had been pushed out of their lies? Why will they never take anything when the red glow is on the water?

7. Why is it that a salmon, having pulled at a bait or a fly, so very, very rarely follows after it and takes it? Fish may follow a greased line fly, boiling at it several times, finally to take it at the dangle, or when the fly is being lifted for the next cast. I have never known them to follow it round and finally take it if they have previously touched it. They may, however, and often do, take a previously touched fly on the next cast. Why is that?

8. If the sunk fly is too big, fish after fish may pull it without being hooked. How do they do that, and why should they be so particular about an extra quarter of an inch?

9. When there is no perceptible change in the weather, or in the water, why do all (or nearly all) the salmon in the river come on the take for perhaps an hour or so, and then go off again as suddenly as they came on, and for no obvious reason?

10. (This question and the next are perhaps peculiar to the Tweed.) March is a sprat month but every year the fish go off the sprat for about a week, generally the third week, and then come on to it again. Is there any reason for this extraordinary fact?

11. In the autumn when fishing the Tweed with a big fly rod and a No. 6 line, I do not remember ever catching a fish before October 15th when I was pulling in line for the next cast. After that date, and almost every season, I have caught

more than half of my fish when shortening the line to lift it off the water. A fish may take on the first pull in, or on any one of them up to the seventh and last. Is there any explanation for that?

12. Why should fish generally take the moment the morning mist begins to rise?

SEA TROUT

1. Even when the Spey is full of sea trout they never (or practically never) take a worm unless the river is big and coloured. Does that not seem peculiar when they will take a worm in clear water in other rivers?

2. In any river the sea trout like small No. 10 or No. 11 flies and only an occasional one is caught on a large fly. Why is that, when on Loch Maree, if there is a wind, they like a dapping fly the size of a golf ball?

3. Good baskets were made on Loch Maree on wet fly before dapping was introduced. A small Black Pennell was the favourite. Now that the loch has been dapped for a number of years, the sea trout are no longer interested in wet flies – except possibly in September. Is that not hard to explain as a good proportion of the trout that rise to

the dapping flies must be caught? Those that are missed are likely to be caught on another occasion. And there must be many trout coming into the loch that have never even seen a dapping fly.

4. If on a windy day they take a very large dapping fly, why then do they ignore an ordinary salmon fly? I fished on the top of the waves, and under them, for three whole days with a big rod and heavy line with flies from size 4 to 5/0 without getting an offer while my friend at the other end of the boat caught them on the dap.

5. Can anybody explain why the Loch Maree sea trout will not take a worm, or even a bunch of worms, whether suspended from a float or left lying on the shingle bottom?

BROWN TROUT

1. Keeping question five on salmon in mind, why is it that brown trout are more easily caught on natural minnows in a loch where there are no minnows than in one which has a lot of minnows?

2. Why does the converse apply to a fly? If the season's fly hatch peters out, sometimes in May, as has been happening on my local

Border rivers, one would expect a fly to be taken greedily as a rare luxury. That is, however, not the case, as I have fished all day, on more than one occasion, with wet flies and nymphs and hardly had an offer.

3. If trout are eating nymphs or spent flies on the surface film it is easy to understand why they will not take a dry fly, or a submerged nymph, because neither is correctly positioned in the surface film. But when trout are feeding on nymphs, say 10 inches under the surface, why will they refuse a nymph that is, perhaps 3 inches or perhaps 18 inches deep?

Although I have been fishing for so many years I regret to say that I am not able to answer any of these questions.

  Suggestions on how to convert a taking salmon into a well-hooked fish are legion, ranging from letting them take a loose loop of line, waiting until the reel screeches, or simply doing nothing until the line swims away. All these methods have their followers, with the last probably being the one most favoured.

  But converting the take to a fly is one thing, while actually spotting the take is something else again – and then what about those takes that we fail to see?

  Many times a companion sitting on a higher vantage point has watched a salmon turn on the fly and eject it without as much as a tremor showing on the line. So in reality, it could well be that during what has, on the face of it, been a totally blank day, the angler's flies may have been fleetingly held by a salmon.

  Graham Booth had just this situation much in mind and offered some valuable advice in the next article.

TAKES THAT GO UNSEEN

by GRAHAM BOOTH, *August 1988*

SALMON FISHING is awash with unexplained phenomena – puzzling incidents that mean little by themselves. But sometimes an unusual perspective can give rise to a theory which seems to fit the facts – at least for some of the time.

It was late March on the Aberdeenshire Dee – the second evening of our week. There had been 21 fish taken from the beat the previous week, all on spinners. I was persevering with fly, unlike my four fellow rods, who had taken four fish so far, all spinning.

With my sinking line and 2 inch Waddington Willie's Gunn I had lost a fish after brief contact on the fourth cast of the day and, in the ten hours since then, had not had so much as a pluck. At the lower end of a good piece of water I raised the rod as the line came round to the 'dangle', to roll the line to the surface prior to making the next cast. To my surprise, the rod remained bent. I was into a fish.

I remarked straight away to my companion who was standing nearby at the time that I should probably lose it as it was hooked on the dangle and I had felt no pull. In effect, the fish was struck instantly. I was proved wrong. Some seven minutes later a brand-new Dee springer of 9 lb was landed safely, securely hooked in the roof of the mouth.

I have often pondered this incident since, and several other related occurrences. These together with the not uncommon phenomenon of going down a pool second or third, behind others using similar (or totally dissimilar) tactics, and taking a fish, have led me to conclude that when fly-fishing for salmon, whether with floating or sinking line, we actually get a far greater number of takes than we ever notice.

I am quite aware that this will come as no earth-shattering revelation to most experienced salmon fly-fishermen, many of whom long ago discovered as much for themselves. More interesting are the implications of successfully following others down a pool.

Several seasons ago, while fishing one of the Findhorn's dramatic gorge beats, I began to suspect that many takes from salmon were going unnoticed. I had preceded Tim

Goode, my companion at the time, down the pool. At the tail of the pool was an enormous rock some 12 feet high, and having got out at the bottom I climbed on to the top of it to watch Tim fishing down towards me.

As he drew near enough for me to see his fly, I suddenly saw a grilse appear as if by magic and take his fly in its mouth from directly downstream. I shouted to Tim not to tighten as the fish was facing him, but Tim was unaware of the take. The next cast a repeat performance occurred, and again Tim felt nothing. Thereafter no amount of covering the fish could persuade it to reappear.

Later in the same week I found myself obliged to fish down a pool known as the Black Pool. The river had risen somewhat, making it impossible to negotiate the waterline, and I had to cast from the top of a rocky cliff 12 feet above the water. I could see my fly working round the whole time.

During this week we took just one salmon each and felt no other takes. I, however, was able to observe two takes (one from a very large fish and another from a grilse) to my own fly while covering the lies in the Black Pool on this one

occasion. The following day I saw another fish take my fly.

With all of these takes the fish simply slid up to the fly from behind, took it in its mouth and then ejected it after a few seconds. In frustration I tightened into the third of these offerings, but not surprisingly I merely succeeded in pulling the fly from its mouth. On no occasion had I felt so much as a pluck to indicate a take.

All five takes occurred during the extremely limited times when I was able to observe my fly and the salmon's reaction to it. I wonder how many more such takes went unnoticed during the far more numerous occasions when observation was impossible.

This brings me back to the Dee fish, hooked and landed purely on account of my good fortune in raising the rod at the right time, unaware of a take. Had I not done so I am doubtful whether any indication of the fish's interest would have registered. Far more probably it would, like those on the Findhorn, simply have ejected the fly.

This had possibly already happened to my companion, who had preceded me down the pool a short time before. Had I not raised my rod when I did, he might have covered the water again himself and caught the fish. No doubt we should have remarked how odd it was that the fish had been covered three times before showing any interest, especially since we were using flies of the same size and similar pattern.

Perhaps this is relevant to something which used to puzzle me when first I began fishing for salmon some ten seasons ago: namely how a salmon gets caught several months after entering fresh water when, on today's hard-fished rivers, it must have encountered scores of offerings from hopeful anglers.

For some inexplicable reason it found the umpteenth offering irresistibly tempting, but surely water, weather or size of pattern or presentation of the preceding flies cannot all have been wrong; if this were so, how can we explain those fresh-run fish which did get caught?

Is not a more plausible answer that our fish did respond to many such flies, but in such a manner that did not register a take with the angler? Why it should eventually take a fly in a more positive manner is a puzzle.

If, however, we assume that salmon give a firm take on a high proportion of occasions, then statistically some would get hooked and some would not. Examined thus, the phenomenon appears, to me at least, somewhat less perplexing.

How might we profit from such a phenomenon? Having discovered, after observing salmon taking a variety of offerings from fly to spinners and even prawns, that often a fish that has taken without being hooked is prepared to have a second and usually a third go, we may assume that during normal fishing we are quite possibly getting more takes than we realise. Moreover, such fish are very likely to come again if given the opportunity, especially if our fly or method of presentation are subtly different the next time.

Rather than move on after going once down a good pool, it might be better to go down the same pool again, preferably with a different fly size or pattern, or method of presentation.

⋟ But just how many takes did that angler of long yesteryear receive to his own rod to put an amazing catch of 22 salmon on the bank before he staggered home for breakfast? That such a feat and others almost rivalling it are actually more than a salmon fisher's wildest dreams, is well documented. But do the figures really represent what actually happened on those golden days? ⋟ Tony George investigated the old catch records and drew some interesting conclusions.

TWENTY-TWO BEFORE BREAKFAST ...

by TONY GEORGE, *November 1981*

NOT INFREQUENTLY have I found myself meditating on some of the great bags handed down from the past, and wondering among other things just how such quantities of fish were ever landed within the durations indicated, not to dwell on the sheer physical energy that would have been involved.

On those far too irregular occasions when one has caught more than one or two salmon or grilse in a single morning, say a handful, the session has seemed remarkably active and full. One moment it was ten past nine and the next five to one.

One can sanction without undue effort the bag of 30 Tweed springers, mentioned last month, caught in a winter's day because such fish would not have been lively, were probably half-frozen, would have averaged only 7 lb or 8 lb, and were killed with the bait on tackle a lot more than up to the job. But later in the season when the water had warmed up they would surely have presented a problem of different magnitude entirely.

With fly-tackle particularly, so it seems to me, excluding a small minority of the most skilled and dedicated, salmon anglers tend on the whole rather grossly to underestimate the actual time absorbed between hooking a fish and wading back into position to resume fishing. The attitude of the majority of salmon anglers is really positively leisurely.

How, then, reverting to last month's piece, was it possible to kill 20 springers within the span of a May afternoon? That is what I should like to know. Or did the afternoon begin at noon and end at 7 p.m.? Or perhaps Captain Straker-Smith was just the victim of journalistic enthusiasm?

I particularly like the story of Miss Mould, veteran of the Helmsdale, who is reputed to have killed 18, all with the fly, between her lunch and her tea. The mental image of this maiden lady, presumably of delicate nurture, struggling to subdue 18 of them between her *vol au vent* and her cucumber sandwich, is one I find totally absorbing.

At least Buckley's bag of 22 with the trout rod on the same river, the Helmsdale, described by Calderwood in the words 'The greatest angling performance of which I have ever heard', was made between 4.30 in the morning and 7.30 in the evening, the whole detailed story, the smashed rod and long walks included, ringing as sound as a bell.

These sensational Caledonian achievements have not unreasonably been matched if not surpassed in Hibernia, as one might expect. Of great doings on the Bush we read: 'In 1873, in six weeks from 15th June to 1st August, Mr Adam McNeill took 444 fish, of which twenty-two were taken one morning before break-

fast. . . .' Of this, and other glorious exploits, Grimble, with his truly wonderful dead-pan humour, observed: '. . . but we have not been able to find out at what time these two gentlemen sat down to table.'

The truth is, I think, that many of these and similar tales have been embellished and polished in the telling at no liability to their owners. One extravaganza for which the owner accepted full responsibility, since he told it himself, is that of Ackroyd's record spring catch on the Conon. Charles Ackroyd was a skilled and successful angler but possessed a notoriously perverse temperament.

Asked how he had made his bag, he replied that the main achievement lay with his gillie who was a 'know-all', always telling him where to fish and what fly to use. So when his gillie said a place was no good, Ackroyd said that was where he fished. When his gillie said a certain fly was useless on the Conon, Ackroyd said that was the one he put on. By following this line of action consistently, concluded Ackroyd, he made the record bag on the Conon.

How could the then Lord Lovat manage to land with the fly-rod 36 fish averaging 14 lb each in a single day on a big fast river like the Beauly? This exploit is believed to have been by the same Lord Lovat who in five days' fishing on the same river between June 27 and July 5, 1864, made daily bags of 27, 24, 32, 33 and 30.

However, it was reported that these latter events took place during the peak of the grilse run of that year, with its implication that they were all or nearly all grilse. There is a world of difference between landing 30-odd grilse probably averaging, at the end of June, less than 5 lb and 30-odd salmon averaging 14 lb.

Gathorne-Hardy, in a volume of the 1890s, throws interesting light on the way Lord Lovat's bag of 36 was made, and probably on the procedure adopted for compiling many other great bags in the past: 'It is said that the late Lord Lovat once got thirty-six fish in a day, averaging 14 lb each, but I have also heard that he had three gillies and their rods with him, and although he rose and hooked all his fish himself, he then immediately changed rods and left his attendants

to land the salmon.' Some such plan must, I think, necessarily have been adopted in order to get the number in the time, as although Lord Lovat was notoriously very hard on his fish, it would have been hardly possible to have landed such a quantity of good-sized fish in such a stream in the time.

When it comes to numbers the Canadians bring even Lord Lovat's scores into perspective. In 1874, Napoleon Comeau was credited with the following catches in the river Godbout of Quebec during twelve days fishing between July 9 and 22: 57, 25, 34, 40, 25, 16, 37, 16, 28, 27, 13 and 20, at an average of 28 a day and an over-all average weight in excess of 10 lb.

Here again, one wonders if the 57, which averaged over 11 lb each, was an individual or a team effort. I recall my friend Tom Briggs catching 27 kelts in one day. Asked why he had not made it a round 30, he replied that he did not have the time to catch any more as he was in action all day.

One concludes that an unknown but not inconsiderable proportion of the great catches quoted by posterity were family affairs by proximity, or retainership, or both; a comment that applies equally to some of the portmanteaux fish, from Miss Ballantine's to Miss Davey's, and also to the ladies of Gordon Castle.

Incidentally, what a shame it is that so many of the great Canadian rivers have now been ruined by hydro-electrification. Slowly but surely, for this among other reasons, the Canadian Atlantic salmon fishery, and particularly the great Quebec fishery, seems to be going the same way the French fishery long since went.

Many years ago, under the influence of the monographs printed for private circulation by Gray Griswold and other members of the controlling syndicate, I conceived a vicarious passion for the Grand Cascapedia, and was greatly disappointed to read subsequently that this river, formerly one of the most prolific and famous, had been hydro-electrified. This kind of thing still goes on, in Canada and elsewhere.

Why the Norwegians, with enough oil and gas to keep them going for centuries, should be intent on ruining the Tana, one of the most famous of remaining salmon rivers in the world, defies credibility.

Apart from the problem of deciphering historical team efforts there is also the danger for the unwary of accepting large bags of spring fish at face value, particularly prior to the 1860s, the decade during which recognition of kelt fishing as a sport declined rapidly following the legislation of the late 1850s and early 1860s.

Some years ago I was challenged by a correspondent in *The Field* about spring fishing in the Tweed during the 1840s. This gentleman produced photocopies of several pages of Earl Hodgson's volume *Salmon Fishing*, in which Hodgson argued by reference to some great spring bags that the Tweed spring fishing of earlier generations had been much superior to what it had become by the turn of the century.

Fortunately, the individual weights of fish were available and I was able, via an analysis of weights, netting-returns, and the general background of the period, to demonstrate constructively that the fish in question, which were all caught in March, were kelts.

Similar unacknowledged (because then perfectly legitimate) records of kelt fishing from the Tweed and the Spey, among other rivers, are quite common, and have been reproduced in good faith by various writers subsequent to the 1870s. I recently acquired some records of the Gwernyfed beat of the upper Wye for the last century. This river was then heavily netted during the authorised season from February to August at numerous stations extending over nearly 100 miles from the estuary to Hay-on-Wye, which is downstream of the beat in question.

Quite heavy catches of fish were nevertheless recorded without comment for March and April of some years at Gwerryfed, but thereafter hardly anything was caught until September or October. Towards the end of the 1860s, however, quaint remarks such as 'put back in' and '10 returned' appeared against these handsome spring bags (which included the odd clean fish), and by the 1870s the kelt records had ceased altogether, just a few clean fish being recorded in the spring, with the main catch in the autumn.

Many anglers will hold an opinion of their own as to what constitutes the best daily bag made in British and Irish rivers. Purely opinion in all cases it is, since the river, the circumstances, the season, the method, and the average weight of the catch, among others, are all important factors.

Does Colonel Taylor's bag of 30 springers with the bait on Tweed, averaging 7–8 lb, rank equally with George M'Culloch's catch of 19 autumn fish on the fly in the same river averaging 20½ lb each? Not really, one might think. A catch of 56 springers by four rods on the Black Castle beat of the Boyne in one day must take some beating, even if they were May fish averaging only 11 lb. However, the permutations are limitless.

High on the list of my own nominations for the accolade would be Walter de Winton's bag of 17 springers, all on the fly from the upper Wye, caught on May 19, 1913. Being so late in the spring there were quite a lot of small springers in the catch along with the traditional Wye big spring fish. The weights are nevertheless imposing: 10, 10½, 10½, 11, 11, 14, 16, 16, 17, 19, 21, 21, 25, 26, 26, 29, 30: total 17 weighing 313 lb, at an average of 18½ lb each. On reflection, yes, a truly sensational day's spring fly fishing.

De Winton's catch would have been beaten by a remarkable one made in one pool of the Welsh Dee, the famous Dwr Craig of the Llangollen-Fechan beat, except for the fact that the bait accounted for the majority of the latter bag. On May 1, 1927, a single rod killed 21 springers weighing 416 lb, an average of 19.8 lb each. Five of the fish fell to the fly, ten to the minnow, and six to the prawn. Jack Hughes Parry did not give the name of the angler, from which uncharacteristic reticence one concludes that it was himself.

If you want to catch a salmon then follow the Barr System. The tackle isn't anything to write home about and doesn't require the services of a bearer to carry.

The philosophy behind the cunning plan is quite simple, as long as you brush aside the advice of that waterside siren who urges the uncertain angler to take a step in the wrong direction . . .

THE SOLITARY SALMON ANGLER
by DAVID BARR, *June 1963*

IF YOU go fishing to kill salmon or to catch more than anyone else, do not read one more word. If you enjoy fishing for salmon, read on with good heart and you will hear about the only – yes, the only – way of fishing for salmon. There is nothing new in the Barr system, but it seems to have remarkably few practitioners.

To begin with, clothing is important. Waders are necessary though if you're young and tough and prepared to get wet, a pair of rope-soled shoes and expendable trousers are far better. The coat should have two pockets and, if it is raining, be comparatively waterproof. A piece of towelling worn like a silk scarf to keep out drips and draughts completes the ensemble. The pudding-bowl shaped hat that seems to have become the trade mark of the fisherman is very much optional. If you have been so silly as to buy one by all means wear it. It adds little to your chances except perhaps as camouflage for bald and shiny heads.

Now for what equipment is needed. Just this . . . Fly rod, reel and line, a few yards of 6/7 lb breaking strain nylon, a pair of scissors and a small box containing a few selected flies in various sizes. That's the lot – except for matches, lots of cigarettes for the tenser moments, and any sandwiches you think you may need.

You will see that the breaking strain of the nylon is not excessive. If the water is big it is permitted to go up to 9 lb, but in any ordinary circumstances 6/7 lb is lavish unless you want to land a fish in under three minutes. Any risks involved are more than offset by the extra pliability and invisibility of the lighter gauge. You will see, too, that I have not included a gaff or tailer. Pulling a salmon out by its tail is so simple, and to my way of thinking, such a basic part of catching the fish that gaff or tailer are rarely justified.

Difficulties sometimes arise if you get into a big sea trout. It is difficult to distinguish between one of these and a salmon, but when they made sea trout they didn't give them such nice comfortable tails. Nevertheless, if you cannot beach your big sea trout, don't let it dishearten you. A really firm and determined grip on its tail and some quick action afterwards will invariably bring the fish on to the bank.

Having equipped yourself as I have suggested, go to the furthest upstream point of the river as early in the day as you can and start fishing. Take no one with you. No slaves, gillies, little men, wives, children. No one. This kind of fishing derives its enjoyment from solitariness. With no one to speak to and to distract you, your horizon shrinks to yourself, the river – and the fish. It becomes a personal battle of wits and skills. And this is where a pleasant loneliness comes in.

There are some rivers (but I have never fished them) where takes and offers are happening almost all the time – where salmon show themselves and react to the fly almost incessantly. I know because I have read about them in this magazine. In the rivers where I fish nothing like this ever happens.

8 5

For hour after hour I fish without the slightest sign of any reaction, except for the occasional heart-tearing pluck from an undersized trout.

In this way there springs up the first of the mental obstacles with which you have to contend. After an hour or two without seeing anything, a little voice says to you, 'You know, the river's quite empty – they've all run through this bit'. It takes an enormous height of morale to beat this insidious little voice and to keep fishing with hope. If you had a gillie with you who would say, 'Ach, this pool's alive with them – I saw eleven here yesterday', you would find it easier to resolve your doubts. But you are on your own, and you have to beat this on your own. When you do so it all adds to the ultimate feeling of satisfaction.

I had better at this stage – having tied myself down to fly only – make my position on this point quite clear. I normally fish on a river where absolutely nothing (except nets and dynamite) is barred. Worms and shrimps are the normal. Those who spin are considered to be the agile and active ones, and those who fly fish are written off as crazy. If we all did

the same thing the situation would be hopeless. By varying the methods the members are scattered nicely over the seven miles with the flies being cast where no worm would work and worms being used in deep pools where no one would dream of fly fishing. I only fly fish because I am quite hope-lessly incompetent at the other methods and can at least cast a fly accurately and far. There is no need, therefore, for anyone to feel frustrated, tense or unhappy about my emphasis on fly fishing.

Going back to the fishing and having choked back the conviction that there are no fish in the river, that unpleasant little voice gets at you again. 'What hope have you of catching a salmon', it says, 'with a fly like the one you are using? It is far too big . . . or too small . . . or too bright . . . or too dull . . .' Worse still, 'That fly's only fishing an inch or two off the top. You must put on something that will get down to them.' If you yield to these insane doubts you are lost. Bang goes your confidence, bang goes the verve that confidence in-troduces into the way the fly travels. Fish your favourite fly whatever its colour; permit your-self only size variations. Say goodbye to the chances of a fish the moment you start ringing the changes. A taking fish will have your fly whatever its variety.

All day long the voice will be at you. 'The angle's wrong. You can't hope to get one that way', or 'You're not fishing any of the tak-ing-places, you're mostly fishing where there's no hope at all', or 'Don't bother to fish this run, no one ever gets one here. The next pool's far better.'

You must make up your mind before you start that you are going to keep moving downstream. Fish everything but never, however much the voice may tempt you, go back and fish over the same water twice, or at least not until you've been once over all the available river. Miss the last half-mile and it's ten to one that you will hear of some half-wit who stared where you finished and caught three.

As you drag yourself along after the first five hours without any hopeful sign of any kind, you must realise that the acute depression that is beginning to envelope you is not the onset of some form of mental illness. It's just that you're getting tired. It is at this time, like a miler on the last lap, that you have to take yourself in hand,

throw out the morbid thoughts and start fishing as though it were daybreak. One day, after five long, utterly unsuccessful miles, I hurled my fly across the river under yet another hopeless tree branch. The fly was wrong; the water obviously held no fish; my nylon was vividly visible. I stared upstream and thought about dinner and the walk back. Suddenly there was a tug and I looked quickly back to the scene of operations to see the end of an enormous boil. I had missed an-other fish.

All these mental hazards are part of lonely salmon fishing – all part of the struggle of catching fish nicely in not very good water. I rather doubt if the system would work in take-every-minute waters. But the final part of the system works in any river.

There is nothing so beautiful to my eyes as a rounded, silver, fresh-run salmon. Even if the fish didn't have such a scarcity value, it would, I know, look just as noble, just as perfect. When you have pulled the fish ashore – when the adrenalin has returned to its proper quarter and your hand has gone back to only its normal unsteadi-ness – try asking yourself one ques-tion: 'Do I very badly need a salmon?' If the answer is, 'No, I don't', take the hook out carefully and drop the fish gently back. It will soon recover and you will have had all the reward your hard work has earned for you.

❧ *Many stillwater fly fishers have expectations way beyond their capabilities or those of the waters they fish. But success is different things to different people.*
❧ *Be happy for the man who has settled for his limitations and enjoys every trout he catches.*
❧ *Be sorry for the angler who feels defeated if he fails to catch his limit or to include a five pounder in his catch.*
❧ *When the realities of what fly fishing was really all about finally dawned on Peter Lapsley, he scrumpled his inferiority complex and chucked it in the waste-paper bin where it belonged. But what effect did it have on his fishing?*

NOW, I JUST ENJOY MY FISHING
by PETER LAPSLEY, *December 1983*

A T ONE time I had an inferiority complex. Although I had been reservoir trout fishing for two or three seasons, I rarely if ever caught a limit – let alone a 'double' or 'treble' limit. In fact, if I'm strictly honest, I quite often caught nothing at all, traipsing home with my tail between my legs, a dry, unweighted fish-bass and an overwhelming sense of inadequacy.

After all, those angling writers who described their exploits on Rutland, Grafham, Chew, Blagdon, Ravensthorpe, Eyebrook and Draycote couldn't be *very* different from me, and they always seemed to need a trailer or a pick-up truck to carry away all the fish they caught.

When I did take a trout or two, they were never the four-, six-, eight- or ten-pound monsters the pundits seemed to catch with such monotonous regularity. They usually weighed about 1 lb apiece – sometimes 1½ lb or 2 lb – and the annual three-and-a-quarter pounder was invariably photographed on the lawn with great ceremony – until one year the dog ate it while I was loading the camera and telling everyone how long the fish had fought and how many times it had almost come off.

Even when I went to the more expensive, smaller, put-and-take stillwaters, one or two of them stocked with vast, double-figure leviathans, I rarely took more than two or three fish, and they rarely weighed more than 1½ lb or 2 lb each. For a long time, my best trout (apart from a dull grey tailless, 8¼ lb hen rainbow which fought like a sack full of wet mice, tasted like cotton wool marinaded in mud and which I preferred to forget) was a four-and-a-half-pounder from Grafham which actually took me on to the backing once and nearly gave me a heart attack.

My inferiority complex stemmed from the fact that I fared so badly by comparison with the pundits who regaled me weekly and monthly from the pages of the angling press, and that I couldn't understand why this should be so.

I wondered whether it might have something to do with my tackle.

I didn't own a carp rod converted to hurtle a size 12 shooting-head 50 yards out into the wide blue yonder, and I didn't need a Transit van to carry the dozens of other rods I was told I needed. In fact, I had only two rods. One was a somewhat 'tacky' 9 foot fibre-glass affair with a foam-rubber handle and with no AFTM number marked on it, which I had bought at the beginning of my first trout-fishing season; the second – my pride and joy – was a 10 foot, 6/7 rated carbon job, a birthday present from the family, which was – and is – a pleasure to use.

Nor did I have a mass of fly-lines. I used a double-tapered floater on the carbon rod and a weight-forward medium-sinker on the other one. With only one reel for each, I couldn't see how I could accommodate slow-sinkers, medium-sinkers, fast-sinkers, long-bellies, lead-cored trolling lines, shooting-heads and dapping lines – especially if I had to have them in an assortment of colours from white and blue through pink and grey to green and brown and in sizes from five to 12 inclusive.

Nor did I have a suitcase full of flies which had to be wheeled to the water on a trolley and which opened up into 24 stepped, 'Ethafoam'-lined shelves, starting with midge pupae (in 138 combinations of colour and size) at the top and working down through nymphs, sedge pupae, corixae, shrimps (in 19 different hues), alder larvae, stick flies, dry flies, traditional wet flies, marabou and streamer lures, to popping bugs, plastic sand-eels and Dog-nobblers at the bottom. My fly-box was a slightly tinny affair containing an 'infallible' selection of 24 lures bought by mail-order, half-a-dozen patterns given to me at the waterside by kindly anglers who had been more successful than myself, and a further dozen or so nymphs and 'things' bought at various fisheries where they had been, at the time, 'fly of the week'.

But the more I looked around, the more clearly I began to realise that most other fly fishers had tackle really very similar to my own. So I wondered whether it was my casting.

To judge from the articles published in the angling magazines and newspapers, a man wasn't a man unless he could punch out the full length of a 30-yard double-tapered line directly into the teeth of a Force 8 gale. I couldn't do that. In fact – and I had measured it to make sure – the best I could achieve consistently was 24 yards – provided there was only a light breeze and that it was coming from the side. And the harder I tried, the shorter the distance I seemed to cast and the more knots I seemed to get in my leaders. Shooting-heads might have provided the answer, but that flattened monofilament backing was horrible to handle, seemed to me to tangle too often and even when my double-haul went right – which wasn't very often – it added only 4–5 yards to the distance I was casting, the line and leader tended to land in a heap and, if I did get an occasional take at 30 yards range, I almost always failed to hook the fish.

Then I began to watch my fellow-anglers again, and realised that very few of them cast better than I did and that, in reality, quite a lot of them were rather worse. So, I wondered whether my constant failure had anything to do with the frequency with which I went fishing. The pundits seemed to go out twice or three times a week, usually in boats. Or they claimed to take 600 fish or so in a year which, when divided up into eight-fish limits, meant that they were fishing at least 75 times in a 30-week season – i.e. two-and-a-half-times a week, on average. I found it difficult enough to justify spending a whole Saturday or Sunday away from the wife, kids, dog, garden, lawn, decorating, telephone and mother-in-law, let alone to excuse myself for monopolising the car for the day and clawing back £20 from the housekeeping for petrol and tickets. So, I was lucky to get out once a week (actually, it was more often something like once a fortnight), and I tended to fish from the bank, saving much more expensive boats for highdays and holidays.

But when I looked around and started to compare notes with other fishermen at the waterside, I found that they had the same problems, too – that very few of them really went out more than about once every two weeks, with quite a lot going rather less often than that.

And then the light dawned. It was an article in *Trout and Salmon* that did it – not one of those 'how-to-do-it' pieces by some well-known name, illustrated with photographs of boats at risk of capsizing under the weight of the fish in them, but a brief and entirely factual account of an International match at Draycote Water. It said that four teams, each of 12 anglers – presumably the best and most skilful that could be mustered from England, Ireland, Scotland and Wales – had caught 262 trout for a total weight of 232 lb, and that this was the largest number of trout ever to have been taken in an International match other than at Loch Leven.

When analysed, these figures were fascinating. Far from all taking limits, these 48 undeniably brilliant anglers, fishing as hard as they could and with all the skill they could muster, had averaged 5.46 fish each – and this was the best they had *ever* achieved in an International competition. And the fish were by no means all three-, four- and five-pounders; they averaged about 14 oz!

The more I thought about this, the clearer it all became. I had been setting my expectations much too high, basing them on sensational and, perhaps, sometimes exaggerated reports in the angling press, rather than on the realities of life. The bag average at the large reservoirs was, in fact, between 1.5 and 2 fish per rod visit, which meant that each time some self-important, self-styled expert took a limit, at least three other people had to go blank in order that the average be maintained. And the average weight of the fish *wasn't* three-, four-, five- or six-pounds, or anything like it; it was between ¾ lb and 2 lb, depending on where you went.

It was evident, too, that the same applied to the smaller, put-and-take stillwaters. The more I looked around, the more I saw that 'double limits' were actually quite rare, that by no means all of my fellow-fishermen took limits, that the fish averaged out at 1½–2 lb – except at some slightly more 'up-market' waters where trout of 2–2½ lb were the norm – and that four-pounders were remarkable and newsworthy anywhere.

So I've mentally scrumpled up my inferiority complex and chucked it into the waste-paper basket where it belongs. Nowadays, I just enjoy my fishing as and when I can get it. I no longer flail away in frantic pursuit of elusive limits or consider myself a failure if my bag doesn't contain a five-pounder. And the strange thing is that I seem to enjoy my fishing very much more, and to be catching many more fish!

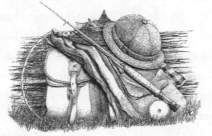

Chapter three

SEEING THE LIGHT

❧ *There's a whole lot more to choosing the killing fly than deciding on the right size or colour, for it is not what the angler sees, but what the trout does, that completes the successful circle.*
❧ *Qualities of light and the direction of the sun are the factors that have the most influence on whether or not the trout find your offering acceptable. Orkney brown trout specialist Stan Headley illustrated the theory with some interesting experiences.*

ASPECTS OF LIGHT
by STAN HEADLEY, *November 1989*

OF ALL the factors which govern the acceptability of any individual fly pattern to a trout at any given time, the most important and fundamental is light.

In a total absence of light, it is unlikely that any member of the salmonid family would ever succumb to an artificial fly in the normal course of events. A worm or maggot could possibly be hunted down in some stygian hole, as all fish have scent-sensing abilities way beyond the understanding of us mere humans. And although members of the trout tribe cannot compete in this sphere of activity with cyprinids or sharks, they are capable of retracing their paths to the spawning redds solely by olfactory means. You try returning to the maternity ward of your birth simply on the evidence of your nose! Throwing camels through the eyes of micro-surgery needles would be an evening's mild entertainment by comparison!

Trout flies must be seen by fish to provoke the desired response.

We spend much time building visual triggers into our artificial patterns to maximise this effect — startling contrasts (e.g. silver on black); fluorescent tags, butts and throats; highly mobile materials (e.g. marabou plumes, hen and gamebird hackles); wriggly tails and so on.

But all these efforts fail in the absence of light. And light is not a constant medium. From sunrise to sunset, light alters in its intensity and direction, the more so when passing through the medium of water. This means, of course, that the flies must appear different to the fish as the light which illuminates them alters.

I have been lucky to have spent my trout-fishing apprenticeship in Orkney. Another man who had a similar apprenticeship was that great literary figure, Eric Linklater. He built what is now Merkister Hotel as a family home, and spent many happy hours on his favourite water, Loch Harray.

I like to think that he also had some inkling into the effects of light on fly fishing, as he wrote, in an essay entitled *Orkney*, 'Light is the only dominating factor in (Orkney's) scenery, and the town-dweller, on his arrival in Or-kney, will screw up his eyes and ask where all the light is coming from . . . There are no hills high enough to intercept it. There are no trees to diminish it. There is, on the entire circumference, the sea to reflect it. And beneath a changing sky, Orkney can change . . . to a radiant panorama of lakes . . . a dazzling chequer-board of grass and ploughland, the shadow and claret of hills . . . And then in less time than it takes to count the colours, the colours will change again . . .'

Who else but a fly-fisherman would refer to that gorgeous heathery colour as claret?

Time and time again, while fishing in Orkney, I have seen the light subtly alter and the successfully lethal combination of colours which has made up my team of flies become just as quickly ineffective. Nothing else changes, simply the light, but the trout now see the flies for what they are, conglomerations of inedible materials, no longer the juicy invertebrate morsel.

For years now, I have encouraged anglers from the South to change their ingrained habits and continually search for acceptable patterns as the trout switch from one preference to another, but, I'm afraid, usually with scant success. Most visiting anglers wait for more obvious signals to precipitate the change, such as a hatch or change of hatching insect.

In my experience, English anglers cannot divorce themselves from the belief that trout flies, regardless of pattern, are imitative, or to stretch a point, bait. Rainbow trout tend to bolster this belief because of their habit of taking the fly slowly and steadily, almost pulling the rod out of the hand of the unwary angler. No self-respecting wild brown trout is so accommodating, but the same brownie is more likely to rise to a wider range of offerings than its transatlantic cousin.

Therefore, to consider trout flies as bait, or that trout consider individual flies as basically edible, can engender a line of thought which usually leads to failure and disappointment.

Let's take a prime example. The bog-standard Soldier Palmer is one of this country's top fish-catchers. In construction, it is basically a bright red or crimson body, brown hackle with a gold or silver rib. In nature, there is nothing that resembles it that features in a trout's diet. In fact, I'll go further. We have, in Orkney, a few very high pH waters which abound with red mites. These creatures look very much like small aquatic red spiders, and are about the closest match to a Soldier Palmer that I have seen in nature. Whereas the Soldier Palmer is a very popular and killing fly on these waters, I have yet to see a fish with any red mites in its stomach. In fact, the trout seem actively to ignore them as a source of nourishment.

Still not convinced? Try this one. Some years ago, Norman Irvine and I were on Stenness, and conditions were indicative of some good sport. Unusually, for this water, we could see some good fish moving in the shallows actively feeding on something we could not see. We searched our fly-boxes for an answer to the problem, but with no immediate result. Eventually, a fish was taken, more by good luck than good judgement.

A quick dig with the spoon

showed the answer – a host of tiny stickleback fry. Charged with optimism, we set out to match the 'hatch' with all sorts of fish-imitating flies – Silver Invictas, etc. No result.

For no apparent reason, Norman put a Blue Zulu on the top dropper, and was immediately into a fish, which, upon administration of the priest, spewed up a host of fry. We ended up taking a quality basket of fry-feeding fish solely on the Blue Zulu. Not one fish took a fry-imitating pattern.

That day, if memory serves me right, was very bright. Another occasion on which Norman and I met trout feeding on stickleback fry was exactly the opposite. We were on Swannay in a very heavy overcast. The amount of light filtering through the cloudy sky was almost negligible, and again good-quality fish were feeding close in, on fry. No lucky fish pointed the way this time. Experience told us that the fish were on fry, so again we went through the imitative approach, and again the result was the same – nothing!

Knowing that claret-bodied flies can be very effective in poor light conditions, and getting desperate, I found a long, slim-bodied Con-nemara Claret and put it on. Before the fish went down I managed to take two good trout, just over 2 lb apiece, and both crammed to the gills with stickleback fry.

So there you have it! Fish feeding on identical items, the important difference being the quality of light, and the trout being very selective in the patterns they would accept. And what produced a result? Not shape of fly, nor size, nor presentation – colour was the answer, and colour relies on light!

Try this little experiment. Select a fly from your box, preferably one with a variety of colours in its makeup, plus a dash of tinsel. Get yourself a light-source – a light-bulb, or a window in a dark room – and hold the fly up to the source of light so that there is a direct line between it, the fly and your eye. The fly will appear totally black, unless there is a floss or woollen tag which will throw back a little colour. Now move the fly around the light-source, above, below and to the side. In every position, different aspects of the dressing will 'light up'. It would be safe to say that, depending upon the fly's relative position to the source of light, it has no set colour, or it has a variety of colours. In fact, directly against a light source, even a Soldier Palmer is just another black fly.

Of course, the imitative fly-fisher will say that this matters not a jot, because his carefully matched fly will still match the natural when in similar relative positions to the light source. Only up to a point, I'm afraid, because most items on the trout's menu are highly translucent, and some even light up like neon bulbs against a bright light source. And matching colour is hard enough, God knows – but matching translucency . . . ?

This is why floating-line fly fishing tends to be more successful when the angler faces the sun. The approaching trout is seeing the true colour of the artificial as the light hits the fly and reflects back into the trout's eyes. With the sun behind the artificial, all the trout will see is an opaque black lump.

There is another aspect of light and its effect upon how the trout sees and reacts to a fly, which should be of interest to those among you who are unaware of it. An integral part of loch-style fishing is the working of the bob or top-dropper fly, in or just on top of the surface film. The reservoir fisher calls this 'dibbling', a term which makes me squirm, I'm afraid, but for the sake of clarity I'll grit my teeth and use it. A major proportion of loch-style trout are taken while the bob-fly is in or on the surface film, but you may have noticed that some anglers have more success 'dibbling' than others. I think I have discovered part, at least, of their secret.

The most successful top-dropper exponents I have come across rarely work the fly directly up-wind. As the top-dropper reaches a point where it can be 'dibbled', the master will angle the fly across the waves to a greater or lesser degree, depending upon the requirements of the trout. The secret is never to cause the fly to 'run' towards the sun; always move it *away* from the sun.

One last thing that is worth considering is the angle of the sunlight and its ability to penetrate the water. Early and late in the day, should the water be calm, means that very little direct light actually penetrates. In such circumstances the water surface becomes a perfect mirror and will deflect all the direct sunlight. Admittedly, some reflected light from the sky and surrounding land will penetrate, but, to all intents and purposes, daylight hours below water are appreciably shorter than above water.

This may seem irrelevant, and only a vaguely interesting piece of observation, but if you are fishing during these periods, it would be well to remember that the fish will be feeding in almost total darkness, and not enjoying the bright and colourful dawn or dusk.

I am a great believer in the use of fluorescent materials for flies during that period of poor light which we call dusk. When I am sure that direct light is not penetrating the surface is the time to slip on a fluorescent Palmer. I will usually work only for a short period – probably that time when only small quantities of reflected light are entering the water – but the fluorescent fly will boost the basket appreciably in that very short time.

Now whether you are prepared to take on all that I have put forward, half of it, or none at all is by and large beside the point. These are theories which have helped me catch fish but, more importantly, they have encouraged me to observe the happenings around me, and study cause and effect. If my bletherings prompt you to take the same attitude to your fishing, I guarantee you'll start making things happen, rather than letting things happen to you. Remember that light not only blinds, it often illuminates!

❧ Once hooked, a fish has to be landed. This can be an art form and a pleasure to share, or it can be a bumbling, thick-eared affair best not watched. There's far more to a successful landing than using the right tackle. It is, as demonstrated by stillwater nymphing expert Brian Harris, all in the hands.

YOU NEED HANDS

by BRIAN HARRIS, *September 1985*

I LOST another big fish this morning. I did nothing wrong but the fish was just too much at the time and in the circumstances. I could have cried . . . but then I feel like that every time a big trout gets away, specially with a hook and length of leader in his jaw. It was one of many . . . too many!

This season, until May, there had been relatively few big trout showing at Bewl Bridge, no doubt due to the very cold weather keeping the overwintered and many-wintered fish deep and out of the way of splashing, heavy lines. The stockfish were about a pound to a pound and a half this season, again due to the cold water temperatures preventing the fish from feeding in the rearing cages. And until this morning, though the fishery record went early this season to an 8¼-lb rainbow – a true Bewl Bridge-grown fish rather than one of the former management's unadmitted giant stockies, and since then a 10½-pounder has been taken – my only decent fish (above 2 lb) so far shed the hook on a big leap.

But this morning's fish was 'something else'! With a chill nor'-wester blowing down Hook Straight onto my casting arm, I had moved into the slight lee afforded by the north shoulder of Brown's inlet, a deep bay where one of the reservoir's many feeders comes in, and scene of many fine battles with big fish, usually taken when the water was low late season and casting into the channel of the stream.

Today, though, I chose to combat the rather fast drift to my left, by using a leaded size 10 olive midge pupa on the point of an extra-fine 5 lb 18-foot, leader, with a leaded size 12 black pupa four feet above it. All was well de-greased and I was casting about 20 yards of weight-forward 6-weight floater across the ripple and letting it belly round, only figure-eighting to collect the slack. Suddenly the line darted, and I lifted a fraction late, so I lifted off, cast to the same place again, let the pupae sink, and commenced to watch the drifting belly on the grey waves.

Suddenly the line drew away and my lift brought a tremendous thump on the rod tip and, without pause, the recovered coils leaped from my left hand and the little Marquis 6 began to howl.

I had an impression of immense power and size, though the fish did not show at all, but drove fast away to my left and deeper and deeper into the stream channel. Just as the end of the flyline flickered into the butt ring and the white braided backing snickered out, there was a sudden wrench and the fish stopped. I felt for it, the little 8½-foot Hardy graphite straining, but though I could detect a feeling of movement, all was solid.

The Brown's Inlet area is a nightmare of old tree stumps and roots and sunken briars, as anybody who has seen it in low-water conditions will know, and the fish had obviously gone into one of them, maybe the dropper having snagged. Eventually, with sinking heart, I put the rod down and waited a minute or so – a tactic that has rescued me a time or two in the past – but the line stayed slack from the rod tip out into the crystal depths. After five minutes I picked up the rod, tightened up again and felt another tiny tremor. I pulled, there came an answering pull, and then nothing. I knew the fish had parted the leader and left

me snagged, and pulled for a break.

Thinking the fish might have been one of several big fish moving in the bay, I set up again, but with a 6 lb tippet this time. Same two pupae. I did not have another take on that outfit, just a stockie when I switched to fishing a small black and gold fly near the surface and fast. Clear water and 6 lb nylon do not mix at Bewl Bridge, I fear.

In September last year, I lost another big fish at Bewl, hooked during a mad session with trout sploshing at craneflies as the west wind drove them out of Copens Reach, on to which the insects had been blown from the surrounding sloping meadowland, towards Chingley Wood and past the ferry point where Copens joins Bewl Straight. If I remember the facts correctly, it was the fourth fish of a six-fish limit that gave me 'the works'.

The fish were taking our floating cranefly imitations well enough, but many were being touched and lost, mainly, I believe, because the presence of so many of the long-legged insects was causing even the fish to behave erratically, and many of those fish lined up in the daddy diner were big ones, come out of their usual fastnesses to make the most of this feast of big mouthfuls.

I remember casting my artificial about 15 yards to where most of the activity was taking place, and I also remember the rise – a bow-wave into the waves that seemed to flatten them for yards around.

When I lifted the rod, the tip was wrenched down again, the whole thing arced into the handle section and the figure-eighted coils of line in my left hand went in a split second, followed by the shrieking of the Orvis CFO 1V reel as line left it

as fast as I can remember bonefish taking 200-odd yards out on the flats of the Bahamas and Mexico's Yucatan Peninsula.

That rainbow – for that's what it must have been – took the 30 yards of flyline and all the backing that reel held, which was all of 85 yards, before it finally broke the tippet, by which time the fish was way out in the depths of Bewl Straight and heading for Chingley Wood.

There was another huge rainbow I lost at Roger Daltery's

Lakedown Fishery at Nurwash Common, in neighbouring Sussex – less than a half-hour's drive from Bewl Bridge. I hooked it in high summer in the Lodge Lake – before Roger had the snags pulled out and the new promontory in for last season – on a dry sedge one evening and it ran to near the end of the flyline, then suddenly dived deep into the old tree that lay submerged in the water at the time. I saw the fish flash as I lifted into the rise, and it was not far short of double figures.

I could go on, but it would serve no great purpose, for most of us who have fished for a few years on still waters will have had similar experiences. My others have occurred at Grafham, Rutland, Draycote and Sutton Bingham reservoirs and at Packington when Tony Chattaway was there. But I remember, too, one enormous fish, this time a brown, that I lost on the Kimbridge stretch of the Test.

The fish had been rising intermittently for most of the September afternoon, but he was right under the far bank – a distance of about 18 yards – and drag proved a problem every time I tried to put a fly over the monster. Then, while I was having a rest after catching several good fish during a late-evening rise to pale watery and sedge, he sloshed again in the dusk. I was tempted for a final fling. And so it proved to be.

I had watched the fish carefully, and put him at about 6 lb. So I replaced my fine leader with one tapered to 5 lb over 14 feet and clinched on a Red Sedge, size 10. And to cut a long story short, the fish took on my second presentation, just as the current gave the well-greased sedge action as drag began to make it wake.

That great brown chased the fly two yards and engulfed it, then leapt clear as it felt the hook and took off upstream with the Marquis screeching. I applied pressure, for just upstream were heavy beds of ranunculus, but I might as well have tried to slow a Pickfords' lorry. The fish ploughed on, deep into the weeds, and then snapped the tippet with a final heavy wrench.

Over the years, as I have said, I have had my share of losses, like the ones so far described, and I have had plenty of success, too,

with big trout coming to net on very light gear and gossamer tippets. Often, as I am sure others will have experienced, the hook has either been found to be held only by a thin slip of skin, or else is out of the fish and tangled in the net. A Bayham Lake rainbow of 9 lb sucked in my sixe 14 Olive Midge Pupae a couple of seasons back up at the island end, and ran me 80 yards first go. I was using an 8½-foot Diamondback for 3–5-weight lines and a 3 lb tippet, for the lake was calmish and very clear.

Yet despite the light gear and little hook, I had that fish in the net in about 20 minutes, without any big problems.

Not all breakages are big fish, of course, and many's the time I have had a smash-take – usually not truly that, but a combination of fast fish action and excessively fast and *hard* tightening by me – and thought . . . 'Damn, big fish, that' . . . only to see, seconds later, a 1½ lb rainbow leaping repeatedly as it tried to shake out my lost hook and trailing tippet. You must have had it happen if you have fished a few seasons.

Playing trout – and other fish, of course – on fly fishing tackle is unlike using monofilament lines and fixed-spool or multiplier reels for bottom fishing and spinning, because the bulk of the flyline and the single-action reel (yes, I know there are multiplying ones, but I have yet to find one I like) combine to present problems not encountered with the other outfits. The line's drag behind a fish swimming fast, or jumping, especially when that line is drowned and in a serpentine configuration after several changes of direction by the fish, can and does shear the tippet, part a knot or open-up or snap the hook.

Usually, too, there is the need to handline the flyline immediately on hooking a fish, to gain contact and initiative, specially if the fish runs towards you. Some fishermen continue to play their fish by hand, and this is, I feel, a bad mistake. It is so easy to be hauling in line at a rate of knots, to keep contact with a wild-fighting rainbow, only for the fish to change direction and – whammo! The sudden impact parts the leader, or the hook fails, or the hold gives.

I get the slack recovered line back on to my reel as soon as I have the fish on a reasonably taut line, and then play the fish off the reel. After all, that's what your reel is for, isn't it! Very few reels these days have chattery ratchet systems that can cause a tippet to snap when a fish takes off for the horizon, and some of the better ones have drags that can also be adjusted for tippet and hook strength.

Then, if the fish suddenly makes a dash, the reel yields line smoothly, keeping just enough strain to retain the barb's hold. On the other hand, a sudden rush can lift a catscradle of line, lying coiled at the feet of the angler, and with maybe a strand or two of weed or grass or a twig in it, to jam in the butt ring and let the fish get free.

Excessive strain is imposed by many fly-fishermen, specially those fairly new to the stillwater scene. They lose many fish through their impatience and the lack of 'hands' – that hard-to-define quality so important in angling (and other sports), that tells the angler how much strain to apply without him having consciously to think about it. At its best, playing a trout on fly tackle appears to the observer to be like a strange dance, each movement carried out with a smooth rhythm in answer to the fish's moves, so that the whole act, culminating in a gentle netting of the trout, is like an art-form. At its worst it is a rough-and-tumble, thick-eared affair of jerky moves by the fisherman, accompanied by curses, stumbling feet, much splashing by both combatants and a final boot up the bank – an igno-minious end for a gamefish. Or a lost fish due to a broken tippet, hook or hook-hold.

I play fish lightly these days, having run through the whole gamut of horsing them and losing too many. You never know how light is the hook-hold, and often a fish ends up in my little Hardy Troutfisher net which, had I given it 'some stick', would certainly not have done so. In short, many fish I net are held only by a sliver of skin by a tiny hook.

Also, I like to fish a dropper, both when fishing midge pupae or sedge pupae patterns, for two rea-sons. Firstly, it lets me fish two dif-ferent colours or sizes of fly, and secondly, it allows me to fish at two depths simultaneously. Often I fish a leaded pupa on the point and a plain one on the dropper. But dropper-knots, no matter which, are often unreliable and shear when the fish pulls on the take, due to the right-angle at the hinge point.

After much experimentation, I believe the upper end of a four-turn water (Cove) knot to produce the strongest dropper, and the long end of a bloodknot to be the weakest, in general. I have also tried attaching droppers above a bloodknot in the leader, by using a tucked half-blood around the leader and then jamming it on the bloodknot. I do not find these much better than the long end of a blood.

Once a fish is hooked on a dropper, I seldom have any real problem; it is the impact of the take and the answering tightening that brings breakages for most an-glers. It is very difficult, specially after fishing slowly by drifting a couple of midge pupae round on the belly without an offer for an hour or more, not to react to a sudden take with a snatch rather than a nice, little lift of the rod.

Finally, rod angle when fighting a trout is important. About 40 de-grees to the horizontal is about right for most situations, but the rod may be held higher if the fish is more than 30 yards away, to try to keep line out of the water, to avoid the fish tangling weeds, sub-merged brush or other snags. A low rod, to apply side-strain to turn a fish away from a dangerous area, or to bring it into closer range, is a good idea. But one should always try to maintain the same strain, which avoids frightening the fish into mad dashes, gyrations and head-shaking. When the fish jumps, ease the strain by dropping the rod tip quickly. I am never afraid of letting a fish swim almost free, towing a big bow line, once I am fairly happy that the barb is sunk. I slack off like this when a fish begins head-shaking, which is perhaps the most dangerous time when a hook can lose its hold, certainly more so than when a fish jumps.

Holding the rod high all the time imposes unfair strain on the fragile tip instead of spreading the load down the shaft, which can then provide that essential buffer to sudden strains produced by the fish.

And don't forget that a rod ex-cessively bent, specially one on which there are either too few rings or on which the rings are badly placed, so that the line forms sharp angles over each one, adds excessive friction to the line, which can pull out a hook, cause it to deform or snap the tippet.

The only time the rod should be held high and the tip bent over is when the fish is being brought over the net, apart from the aforementioned long distance between rod and fish, or keeping line out of snags.

Generally, because most of my fishing on stillwater involves nymphing, with the line bellying downwind from the rod tip, I know on which side of the fish's mouth it is hooked, and can safely apply pressure from that side and ease it somewhat when the pull is from the other side as the fish swims the opposite way.

&▲ *I learned how to spot fish the hard way. Many was the trout I walked past unawares only to see it dash downstream when the pool was given up as having not a single tenant.*

❧ *My problem was that I was looking for the whole fish and not the*
give-away glimpse of a nose, tail or fin peeking
from behind a sun or weed bed.

❧ *And many are the fishery owners who are berated at the end of a fruitless*
day by a disappointed angler who accuses them of failing to stock enough
fish. They were there, but the angler was too intent on casting than looking,
mistakenly believing that sooner or later a trout would take his fly.

❧ *Spotting fish hidden beneath a sunlight-marbled surface is a skill and a*
technique that can be learned and practised like anything else in fishing.
Jon Beer is a master at the art and he gives away some useful hints
for those who are looking but cannot see.

THE EYES HAVE IT
by JON BEER, *June 1988*

I DO NOT know the statute of limitations in the crime of poaching. Many years ago I drove several hundred miles for a job interview in Plymouth. I did not get the job. In fact, so rapidly did I not get the job that I had time to spare in the afternoon and took a leisurely route home across the moors. I was a bit cross, and I was muttering things when a dip in the small road brought me to a small stream bordered with close-cropped grass. There was no-one in sight.

I got out and looked at the water. It was very clear and inviting. I had a small rod in the car. I rather thought that if I were to see a fish I would be unable to resist a cast or two. I looked very hard. There were trout everywhere, hovering above the bottom and then flashing away from me as I walked the bank, leaving tiny puffs of silt in the current and slipping under the big brown stones in mid-stream. So be it: I would have a cast or two.

Looking guiltily over my shoulder, I skulked a little way downstream where the banks were fringed with a few stunted trees and the stream dropped down a low waterfall into a small pool beside a large rock. I hid behind the rock and flicked a fly up to the bubble and froth where the waterfall emptied. The hungry moorland fish grabbed the fly as if there were no tomorrow – which, for a couple of the fatter ones, there wasn't.

I was watching the steady progress of the fly down the line of bubbles across the pool when a voice, quiet and very close, said:

'Any luck?'

How he had come upstream with his dog so quietly I did not know – or care. I was too preoccupied fashioning a convincing, but innocent, explanation for the trout rod in my hand. I blustered something about '. . . not really fishing, more trying the little rod out – don't suppose there are any fish in the stream anyway . . .' Frankly, it sounded thin – particularly as I had a brace for supper in my pocket. Then I saw on his face that expression one might use for a small boy fishing in a bucket – more amused pity than anger.

'Well,' he said, 'I've walked up this river bank most days for eleven years and I've never seen a fish – but good luck anyway'.

Pretty soon we had established that he was not a bailiff. I showed him the two nice fish and we walked together up the stream to the car. On the way I tried to show him the fish that were still there in the clear run above the pool. I pointed to a small trout in midstream. 'See it?' I asked.

'How?' he asked back.

I was nonplussed. How do you explain to someone how to see? But he was disconcertingly right: seeing fish beneath the surface is just a technique – a skill that can be learned and practised like anything else in fishing.

Why bother? There is a great deal to be said for *not* looking for fish. If you can see them then it is equally true that they can see you. In fact, they can see you much more easily as you are up in the daylight and they are in the relative gloom of the river with a half-silvered mirror (the water surface) between you and them.

There are, however, several good reasons for spotting fish before you start fishing. The first is illustrated in my illicit fishing on Dartmoor; we all fish better when we know that there are fish to be had, when there could be a take at any second, and when we have confidence that there is something scrutinising the fly. Conversely, it is quite possible for a compulsive fish-spotter to get dispirited if he doesn't see any fish – although they may still be there.

Of course, it is not necessary to

see fish below the surface to know that they are there. The sight of a rising fish concentrates the mind wonderfully, but not all fish will be rising (particularly the big ones) and it may be possible to find better, more accessible fish with a careful search of the water.

At the very least, you will look for any non-rising fish that might take fright and disturb the one you are going for. It is all too easy to concentrate on a rise across the water, step carefully into the water only to be startled by a whirl of silt a foot away from your wader as a bigger fish dashes off to wreck the tranquillity of your quarry.

I have to confess slight reservations about what I have just written. It is obviously very sound advice, frequently given, to search and fish the closer water before going for the fish further away in case you disturb the nearer fish. What is not so obvious is how you avoid disturbing the nearer fish if, eventually, you want to go for the one across the pool.

It has always seemed to me that catching the nearer fish is just as likely to disturb the pool as wading carefully through them – and if you don't catch them, which is most likely, you will either have disturbed them anyway or be in the same position as when you started. Better, I think, to try to find some other approach to the rising fish across the pool.

All too often the larger, wiser fish are not those which are rising. If you are after these specimens it will be necessary to watch them carefully and discover what they are eating and their patterns of behaviour. A larger fish, particularly in slower water, will often be taking the natural fly some distance below its habitual station. The trout rises slowly in the water, drifting back with the fly, before committing himself. The angler casting perfectly to the point of the rise may be casting several feet behind the waiting fish.

Seeing the fish beneath the surface may be a luxury in dry-fly fishing, or when the fish are rising. It is vital when fishing a nymph or a wet-fly upstream, when there may be little or no evidence on the surface, that the fish that has taken the fly and is about to spit it out again can be seen.

We see an object when light from the sky is reflected off it into our eyes. Relatively little light enters the water, much of it being reflected away at the surface. Of the light that does enter the water much of it is absorbed by the water itself or by the particles of silt and whatnot, which is why you can't see fish in a brown flood.

More is absorbed by the fish itself, as trout, like most fish, are darker on their backs than on their bellies. The little light that is reflected from the fish then travels up through the water, passes through the surface and from there can enter the eye of the angler.

If that were the only light entering the angler's eye there would be no problem; the eyes would adjust to that small amount of light and we would see the fish as clear as day. Unfortunately, the little light from under the surface is competing with huge amounts from everywhere else, particularly from the sky and reflecting from the surface of the water. The eyes adjust to this relatively bright light and our view of the fish under the surface disappears in the same way as our view of a moonlit garden seen through a window disappears when the room light is switched on.

Freshwater pearl fishermen see perfectly into the water by looking through a glass-bottomed bucket pushed into the surface of the water. The competing light from the sky and reflecting from the surface is cut out by the sides of the bucket and only the dimmer light from beneath the surface enters the eye. Result – a perfectly clear view. I don't recommend this solution to the fisherman. It disturbs the fish somewhat!

The fisherman can do something to reduce the competing light entering the eye. A hat with a large brim will cut out a lot of the sky. A large brim will also cut out a lot of rain down the back of the neck. This is the headgear I use and I can report one drawback – folk laugh at you. Some people prefer a light cap with a large peak, American style, but a surprising amount of light can enter from the side.

If a hat is too hot, try an eye-shade. These are usually white (for tennis) on the upper surface and could have been designed to scare fish. Try dyeing them. For people who really get hot-headed in a hat,

Orvis sell a 'Solar Helmet', a sort of mesh *sola topi* with an electric fan in the brim, powered by a solar panel perched on the top of the helmet, and with back-up batteries (not included) secreted under the crown. A word of caution: folk will laugh at you, and one can hardly blame them.

The other source of competing light, reflecting up from the surface of the water, is more of a problem because it is superimposed on the light coming from beneath the surface.

We see reflected light as an upside-down scene on the water. If that scene is very bright, e.g. the sky, there will be an overwhelming amount of reflected light and little or nothing will be seen below. If the angler changes position until there is a *dark* reflection on the surface he is trying to peer through, the light from below may be able to compete. A dark cloud is better than nothing, but a high bank in deep shadow is best of all.

Light from the sky 'vibrates' in all directions. We cannot see these 'vibrations', but some creatures, many insects for example, can. When light is bounced off a shiny surface (a water surface, say) most of that reflected light is vibrating in

just one direction, horizontally, having been 'polarised'.

The glass of polarised sunglasses will only allow light vibrating in one direction to pass through it, and all other light is cut out. When glasses are made the lenses are mounted to cut out horizontally polarised light – the light reflected from the surface of the water.

If you turn the glasses on their side, the reflections will miraculously re-appear. This is worth bearing in mind as you peep round a tree to view the water. The head is rarely held vertically (the way the glasses were designed) and will not be cutting out as much reflection as they can, but try tilting your head from side to side to get the best possible effect.

There is a penalty to pay for this reduction in reflected light. The light from below the surface is unpolarised, vibrating in all directions, and so the glasses will cut out about half of this valuable light. This is a small price to pay on a bright day with clear water, when there is plenty of light coming from beneath the surface. As the light drops in the evening, or on a very dull day, there comes a time when this reduced light from below the surface is too little to be of any use, and you are better off re-moving the glasses and coping with the reflections in other ways.

Polarised glasses cut out about half of unpolarised light, so they look 'grey' to us. Polarised glasses with some colour tinting will be removing even more light without any advantage, so avoid these. There are super models with small magnifying lenses beneath the polarising lenses.

If you prefer to wear a hat with a peak, rather than an all-round brim, it is well worth buying the glasses with broad sides, like blink-ers, to cut out side light. I once had a pair so surrounded by shields that they were virtually goggles, and any exertion or excitement, like hooking a fish, would cause them to mist up, leaving me befog-ged in a small white world.

So, you have done everything possible to get light from below and cut out light from above. Your brain has to do the rest. Perception (seeing things) does not work pass-ively like a camera; the brain ac-tively constructs a world of objects from a few patterns of light and colour falling on the retina at the back of the eye. You had to learn it at birth, and the angler has to learn to do it all over again. As a

first exercise – and to show you that perception is active – take a look at the frame-work on this page.

Most people see it first as a box seen from slightly above and slight-ly to the left, with the face marked with 'O's nearest the viewer.

But it can just as easily be seen as a box viewed from slightly be-low and slightly to the right – with the face marked with 'X's nearest the viewer. After a little time you should be able to see both boxes, often switching from one to the other and back again. Your brain has constructed two different ob-jects from the same pattern of lines entering the eye and falling on the retina.

Now practise. Practise holding one of those perceptions; run your eye over the box without 'flipping' to the other box. Now deliberately 'flip' the perception and practise holding and looking at the other box. (If you find it difficult to flip deliberately, try looking at the face that you want to have in front.)

You are practising to hold just one perception when two are poss-ible. This is *exactly* the problem you encounter when seeing through the water surface; the scene under the water and the reflections on the surface are superimposed. Your brain can construct and hold one or the other, but it will usually flip to the reflection as that has more light and detail.

Now practise by the water. Make it as easy as possible to start practising before moving on to more difficult conditions. Start with the water's edge, preferably viewed across a small river or pond, say, five yards away. Find an object on the waterline – a large stone perhaps – and follow it down beneath the water. Look at neighbouring features on the river bed.

Now 'flip' the perception to the reflection on the bank at that point. If the bank is in deep shadow and the water is smooth there will be very little reflection, but look for the reflections of light objects, such as grass-stems and stones.

Now flip back to the perception of the bottom underneath. Extend your view into deeper water, moving your attention from one object on the bottom to its neighbour.

When you can do this easily you can practise under increasingly difficult conditions. Looking through the surface gets more difficult as the water surface is disturbed (bathroom windows depend on

this) and as the angle between the line of sight and the water surface gets smaller (when the angler crouches down behind cover). As this angle gets smaller, more of the daylight is reflected at the water surface and, to make matters worse, the light reflected at these angles is only slightly polarised so that your glasses become ineffective in cutting it out.

Any skill needs practice. I am lucky. I live next to a small river and have a chance to watch fish on station outside the kitchen window. Even so, I find it a lot harder to see these fish in March than later in the season, when I have been peering into the water for several weeks. The solution is to start the season early.

Before you feel tempted to cast a line, take the time to walk up the water you will fish later on. The low angle of sunlight and heavier water of early spring will make fish spotting difficult, but it will stand you in good stead later in the season. You will also have the leisure and the new skill to study the changes in the underwater features of the river that the floods of winter bring about.

I once spent several early mornings in June watching a large rainbow patrolling the reed margin of a small lake. The only way I could devise of casting to him in the clear, shallow water was to lie flat on my back on a small boat jetty that reached out beyond the reeds. I could watch the fish cruise past from behind the reeds. I then had about six minutes to wriggle on my back along the jetty before his circuit brought him back to the spot. I had flicked a slow-sinking fly into place and was awaiting developments when I felt and heard footsteps on the boards of the jetty behind me.

Etched against the bright-blue sky was my uncle, John, who is no fisherman and, I hope, will never read these words. On that perfectly still morning he could see right down into the water, he told me. There were no fish . . . no, no, he told a lie; there was a fish, a huge one, coming towards the fly.

Uncle John pointed to it excitedly, in case, perhaps, I was tired of lazing on my back on the jetty and wished to get up and have a look myself. 'Here it comes,' he called. 'Oh . . . no, it's swimming away again.' I cannot blame the trout, he was not to know that the figure waving against the sky was quite harmless to fish. The moral: when

possible, look into the water without fishing, then fish without looking into the water.

Sometimes, the first sign you will see of a fish is a puff of silt as the startled creature tears off across the pool. Better that happen now before you come to fish the place in earnest. Identify the spot relative to a bank feature before the silt disappears – you can look for the fish on your way back to get the rod.

The business of marking a spot in the water where a fish has been seen is another tool in the angler's box. It is not enough to see the thing; you have to be able to find it again.

Similarly, it is much easier to see a fish if you know where it is, from a rise or a bulge of water at the surface. On stillwaters the rings of the rise stay more or less stationary and you have time to look around and fix the spot (in line with the willow, three yards out, say). On a river the problem is deceptively more difficult as the rise moves downstream and, however much you try to resist it, your eyes move with it.

Technically, this is called the 'optomotor response', present in all creatures with good eyesight. The eyes over-rule your wish to stare at the same spot in the space because their job is to provide you with a good, steady image of an object on the retina – and if the object is moving downstream then, by golly, they will move with it whether you want them to or not.

If you want to demonstrate this phenomenon to yourself, ask someone to move their gaze smoothly from one side of the room to the other; it can't be done. If you look closely at their eye movement you will see the eyes flicking from one stationary position to another, a series of jerks around the room.

Perhaps the eye muscles can only supply this jerky movement? Not so. Now get them to follow their moving finger as they sweep it through the same arc. The eye movements follow the finger smoothly, because the eyes are holding fast onto a moving object. In both cases the eyes are trying to provide as steady an image as possible.

Because of the optomotor response, most people trying to fix a rise will place it downstream of where it occurred. As soon as the rise is spotted, either look directly above it to the bank or, if you have mastered the art of focusing atten-

tion on the reflections, fix the position of the rise on the reflection (which will not move). Then you can fix that position on any handy bankside objects.

I have suggested how you can practise looking beneath the surface; but I haven't suggested what you can look for. Fish, of course, but a fish alive in the water looks nothing like the pictures you see in the pages of this magazine. I keep stressing that our perceptual system is active; it *constructs* an object from a background of light and dark lines and blobs. Seeing a fish starts with finding tiny clues to its presence.

Look for movement. Obviously a dead give-away in stillwater, even in flowing water objects beneath the surface move very little and always to a regular pattern. You have learnt to ignore the surface, with its hypnotic tendency to grab the eyesight and carry it downstream with the optomotor response. Now look for any movement across the current or, even more significantly, up against it. These can only be animals with their own propulsion, and that is almost certainly fish (although dabchicks can make your pulse race – they look enormous).

Weeds hanging in the current move from side to side and can suggest fish. Watch a while for a regular rhythm to the movement; irregularity means fish. Similarly, a flexible object that *isn't* moving with the rhythm of the weeds can be a fish.

Because the eye is attracted to movement, the first sign of a fish may be a fin or, more usually, the tail. Trout-tail movement is rhythmic, like weed, but differs in two ways: first, the trailing edge of a trout tail is more or less vertical in the horizontal world of weed in the current. As the tail has no silvery scales to reflect the light the trailing edge can stand out as a dark, vertical line.

Second, the rhythm of a trout's tail, as it holds station, is usually faster and somehow more purposeful than the languid movement of weed. If you find a rhythmic, languid movement *and* a dark tail line then you could well have found a chub which has a much more 'limp-wristed' action to its rear end.

If you suspect a tail, look upstream for fins and a mouth, which can also be opening rhythmically to reveal a white interior (a great white cavern confirms a chub).

The pereptual system should have done its work by this time and you will be able to see the fish. Even now it can miraculously disappear before your eyes, particularly if it is hanging in mid-water on a sunny day.

The reflecting surfaces on a fish's scales are aligned in such a way as to reflect light from the side. On a sunny day, with plenty of light bouncing around down there, the fish seen from the side is a mirror, reflecting the surroundings and becoming, seemingly, transparent. Under these sunny conditions it can still be given away by its shadow on the river bottom.

Seen from above, the scales do not reflect the light; it would be a bit of a give-away if they did, although they might possibly blind a predator by dazzling it! This difference means that the whole fish is commonly seen as a rather thin, dark line moving across the river, the sides having disappeared leaving only the darker back visible. When the fish twists over to scrape a shrimp from a stone, or take a nymph, the mirrored side is momentarily uppermost and we get the 'flash' or 'wink' of a taking fish – another dead give-away.

Seeing fish is immeasurably easier when you know where to look, but a detailed examination of all the favoured lies of trout is a book in itself. Besides, now you can see the things you can write the book yourself.

Finally, a word of caution. I get so much pleasure from watching the fish in the stream that runs past the house that by watching them they have become individuals – and who could bring himself to deceive and hook a friend? And so I have had to give up fishing this stream.

> ❧ *Why is it that as we grow older, nylon becomes thicker and hook-eyes so much smaller, and why do the two always manage to combine as the light is failing and on the one evening of the season when the trout are just begging to be caught?*
> ❧ *'Sheer age, old lad,' said the optician. Not a bit of it. I could see as well as I could twenty years ago. The obvious answer was to take two rods. One to fish with until the fly managed, as they always do, to grab hold of a passing tree, the other to complete the evening until the second fly found a similar home.*
> ❧ *David Barr was not so proud and took his optician's advice but then the saga of the Polaroids began . . .*

A QUESTION OF VISION

by DAVID BARR, *September 1981*

AS I GROW older, I find that I am suffering from two inescapable defects. I cannot easily tie knots or untie tangles without the help of glasses – nor can I see a tiny floating fly bobbing along the stream towards me, ten yards off. I became aware of my downhill slide some years ago on the banks of Eyebrook Reservoir.

It was dusk, the fish were rising and I was changing to a dry Sherry Spinner. I could not tie it on; hold it to the sunset as I would, it was not possible. The optician, next day, told me why – and made me my first pair of reading glasses.

It took a little longer to discover the next defect – when watching Match of the Day, in fact, and wondering why they were playing without a ball. So now I have glasses for that too. I know all about bi-focals, but I am of a mind to fight these things. My obstinacy leads to the presence in my fishing bag of putting-on-the-fly glasses and spotting-the-fly-in-the-water glasses. This in turn led to a magic pair of Polaroid glasses, ground to my prescription.

These glasses opened up every kind of exciting fishing pleasure and put me right on top of the local success league. I see fish with them that no-one else believes exist; more importantly, I can pick and choose, passing over the undersized fish and concentrating on worthier targets. I cannot understand how anyone can fish without them. Furthermore they are life-savers when wading. The river in front of me opens up as if under a search-light. I can see the sudden holes and the menacing rocks in my path.

Tragically this vital piece of fishing equipment, after a too adventurous season, recently met its Waterloo.

The first drama occurred in July when I was fishing the Dee, standing in fast deepish water. My feet were firmly implanted on a gravelly run, three feet deep. I was casting, a little despondently, a long line over a fish that would break the surface each time the fly passed over his lie – purely, I thought, to encourage me.

It was not this obdurate salmon that was absorbing my attention; it was the cloud of living, buzzing flies that had decided that my face was a haven on which they would all like to spend their leisure moments. I developed a cunning diagonal sweep of the hand that swished my enemies, as they retreated, two or three at a time, into the water – and into the mouth of a tiny brown trout which must have felt that at long last he had found a place where he could grow into a takeable fish.

All this I could see, as though in a large clear bowl, through the Polaroids – until my cunning sweep missed the flies and dislodged the glasses, which fell with the appearance of a final Goodbye, into the current. At that moment I realised that without them I could see no sign of the clear gravelly run – and not a sign of my tiny trout.

I stood still, wondering about the price of a new pair and realising that I might be in the middle of my most costly morning's fishing. At that moment the sun came out. I leant forward until my nose brushed the surface of the water and there, four feet ahead of me, lying on the gravel, I could see two black circles.

I wound in, slung my rod onto the bank, and slowly submerged myself. By great good fortune my clutching fingers touched, then grasped my treasures as the water poured inside my waders.

With such a warning I should have grown trebly careful, but worse was to follow within the fortnight – in fact on the last day of the holiday, on the Spey beat called Carron. I had just landed my first fish of the 12 days' fishing. I was sitting on the bank, feeling fulfilled and pleased with myself and as a precaution, decided to re-tie my fly.

Off came the Polaroids, on went my fly-tying glasses, the fly was methodically knotted to the nylon, and I moved to the next pool in search of No. 2.

That night, packing the car, I noticed that the Polaroids were not in the usual place, but never gave it another thought. Only when I was safely back in East Anglia did I start seriously to worry, to fire my memory, and realise that I must have left them on the bank where I had caught the first fish and changed the fly.

An inch of rain, at least, had had its due effect on the river and my treasure, I realised, must have been swept downstream to Delchapel or even the pool below. Even so, I thought it worthwhile to write to the Carron gillie, tell him when the Polaroids had last been seen and offer a suitable reward. Some benevolent power must have been watching over me. Four nights later a gentle Scottish voice, on the telephone, told me that the glasses had been found and posted to me. It was very good value for £5.

There, by any standard of providence and responsibility, the adventure should have ended; this was not to be the case.

One late-season evening on the Babingley, packing up and hastening towards a beer at the Ffolkes Arms, I allowed myself to be diverted by some homing woodcock, finally got into the car to drive to the refreshment, and remembered, halfway, that I had left the Polaroids and the scissors on the car roof. With a sinking heart I drove back, to find that the very worst had happened. I tied a yellow ribbon on my scissors. They were easy to find. They acted as a marker for the Polaroids, shattered where I had backed over them. They were not even insured.

I fished the season out, without their kindly help – and with much of the joy gone from each evening. Seeing the fish is one of the bonuses of clear-water streams; though they are perfectly visible looking down at them from the bank (before they streak into the weed beds), trout are wholly invisible standing downstream of them in the water, with the waning light a mirror on the surface.

One evening I caught 15 undersized fish, which had risen and imitated two-pounders; luckily I was able to put them back without damage.

The optical industry is not adjusted to this specialised market. My very charming optician discovered that no-one was any longer grinding personalised Polaroids. She was on the brink of contacting America (where they do it all the time) when she found a pair that fitted my prescription. If I can only chain them to me, my fishing happiness – and safety – is, once again, assured.

• *Why is it that while the angler on one bank will rise and hook fish after fish, another on the other side will fail to raise a fin?*
• *Barrie Welham had made the fatal mistake of promising someone a fresh trout and was busy thinking out a suitable apology when he turned age-old advice on its head.*

THE AREA OF DECEPTION
by BARRIE WELHAM, *July 1956*

WHEN I FIRST started fly fishing I was taught the rule; always avoid the sun on your back. The idea be-ing to prevent one's shadow from falling on or near the fish in the water and so scaring them. I accepted this quite happily then, but now I think that at times the sun can help rather than hinder.

It is still important that your shadow should not fall upon the water which you are fishing, thereby betraying your presence. But when your shadow is short, as it will be when the sun is high, or when you can keep it off the water by any means at all, it is sometimes advantageous to fish with the sun on your back.

To justify this let us consider for a moment the human eye. For want of a better comparison we have to accept that certain conditions affect piscatorial vision similarly to our own.

When the sun's rays directly strike our eyes it blinds and dazzles us, but as you turn your head away from the sun vision becomes clearer and clearer until everything comes into sharp focus. If you look at the surface of a river against the bright sun it is difficult to make out detail. But stand with the sun behind you and everything is needle sharp.

This being true for our eyesight, could not it also be true of a trout's view of a fly on the surface? At least, that is how it struck me one day while sitting on a very nice trout which scorned my every of-

fer; although he hardly missed a natural. I had shown him three different patterns each in two sizes and the best response I had was when he tilted to look at the fly and then moved back.

Then I thought; if my eyes cannot discern detail against the sun, why should not that same sun's glare affect this trout's vision? If it does, then there must be one area where it will be almost impossible to see a small object at all, and another area where this small object will be very blurred and difficult to distinguish. So even though this trout is very wary if I could put my artificial in this fogged misty area he may not be able to differentiate between it and a natural.

Since thinking this, while sitting by that wary trout, but being unable to try out the idea through being confined to one bank, I have had many opportunities of putting it to the test. While it never pays to be dogmatic where fishing is concerned I have proved to my own satisfaction that by placing a fly where the sun blurs the trout's vision it is more likely to deceive him. This area of deception is between the area of maximum glare and that area where crystal clear vision begins.

Fishing the Test one day I watched a good fish rising steadily. I tried him with everything in my box, but he disregarded all my artificials, and kept sucking down the naturals. It was not until I removed my polarising glasses that the glare of the sun reminded me of the area of deception idea. I could not cast a longer line to place my fly across his lie into this area for fear of scaring him with the gut. Instead, I hurried away across the river.

Keeping very low, I crawled into position for a cast, kneeling on the ground. The sun was now on my back and I had very clear vision indeed. The first cast was a little short, but landed near the spot which I felt would be directly in line with the fish and the sun. The next cast sent that little Blue Quill, already refused so many times, a little farther up, into just the place I wanted it. It had moved barely six inches when it disappeared in a powerful suction dimple. I raised the rod and he was on. Eventually I landed a nicely shaped fish of three pounds.

A little later that year I was on a river in Hertfordshire. Quite late in the afternoon I came to a deepish run. It was a longish stretch and fish were rising throughout the whole length. I had not had a fish so far, and I had done something which I always regret – I had promised someone a fresh trout.

I cast to several fish, not putting them down, but moving on from one to another. I never rose a fish. Then I thought of the 'area of deception'. Once more it meant crossing the river and a long walk, wasting precious time. When I got back the sun was low enough in the west to make the shadow problem a very real worry. By good fortune some handy trees cast shadows which I could utilise, enabling me to cover some of the fish. I had a brace and a half, two over 15 inches and the other over 16 inches, before the sun left the water.

There are lots of loopholes in the theory and it is impossible to work out all the angles exactly. But it might help to explain those frequent occasions when two friends of similar ability, fishing opposite banks, have a good bag and a blank respectively.

It pays to be properly dressed when fishing, but not to appear a picture of sartorial elegance, or to give the impression of being someone who knows more about the game than he probably does. It's more a question of being dressed for the day. No one can enjoy his fishing after that first icy trickle has found its way between collar and neck, nor suffering to the point of collapse under the weight of a heavy waterproof on a sweltering day.

But people react in different ways to extremes of weather, as Bruce Sandison discovered.

THE HABIT PROCLAIMS THE MAN

by BRUCE SANDISON, *March 1980*

'FISHING IS a delusion entirely surrounded by liars in old clothes.'

This world-shattering fact was first revealed to me on November 28, 1978. You may wonder how I can be so precise about the date. Indeed, you may ask, what sort of twisted mind stores away such trivia? The answer is simple. I got this piece of information from my desk calendar. It's one of the type that greets you each morning with a different and uplifting message.

For instance, as I write, towards the end of 1979, I note that on January 2, 1980, I shall learn that 'A change in the weather can often create a new world for us.'

Now that's more like it. You see, although I do at times tend to tell little lies about certain aspects of the fish I catch, and although I

really should do something about my shabby fishing gear, I object to being confronted with the truth in such a brutal fashion. Anyway, I never delude myself – well, not often. So while I do not agree with the first statement, I can confirm absolutely the validity of the second. As far as anglers are concerned a change in the weather does often create a whole new world for us, and certainly at that time of year a change in the weather is the thought uppermost in every angler's mind.

My calendar doesn't say who wrote either of these quotations, but I should think the first was penned by some disgruntled pessimist – the type of angler who knows all, but catches nothing. You have probably met him. He is the one at the bar who can recite the life-cycle of the brown trout backwards; re-late riveting tales of skilfully caught monster trout – caught by himself, of course; knows all the 'right' people; has access to all the best waters; and has decimated the fish stocks of some of the finest rivers in the world. When you finally per-suade this God-like creature to be your guest on your private beat of the Tay, don't be surprised. You will spend half the day climbing trees to retrieve his casts and gen-erally have to wet-nurse what is as-suredly an inexperienced beginner.

It becomes easy to understand how a man like that can be responsible for such a jaundiced and sarcastic statement. The fact that he chooses to remain anonymous means he is still out there, somewhere, and doesn't want to be recognised. However, that should be easy. He'll be the one in new plus-fours and natty deer-stalker – no old clothes for him!

For myself, however, clothes do play an important part in fishing. Their choice is about as important as having the right fly. Particularly up here in the North of Scotland. Open-necked shirt and slacks may be fine for Easter in Hampshire, but would be utter madness for April on Orkney.

Last spring a friend invited me to spend a day on the Helmsdale. It was to be my first visit to this magnificent Highland river, and I fervently prayed for reasonable weather. As it transpired, we had a fishless, freezing day, dogged by weal-raising hailstones and forty-mile-per-hour blizzards. Never-theless, it was a most enjoyable day and I suffered little discomfiture due to the weather. I had gone prepared: String vest, woollen shirt, two woollen pullovers, heavy tweed sports jacket, fishing coat and anorak. Down below were three pairs of socks, pants, tweed trousers, two pairs of over-trousers and boots.

The whole was loosely rounded-off and decorated with gloves and an 8 foot long hand-knitted scarf. As far as I was con-cerned the weather could do its worst. Safe within my cocoon I was completely impervious to it.

Of course, people react in differ-ent ways to the cold. Many a time I have come across some hardy Highlander, hatless and snow-smothered, kilt blowing free in the gale, earnestly fishing away. As I waddle by, pitching slightly in the wind, I manage to catch his inevitably cheery greeting.

'Grand day for it, eh! Any luck yet?'

The remainder is whisked off in the teeth of the storm.

My wife suffers most dreadfully from the cold. During the early months of the trout season a glance at her face is a more accurate indicator of fishing conditions than any thermometer. Over the years she has accumulated a vast array of trousers, jackets, rugs, plaids, scarves, hats, blankets and gloves with which she positively festoons herself. I almost have to 'build' her into the boat, layer after carefully-wrapped layer. All that generally remains recognisable at the end of this process is the protruding cigarette and faintly discernible outline of her fingers rapidly manipulating rod and line. I wouldn't mind so much except for the infuriating fact that she always seems to catch more fish into the bargain.

However, summer does eventually come, even up here in Caithness. The wind drops, we take the heavy ballast stones from our pockets, adopt an unaccustomed upright posture and stride over the hills in our never-ending search for trout. With clothing as light as our hearts we haunt the beautiful hill lochs throughout the long summer days. In June it never really gets dark. At times we stay out all night and share some magic tarn with a curious otter or lonely red-throated diver. Sometimes it is so hot that fishing becomes impossible and swimming a necessity.

I remember one blistering August afternoon on a remote hill loch. After carefully stacking my clothes, I was wallowing about in the warm shallows when a large trout rose towards the middle. I scrambled to the bank, grabbed my rod, and since most of our lochs are fairly shallow, gingerly waded out. With the water lapping my chin, arms and rod above my head, I cast and hooked, played and landed a magnificent 2 lb wild brown trout.

I feel that this story illustrates the truth of the change-in-the-weather theory. Unless I had been swimming, I would never have been able to cover that fish, and I wouldn't have been swimming unless there had been a change in the weather. Anyway, it was the only fish caught all day.

So whether or not you happen to suffer from delusions, have a tendency to fish strangely dressed or undressed, or are even guilty of telling the occasional little lie, a word of warning: Before attempting any bare-bank fishing make sure of your casting technique. Otherwise you might be quite surprised by what you catch!

🙠 *And who could ever put it better than John Garthmyl!*

THE WELL-DRESSED ANGLER
by J.G., *February 1975*

When you're fishin', huntin', shootin'
You must wear the proper suitin'
If you want to do your thing in proper
*   style.*
And at least you can make certain,
When at Moss Bros or at Burton,
That you clothe yourself above the rank
*   and vile.*

There are other kinds of sportin'
In which some men go cavortin',
Such as rabbitin', and rattin', and
*   the like,*
Where it doesn't really matter
If you're dressed in rag-and-tatter
And turn up at the meetin' on a bike.

But when paddlin' after otters
You must wear your knickerbockers
And display your calves in stockin's
*   bright of hue.*
And it's wrong to go out huntin'
In the clothes you pole a punt in,
Or those you go in, rowin', as a Blue.

If you want to bring the fish up
You'll wear knickers like a Bishop,
And natty, tasselled garters like a
*   Knight.*
If your breeks show signs of fallin'
(And the thought is quite appallin')
You'll belt up like an Earl to hold
*   'em tight.*

But I realise now I'm older
And my knees are getting colder,
And a little bit of comfort is my wish,
That the clothes one wears while fishin'
Though they're in the sportin' fashion,
Are no damned help at all in catchin'
*   fish.*

All the feathers in yer titfer
Ain't no good – No! not a bit fer
The successful pursuance of your art,
For unless you've got the knowledge
That they do not teach at college,
It ain't no good just dressin' for the
*   part.*

Chapter four

THE STILLWATER
REVOLUTION

❧ *Up to the early sixties, stillwater trout fishing was a sport for those living in traditional brown trout areas but then, with the opening of drinking-water reservoirs in the Midlands, came the opportunity for anglers who had never picked a fly rod up in their lives to turn to trout.*

❧ *Information for these newcomers was at a premium. Little was known about the right tackle, flies or the tactics to use. Those anglers who did know their stillwater fishing became overnight celebrities.*

❧ *Many of these new trout fishers were very knowledgeable coarse anglers and simply transferred their methods to the new sport. The result was little short of a revolution, with new ideas overtaking old ones almost by the day.*

❧ *Northampton produced many of those early stillwater fishing pioneers. Cyril Inwood ranked high among them and there's little doubt that his series published thirty years ago had a great influence in the still infant sport.*

FLY FISHING ON LAKES AND
RESERVOIRS
by CYRIL INWOOD, *November 1960*

ALTHOUGH I hope that readers will derive some benefit from what follows, I would like to make it quite clear to the beginner that with the best intentions in the world no man can guarantee results in stillwater fishing.

Trout are wily and unpredictable, and every angler who fishes lakes and reservoirs will know the disappointment that can end a day started with high hopes. The absence of shallow runs, deep pools and eddies which are a natural assistance in river fishing makes a different approach necessary. And that is only acquired by experience.

On most of our lakes and reservoirs the rule is flies only. Although arguments can be brought against this policy I will confine myself to the various aspects of fly fishing.

To enjoy success combined with comfort the first and most important thing is choice of tackle. With no hesitation I would say that a good two-joint rod with a lockfast ferrule and bridge rings is the most satisfactory. With continual casting suction ferrules are apt to work loose and twist round, interfering with the smooth flow of the cast.

Length of rod can be a controversial point among trout anglers, but many of us find a 10 or 11 foot rod most suitable for bank fishing. I realise that not everyone will run to the expense of several rods, so when buying remember that a trout rod does much heavy work, a good reservoir angler casting 20–25 yards and sometimes more. My advice, therefore, is a good quality rod, and the outlay of a pound or

two in the first place will probably save some heartache and a good deal of pocketache later on.

The choice of length is really dependent on the strength of one's wrist, a longer rod obviously being of greater help in casting long distances. So buy with your own comfort in mind. Otherwise you may find your wrist and arm aching long before the day is through, resulting in a loss of interest and fish.

From many makes of reel individual choice can vary, but I like a 3½ inch diameter reel of well-known make. This will take a No. 3 double taper line and 50 yards of 12 lb silk or nylon backing without risk of line-guard friction which can spoil the line by rubbing off the dressing.

There are, too, many makes of lines from which to choose. Some anglers prefer a balanced line, presumably because it is easier to cast and also enables one to cast longer distances, but I dislike these on the grounds that they do not float so well. And they have a tendency to go down rather heavily which puts the fish down, cancelling out any advantage gained by longer casting.

In choosing waders, either thigh or breast are suitable, but it is certainly advisable to make sure the boots are studded. I have seen anglers come to grief when fishing from dams (these are rather steep on some reservoirs) and the slippery surface in wet weather is something of a hazard when wearing smooth-soled boots.

The selection of a landing net too can be more important than one would at first think. A large one of sea trout size is advisable as many reservoirs hold fish of 10 lb or more. Too small a net may result in the loss of the fish of a lifetime. Most flick-up nets have a clip for attaching to the belt, but these can be unreliable as when wading through weeds the clip may become disengaged, and the loss of the net unnoticed until required. I find the best plan is to push the handle right down the belt thus making it both safe and at the ready.

For a three-fly, tapered cast, I make up my own by joining one yard each of 5 lb, 6 lb and 7 lb breaking strain. This is quite satisfactory unless fishing waters like Chew Valley when I use a straight cast of 7 lb or 8 lb breaking strain.

Single-fly fishing calls for a straight cast of from 5 lb to 8 lb according to the size of fly used. I usually have my straight casts 12

foot long. This enables me to get well down without sinking line and avoids having any thick line, which tends to scare off fish, near the fly.

Selection of flies to use in any given month will probably present a problem to a beginner. I will give an indication of my own choice of lures which I take with me each month through the season. I hope it may prove helpful.

Ready-made flies are, of course, on sale at all tackle dealers. Some of these are rather more ornamental than useful, and the novice will grow more selective with experience. Many practised anglers tie their own flies and a good many of my own are made as a result of studying the contents of a trout's stomach. I'll go into greater detail about that later.

Most reservoirs are open for fishing in early April. At this period the flies to use are Black Lure, Alexandra Lure, Alexandra and Silver Butcher size 14 to 6, also Black Spiders, Corixa and Worm Fly. Some of these I use leaded, that is with fine lead wire whipped on to the body before dressing. This is to aid sinking, and it is useful at times on Nymphs in sizes 10 to 6.

The foregoing flies are my choice although the following can be used with some success: Peter Ross, Dunkeld, Claret and Mallard, Blae and Black, Coch-y-bondhu (size 6), Wickham and Greenwell's Glory.

In May all these flies can be used, with the addition of the following: Black Hawthorn, Green Nymph, Alder, Invicta, Grannom Buzzer Nymphs, Chironomus Tentans and C. Viridis.

June brings additions to the fly box in the shape of the Dragon-Fly Nymph, Green and Blue, Black Gnats dry and wet, and Coch-y-bondhu (14's) dry.

July is not as a rule a good month, the water being warm and clear, and the sun too hot; a grand time to be out but more often than not with poor results. Flies to try in this month are Worm Fly, Corixa, Invicta, Dragon-Fly Nymphs, Green and Blue, small Green and Brown Nymphs, Alexandras (14's), small Butchers (14's), Coch-y-bondhu (14's) and Grannom.

August and September are similar in most respects, requiring Worm Fly, Corixa, Invicta (14's), Wickhams, Coch-y-bondhu, Mallard and Claret, Black Lure, Alexandra Lure, Alexandra and Butchers (14's to 6's). Dunkeld, Buzzer Nymph, Dragon-Fly Nymph, Green and Blue, Greenwell's Glory, Grannoms and Brown Nymphs (14's to 6's).

LET SWALLOWS SPOT THE RISES
by CYRIL INWOOD, December 1960

LAST MONTH I gave an inventory of flies to be used. Now let us have a look at the best methods to present them in various conditions.

April in any average year is cold and windy, and if nature follows the orthodox pattern, showers and fleeting periods of sunshine are also prevalent, and often during this alternate dull and bright weather there are hatches of fly.

Whenever possible, keep the prevailing wind behind. This obviously facilitates casting and is in any case more comfortable. Tackle up with a 6 lb level cast and a big brown or black nymph size 6 and leaded. Rub some mud or clay on the cast or put on small split shot to aid sinking.

Knowledge of the water being fished is a decided advantage, but try to locate a point at which the bed rises out of deep water, or a shelf six to 10 feet deep. Wade out carefully, and when the water begins to get deeper, start to work the line out about 15 to 20 yards. Wait a little to allow the nymph to reach bottom then begin to work it in very slowly.

Most nymphs don't move fast. Retrieve the fly until it is only a few yards from you. This is a method that can pay off well, and is at times deadly. If the response to this is slow, change to a nymph that has not been leaded and work it near the surface. Alternatively try an Alexandra Lure, letting this go well down and retrieving it at a much faster rate.

The changing moods of April can bring mild sunny spells and frequently this warmer atmosphere will bring a hatch of Blae and Black. This is the time to change to a tapered cast with two droppers, tying a Blae and Black on the point and Greenwell's Glory next. For the second dropper I use a fly I tie myself which I call a Black Starling, and which I find to be a good killer. (I will give the dressing in a future article). These flies should all be size 14's and worked near the surface.

Dull cold and windy days are all too frequent in April and it is on such days I like to use three silver-bodied flies – Butcher, Alexandra and Silver Magpie, all size 14's. This last fly is a particular favourite of mine on water that also holds coarse fish. The lovely green sheen of this fly seems to make it a surer killer than the others, probably because it is mistaken for a small roach or rudd.

Late April will bring hatches of Hawthorns and Olives. When the Hawthorns are blowing about, use three wet flies on one cast and retrieve at a normal pace. If this fails to attract fish, change to a 5 lb level cast using one fly. Grease the cast to within a foot of the fly and float it flat on its side like a natural, twitching the line to move the fly in a spasmodic movement.

If Olives are hatching, change the cast to a level 6 lbs, put on a size 8 Brown Nymph and fish just below the surface moving very slowly. Alternatively use three flies on a tapered cast, a Golden Wickham on the point and top dropper with a Greenwell's Glory in between.

When twilight begins to fall I invariably move to deeper water, such as where there is a deep shell, a deepish bay or the wall of a dam.

As a rule I already have the 14 foot rod assembled for this period of the day with a straight 7 or 8 lb cast greased right to the point.

This is the time big fish seem to move in. Using a size 6 Coch-y-bondhu or Alexandra Lure, I stand perfectly still and quiet and cast a short line. Not more than two or three yards touches the water, I let it remain a few seconds, and bring it towards me very slowly, raising the line off the water so that only the fly makes a wake. This I have found to be highly successful, often taking the limit in the last 15 minutes of fishing time after being without a fish all day.

Although nothing is certain about this climate of ours, the month of May should bring warmer days, promoting weed growth which in turn brings plenty of insect life. The predominant hatches are now Olives, Alders and Buzzers or Grannom, and before starting to fish, a little bird-watching will probably pay dividends. The birds to look for are swallows, which can spot a hatch of fly far quicker than the angler, and will be swooping in considerable numbers to the various points of hatch rise to pick the flies off the water.

Make for these places and determine which fly is hatching. If it is Olives and fish are rising but the water flat and calm, try a dry Olive or Wickham, an alternative being a Brown Nymph fished just below the surface. Accurate casting is essential to place your fly in the ring before the fish moves off. With a ripple on the water a three-fly cast (Wickhams and Greenwells size 14 or 12) as used in April, might be tried to advantage.

Around a Buzzer hatch I use different methods, fishing three Brown or Red Nymphs on a tapered cast for rough water, or a single on a straight cast for calm water, fished dry. When using the single fly bring it in about a foot at a time after letting it rest a few moments. Do this with a jerky movement making a wake. This can be quite productive late in the evening. Worm Fly and Corixas may also be used in this way.

Should the day be rough the

hatches will blow to the opposite bank and the succession of waves will stir the bottom. Move round then and fish into the wind, not trying to use a long line but fishing across the waves a few yards out moving along the bank. Often it is not necessary to wade, and fish will take right up to the feet. Flies to use are Alexandra, Butcher, Wickham, Greenwell's Glory, Dunkeld, Invicta and Worm Fly.

June, with the usual reservation for the unexpected, is usually a most pleasant month for trout fishing, from the pure pleasure of being out to the improved chances of sport. The weeds are up, water in the shallows is warmer and into both the fish will move to feed. As mentioned previously, the wind direction and birds will help to decide the best approach and if any Olives are hatching fish as in May.

This is the period for the Coch-y-bondhu, and many of these are blown from the tops of the weeds. Wading into the weed bed you will see trout taking these flies along the fringe and the best

method I have found is to put a Cochy dry, on a 6 lb, 12 foot cast. A small hackle tied at both ends of the fly will help to keep it up. Cast about a foot from the edge of the weeds, no more, and wait for the take.

Trout, of course, are no fools and the majority will take you straight into the weeds where in all probability you will lose them. If, however, you watch your line after a take, and it moves out a foot or two, strike and then give the fish line to fight it out in the open. Have your landing net ready and give the fish the butt to bring it straight over the weeds into the net.

In my best year fishing this way I took 98 fish ranging from 1 lb to 5 lb 11 oz, but how many I lost in the weeds I do not know.

Flies to try in June are Worm Fly, Black Lure, Peacock Lure, and Black, Green or Brown Nymphs tied to 14 hook on 5 lb 12 foot casts. Fishing these near the surface will pick up the odd fish or two when sport is otherwise slack.

&* *Richard Connell was already a knowledgeable stillwater fisherman when he took over the reins of Ardleigh reservoir and his anglers benefited greatly from his experience gained north of the Border.*

&* *Written over thirty years ago, this article contained much of what is regarded as new thinking by today's stillwater fishers.*

&* *Fishing for trout in stillwater for Richard Connell was anything but the pulling back of a lure until something stopped its progress, and his advice on how to read the rise is as valid now as when it was offered all those years ago.*

READING THE RISE IN STILLWATER
by RICHARD CONNELL, *July 1960*

FISHING A river an angler observing a rising trout can normally be reasonably certain of its position and the placing of the cast required to bring his fly within its vision.

Fishing a loch it is often not realised that a trout may, within seconds, be yards away from the rise. The advice, so often extended, to drop the fly within the ripples of the rise will assure failure in many instances. The cruising fish, intent on water ahead, won't see it.

My own loch has a high bank overlooking weeded shallows, with some very deep water. On calm days with the correct light I have been able to conceal myself and watch the rising habits of fish up to 3 lb. I discovered that in many cases it was possible to tell from the shape or pattern of the rise ripples and the manner in which they erupted upon the surface, just how the fish was moving. I could tell if he was definitely on the cruise and his speed and direction, or whether he was operating from a lie on the bottom and interested only in a small area of the water.

A cruising trout feeding on or near the surface, generally comes up in a smooth unhurried arch. He may break with his snout. Sometimes (particularly if large) he sucks. Always the ripples will break strongest from that spot and move with greatest energy in the direction of travel. There will be a tendency for the rise to 'point' the way the trout is going. The ripples will be close together at this 'point,' the gap between circles widening towards the tail. The greater the speed of the fish the more elliptical will be the shape of the rise.

Occasionally a secondary disturbance will occur after the first break. This is caused by the tail coming up as the fish drops down again. It serves to emphasise the position of the trout's head. It can, however, confuse the pattern of the rise if the first break was not seen, by creating a second 'point.' An exaggerated description of the pattern of a cruising fish's rise would be a rise within a V, the apex of the V pointing the direction of travel.

Most fish move rapidly for a yard or so immediately after the rise, steadying to a speed of about one foot per second. They will range over astonishing distances. The larger fish I have followed sometimes for over 200 yards before they turned.

The angler presenting his flies to such a trout, having 'read' the rise, must decide upon a point which will be two to three feet in front of the moving fish when his cast lands. He will consider, in calculating, the speed and direction of the trout and the time taken to place

his flies. In landing the cast ahead of the fish, be careful to keep the line from landing over it.

From the bank mentioned I have directed the activities of an angler fishing from the narrow path below. Flies landing in front or even slightly to the side of a moving trout were always investigated. Anything behind seldom made any impression – unless very close. Flies landed on the trout's nose either caused him to grab at once or put him down.

Trout moving up from the bottom worked in most cases in water of two feet or more. Often they moved where it was quite deep. Such fish come up very rapidly, returning in a flash to the original position on the bottom. Often the fly which attracted will be missed. This is frequently the fish which the angler rises two or three times in succession without hooking. The suddenness of the eruption and the rapidity with which the burst of the tail follows the break, forming sometimes a double rise, are good indications. An oily swirl will form in the centre of the rings. Flurry and splash may be associated with the rise.

The pattern will be closer to the conventional round shape, the rings being much more evenly spaced than when pushed by a forward moving fish, which stays near the surface. An angler recognising this rise must place his cast where the break occurred. The trout, having returned to his lie, will have his eyes on the same area of surface.

Fishing from a boat the drift speed must be considered. It is essential, having decided moving fish or resting fish, speed and direction, to react with rapidity and accuracy considering all factors.

I do not suggest that every rise can be classed under the two types described or that on every occasion the angler will be correct in his deductions.

A certain proportion of the fish observed rising followed varied and individual courses, which no pattern in the rise could predict. Generally, however, the principles are sound and an angler applying himself to such a study may well observe details which so far have escaped me, or evolve sound principles of his own.

It is the rapid assimilation of detail and the interpretation of its significance, in relation to the movements of the fish, which are important. A most valuable 'sixth sense' can be developed.

He who troubles to learn the art of 'reading the rise' will appreciate its value, not on days when fish are moving freely so much as when the odd fish only is showing and a catch depends upon making the best of the few opportunities.

 Probably because it was moving on at such a pace and the thirst for new knowledge was so great, stillwater fishing threw up more than its fair share of add-water experts who, with just a few seasons under their Barbours, offered themselves as authorities.

 Trout and Salmon has always steered well clear of these nine-day prophets, relying on angler-writers with extensive knowledge or authors who really did have something genuinely innovative to reveal. Charles Jardine, author of the nexr article, was such an angler and his pieces have inspired, informed and entertained readers for some time.

❧ Dry-fly fishing on stillwater, although thought of as an entirely new approach in the late eighties, was by no means a new method, having been practised in traditional trout-fishing areas for many years. But as ever, Charles Jardine had new things to say and knew how to say them.

STILLWATERS AND THE DRY FLY

by CHARLES JARDINE, *January 1988*

IT IS now 25 years since my baptism with a fly-rod. My world then revolved around a diminutive chalkstream, and its reflections portrayed another age – cane rods, sometimes gut casts (if pocket money was short) and the undeniable penance of silk lines, which to young eyes always sank at the wrong time and required interminable care and doctoring. Then there were the delicately fashioned flies of Ogden Smith in the now curious sizes of 000, 00 or 1: also a singular tranquillity broken only by my father's exacting tutorship. Above all, there was a new-found love – the dry-fly.

As with all neophytes, my thirst for knowledge was vociferous, no piscatorial stone being left unturned, and, gradually, I became aware of other vistas. The 'revolution' was, of course, on the horizon.

Grafham, in many ways, was the turning point, fly fishing life perhaps never being quite the same again. Suddenly new words filled my piscatorial vocabulary: rainbows, buzzers, lures, streamers, sinkers, fibreglass and shooting-heads. Inexorably I was drawn into this web of innovation and monster trout of 3 lb–4 lb, reliving every descriptive 100-yard run of reel-burning chaos.

Amid this mental Nirvana a door slammed shut. I read somewhere that river anglers seldom made good reservoir fishers and that their tackle, attitudes and methods were wholly unsuitable for large stillwaters. Crestfallen, I retreated and continued my love-affair with floating fly and river delicacy, shunning any unfriendly reservoir.

That was many years ago. Nowadays I hold almost equal affection for both still and running water and freely admit that the complexities afforded by large reservoirs require a tactical agility and understanding on an entirely different plateau from stream fishing.

But the one presiding element is that I have always fished them *as* stillwaters – the two waterborn philosophies never appearing to meet. Recently, however, instances have occurred to alter this opinion. I am now convinced that certain circumstances on reservoirs can benefit from a river-orientated doctrine – especially concerning the dry-fly.

It was to be Blagdon's north shore, with a southerly wind blowing left to right, that convinced me and evaporated a 20-year-old burden. Caenis were responsible. All along the conveyor belt of tiny white spinners undulated the trout, their familiar erratic 'gulps' furrowing the surface film. True to stillwater form, I opted for a Grey Duster, then something else, then a 'white thing' and then a 'black thing' and so on. Increasingly, the familiar frustration was leaching into every unco-ordinated cast of defiance.

Eventually I stopped, and mentally pictured what I would do given this problem on a river. Immediately, I retied my leader, discarding the 4 lb nylon in favour of 2 lb and, tying on a size 22 hen

wing, singled out an individual fish and cast, accurately. Six fish later, I felt that perhaps I was getting somewhere. That was five years ago and it would, of course, be folly to claim anything new or innovative about dry-fly use – indeed, there are few anglers who either do not fish or at least carry, floating patterns. Both sedges and 'daddies' are considered high spots in our stillwater tactical calendar, but it appears there is always a sense of surprise when a buoyant artificial is accepted by the trout. Why?

In river terms, a rising trout is viewed, logically, as a surface feeder, the angler merely evaluating to what extent this may be – either in, on, or just underneath the surface film, and acting accordingly. The stillwater angler generally sees this same fish as a candidate for a lightly dressed pattern, usually a midge trapped in the surface film. The chances are that he is often right in this assumption, but I do wonder just how many potential dry-fly situations are viewed in this way and, of course, missed.

Similarly, the actual patterns used on stillwater normally conform to the refugees from river

THE BEST OF TROUT AND SALMON

worlds, save the Sedge/Caddis. There appear to be few calculated dry representations of specific reservoir forms, and golden opportunities, I am certain, are also missed because of this.

If we again look at the stream fisherman's credo of 'If it interests the trout while floating, match it, at least tolerably' – which may necessitate hook sizes from 28 to 12 – we begin to see the real potential of dry-fly on stillwater, with its vast and varied insect population. How well I remember reading that adult midges (chironomidae) were very rarely taken by trout! Suffice it to say that the past two seasons have seen this type of pattern in my top ten of all-round effective patterns.

I could go on quoting instances of the floating-fly's potential and theory and perhaps labour the point, but, before touching on various methods, usage and tackle, it is worth mentioning one dry-fly tactic which is now almost 'traditional' and for years has been a favourite with Grafham anglers. 'Hopper fishing', in essence, is fishing from a moving boat with either a single Sedge or two Sedges or Daddy-longlegs patterns, short-lined and held static in the surface

film – imitating a trapped adult. This method also gained popularity at Bewl Water last September, accounting for many memorable bags of fish. It is, however, the mere tip of an enormous iceberg.

My choice of tackle for fishing dry on stillwater is influenced by my river fishing and by how trout feed on surface fly. Line weights above AFTM 7 can be excluded as their thicker profile will often scare a surface-feeding fish or lead to problems when one is hooked, the extra drag through a larger surface area seldom protecting the necessarily fine tippets involved. For preference, and when conditions allow, opt for AFTM 5s and 6s. Naturally the line must float! Indeed, the higher the better. It seems to matter little whether you use double-taper or weight-forward – I personally prefer a WF or, better still, a long belly for both their accuracy at range and their running line that offers less resistance to a hooked fish.

Rods are emotive – one man's meat definitely being another's poison. I leave the choice to you – but obviously it must accommodate the light lines and function correctly, the criteria being a fastish tip-middle action that will not only

138

THE STILLWATER REVOLUTION

react quickly, set a hook at range, but protect fine nylon in the process. Length, however, is important. Normally, I use a 9 foot 6 inch or 9 foot model, both of which fit the dual bill of boat and bank-fishing. I have found there is seldom any advantage offered by longer rods in boat-fishing and some distinct disadvantages when on the bank – strike delay and inaccuracy being just two.

As in nymph-fishing, leaders are a crucial part of the tackle system. I do prefer, though, limp nylon as opposed to stiff, but thereafter my leader is similar to a nymph set-up, varying between 14 foot and 16 foot or, if two or more flies are employed, up to 24 foot. The two essential criteria are good turnover and that the tippet section sinks – but you may find it far better to reduce length in order to achieve a straight and accurate presentation than a coiled mass of nylon with a dry-fly sitting gallantly in the middle. That the tippet sinks is crucial in order to avoid any potential fish-scaring nylon flash, or shadow. I confess to having rejoiced over the invention of braided-leader butts, the dry-fly fishers' answer to a prayer. They are, by no means, essential, but help in both presentation and shock-absorption.

There is little else needed except good flotant (Gink or Permaflote), nylon sinkant and the usual paraphernalia we all insist we must have (but seldom need), for a day's fishing.

On the three tactics I use for stillwater dry-fly fishing – static, twitch and drifted – the most useful is probably the static – in river terms the 'dead drift' or 'drag-free float'. It constantly surprises me how few people realise that a dragging fly and its uselessness is not confined merely to rivers. Stillwaters flow, not, perhaps like rivers, but currents which are created by wind or undertow can render a fly equally fishless and laboured with drag. This, of course, necessitates a constant appraisal of the flies' antics.

Thereafter, the method is simplicity itself and is by no means confined to times of rising activity.

Trout – especially rainbow – appear to be curious by nature, and will often inspect and accept a floating artificial simply out of conditioned reflex, rising through water levels to do so. It must, however, be stressed that it is not a 'chuck and chance it' operation – weedbeds, stream inlets, indeed any likely nymph-holding areas are obvious options if no trout are rising.

Whenever possible, match the insect in evidence. If this is a 'multiple hatch', as it often is, then choose the dominant species and ring the changes from there. The permutations around this alone are almost limitless, as is the time of day for fishing dry. Personal experience can be the only guideline. However, one instance typifies this form of fishing, and again Blagdon was responsible.

Dawn on any reservoir is a special and evocative period; the stillness of this particular one was broken only by the odd dimple far out on the mist-laden surface. Everywhere at my wadered feet lay the dead fruits of the previous evening's harvest – spent grouse-wing sedge. So it seemed logical to try an artificial in this guise. Carefully wading out of the water. I

knotted on a delta-wing Spent Caddis and prepared to re-enter the water. To one side of me, along the shoreline in no more than a foot of water, a brown shoulder broke, crumpling the surface. On my knees I cast, half across land, half on water, and the fish took and presented me with my best ever West Country brownie (comparatively modest for there) at 3 lb 2 oz. This leads to many questions, one being why we don't try as many spent flies as we should.

Dawn, throughout the summer, will reveal the spent forms of a previous evening emergence, and all are at their most vulnerable to the trout's attention. Incidentally, I now carry as many spent types as fully winged adults. But I realise that of all static forms of dry-fly fishing this is perhaps the most demanding mentally. It is positively agonising waiting for that one moment of truth, or refusal, and resisting the urge to lift off and try again.

The twitched or skated fly relies on very basic criteria: first, sufficient ripple to disguise any minor imperfections and secondly that the type of insect imitated actually engages in such energetic pursuits.

This fact alone confines one to Sedges and the occasional Daddy-longlegs (though I have consistently found a dry Daddy is best left well alone): thirdly, the pattern must be buoyant. Hairwinged patterns such as Elkhair Caddis, Humpies/Goofus Bugs and so on are all extremely good for being bounced and tumbled through the waves. It does, however, largely preclude our more delicate insects such as upwings (caenis, lake and pond olives etc.) and adult midges. Twitching such patterns can seriously detract from their static charms. The method is simplicity itself and much the same as fishing a Muddler through the surface. But you must take a rest now and then: watch any sedge on its travels for propagation or egg-laying purposes and you will soon see that nature indicates the method you should use.

The drifted dry-fly is slightly different again, but echoes more the static method than the vigorous 'twitch'. It is entirely a bank-bound pursuit, for all one does is to walk the dry-fly downwind, thus not only covering great expanses of water but presenting the fly drag-free on all occasions. Angler-free banks are essential!

The remaining, but perhaps less familiar, sucessful ways with a static dry-fly are as follows:

First a method which evolved last year and owes its parentage to the 'Grafham Hopper' ploy, though the offspring is rather different. It is a method which utilises a moving boat drifting broadside but, rather than 'short-lining', the angler should adopt a long-range strategy of 'fine and far off'. It is, in essence, simplicity itself. All you need is a long leader (upwards of 20 feet) with two droppers – a dry-fly on the point, a buoyant pupa on the dropper and another dry-fly (possibly fractionally larger) on the bob. Positioning may vary, but ideally there should be at least four feet between fly positions. Your flies are either cast downwind to upwardly moving and/or feeding fish, or cast in the normal long-lining style in the general area of expected activity. Thereafter, all you have to do is to keep in contact with the flies. This, of course, depends upon the speed of the boat and the wind strength, so retrieve rates must echo these. Often a steady figure-of-eight is all that is required. Occasionally an easy stripping motion might be necessary, the one essential being that

angler, line and flies are in contac-
with one another – a slack line is
useless for this style.

The idea behind this method is
to present the flies naturally buoyant but avoiding any line wake –
hence the suspended nymph. A
buoyant Buzzer is ideal as is the
Fraser Booby Nymph – even a tiny
greased Muddler would suffice.
The middle fly is really only a supporting actor to the two dry-fly
stars – and thus sacrificial. Takes,
or better still rises, are subtlety itself
– no bravado, seldom a flurry –
usually a tiny dimple or, at best, a
brief ring of a rise. Alertness is essential, as are good polarising
glasses and a peaked hat or cap. Although this method works well
when sedge/caddis are about, it is

at its deadliest when adult midges
come out to play.

One last thought on static flies –
indeed on dry-fly fishing on stillwater. Never be afraid to fish small.
So often there is a mental barrier at
size 16. Last season at Bewl Water
saw evenings when I fished exclusively with Micro Caddis and
Midges on sizes 20 and 22 and had
heart-pumping moments to show
for these delicate eccentricities of
mine. A small wire and barb will
hold every bit as well as its larger
counterpart and trout, the supreme
judges of our fly-tying efforts, appear to accept them with an almost
casual positiveness, often carrying
on for many yards, making striking
– as it always should be when fishing dry – a mere lift of the rod tip.

❧ *By the mid-seventies, many stillwater trout fishers had already made the
decision to leave the lure box at home. True, lures caught trout but the
method produced little of the delights of watching a trout
sip in a fly off or close to the surface.*
❧ *What fly to use was important, but the way they were offered gave those
anglers who understood the subtleties of accurate presentation
far more consistent results.*

❧ Keeping the fly in the vital eye-to-fly position for as long as possible by greasing either the fly or the leader was something still quite new, but not to John Goddard, who offered some sound advice on when and where to apply floatants.

TO GREASE OR NOT TO GREASE?

by JOHN GODDARD, May 1975

I AM SURPRISED at the comparatively large number of still-water trout fishermen I have encountered over the last two or three seasons who seem unaware of the importance of oil or grease, or the lack of it, on their flies or leaders. In fact, these floatants can often mean the difference between success and failure, and are vitally important under most conditions.

Several different brands of line grease are available, but my preference is for the plain Mucilin in the little green tin. This is supplied with a felt pad for application to the leader, but it should be used sparingly.

Oil or floatant for flies is offered either in bottles or aerosol-type sprays. Again, my personal preference is for the preparation first recommended by Richard Walker in *Trout and Salmon* two or three years ago. It is in liquid form and is best kept in a wide-mouth screw-top bottle, so that the whole fly, no matter how large, can be dipped,

preferably some little time before use to allow it to dry out thoroughly. Flies treated with this oil float beautifully for several hours.

Several preparations can be obtained for degreasing leaders or flies, from ordinary liquid glycerine to thick mud from the edge of the water, which will suffice if nothing else is available. Liquid detergent is good, but I prefer glycerine mixed with Fuller's earth.

A basic error made by many anglers is to apply grease too liberally to the leader in an effort to ensure that the dry fly does not become waterlogged. You should always apply it lightly, and always leave the last 6 inches completely free of grease. Some fishermen do not realise the disturbance a greased line creates as it is retrieved on the surface. Under calm conditions this will be immediately apparent, but in rough water it is not noticeable to the angler, though it is to the trout.

The same applies when you are using wet flies or nymphs on a floating line. If you need to fish these at any depth, it is essential to degrease both flies and leader before you start to fish. It should also be appreciated that the application of grease to different sections of the leader can predetermine the depth at which the various flies on it will fish.

For example, from midsummer onwards when a lot of sedge-flies are about, an extremely effective method is to use in conjunction with a floating line a dry Sedge pattern on the dropper with a Sedge Pupa artificial on the point. In this case the leader above the dry fly is greased, while the remainder down to the point fly which must be retrieved just below the surface is thoroughly degreased. Or you may wish to retrieve a dry Sedge, Invicta or similar pattern in the surface film. This can be a killing method when trout are feeding on the adult sedge, for they will often ignore a dry Sedge fished on the surface, but readily accept the same pattern fished in the film. They seem to take this for a sedge-fly hatching. To ensure that your

chosen pattern fishes in the correct position, you must degrease the leader and sparsely oil the artificial. Too much oil and it will float too high, too little and it will sink too far below the surface.

To illustrate the importance of this aspect of fly fishing, let me recount an incident I was involved in last season. The time was early July and I had arranged to take a friend for a day's boat fishing on one of our larger reservoirs. Fairly new to this style of fishing, he asked me to guide him on which patterns to use and how to fish them. Few fish were rising and anglers were having most successes to deeply retrieved lures.

Observing several sedge-flies fluttering in the margins, I felt it should be possible to take a few fish on the surface despite the complete absence of rises. Under these conditions it would be necessary to attract the trout to our flies, so it was essential to use a large dry, well-oiled Sedge on the dropper with an Invicta fished just below the surface on the point. I explained this to my friend and advised him to grease the leader above the Sedge. We then started a nice drift over water not too deep, where the trout should be able to see the disturbance created by the Sedge on the dropper even if they were lying near the bottom.

Sure enough the method was successful, and during the next two hours I boated four nice trout and rose several others which came short. The disturbance created by the Sedge attracted them to the surface where most accepted the Invicta. Despite the fact that he was fishing the same method with similar flies my companion rose only one fish. I checked his flies, leader and even the distance between flies, but could not account for this. We also changed places in the boat, but all to no avail. Eventually I suggested we exchange rods, and the reason for his lack of success was immediately apparent. The flies were fishing incorrectly as he had greased the leader between the two flies instead of the section only above the Sedge on the dropper, I corrected this for him and within five minutes he was delightedly playing a fine plump trout.

This clearly demonstrates the extreme importance of this aspect of fly fishing.

From a situation reigning only a few years earlier when stillwater anglers used all methods and techniques to deceive their quarry, the mid-seventies saw a gathering together of like-minded fishers who denigrated methods other than the one chosen by themselves.

The nymph, and later on the dry fly – and the smaller the more respectable – was the 'only' way to catch stillwater trout.

Lure pulling for certain was something done by the less than able.

Such a blinkered viewpoint was certain to bring a response and readers were not to be disappointed. Ron Burgin, now a fishing guide in New Zealand, was sure that bigotry was dangerous for the sport.

RESERVOIR ETHICS

letter from RON BURGIN, *November 1975*

OVER THE past few years there has been much heated argument about how an angler should set about taking his catch from a trout reservoir. There are certain groups: Dry-fly purists, nymph and wet-fly fishermen; and, of course, we have all seen the lure fishermen stand at the water's edge like a demented heron, thrashing the water to a foam. Each group at one time or other has been stood to attention and shot at.

No angler can honestly call himself a trout fisherman unless he manages to obtain a certain degree of proficiency in each of these methods. Anglers who stick to one method and argue that that particular method is the only correct way to catch trout must surely have many lean days. I constantly go out on to public reservoirs and see the same people employing the same methods week in, week out. Occasionally they have a good bag of fish, but because of their rigidness of method they cannot be consistent. All methods are killers – on their day. We all have our preferences; mine is to catch a nymph-feeding trout on a floating line, but the important thing to remember is that trout feed according to their mood, not ours.

Having said that my favourite method of catching fish is nymphing, I must add that 205 or the 253 trout I have caught this season (up to August 23) have been on a lure fished on a sinkling line of one form or another.

Recently, Bob Church was ribbing the dry-fly purists, and I must say that for the most I agree with Bob. When the trout want the fly on the surface of the reservoir the dry fly is an easy and effective method, and not as difficult as the purists would have us believe.

Most of my fishing is done from boats, as I find it most rewarding, but not necessarily easier than bank fishing. The main difference between the two is the duration that the trout are feeding in front of you. Trout for most of the day, apart from dawn and dusk, tend to stay away from the banks. This reduces the bank angler's chance of covering a fish, but it does not necessarily mean that the fish are harder to tempt. As I live 50–80 miles from the reservoirs I fish, early-morning sessions are rare, and so I follow the fish to the middle of the lake.

I think that anglers condemn particular methods before they've tried them and are ignorant as to their correct use. Mr Geoffrey Bucknall recently cried out about the use of lee-boards and drift-control gear on boats. These devices are used to enable a sink line to do the job it was made to do: to get to the depth the fish are feeding, but still be able to drift and cover fresh ground, just as the wet-fly fisherman does fishing loch-style. Surely people like Mr Bucknall wouldn't suggest that we ban drogues because they help present the flies properly with a floating line?

If the object of angling was just to wet a line or have a day out, why do anglers get so frustrated and jealous when the chap next to them is filling his bag with fish by a particular method they don't agree with? Everyone would be much happier with their efforts and rewards if they forgot old prejudices, became more flexible with their methods and took the potential of each day's fishing as it stands. They should not pre-judge the day's events.

I am afraid it would take a long time for anyone to convince me, be it even one of the so-called experts, that there is only one way to catch fish. Through being flexible in my methods, whether it be a floating line, sinker, nymph, dry fly, or lure, I have taken 253 trout in 36 trips (over seven fish per outing) this season, with a rainbow of 4 lb and a brown trout of 5 lb 7 oz, all from public reservoirs.

❧ But William Beveridge saw things in a different way and appealed to fellow anglers to opt out of what he feared was deteriorating into a fly fishing rat race.

TIME TO TAKE STOCK

letter from WILLIAM BEVERIDGE, *January 1971*

IN THE last year or so I have witnessed with great disappointment the change in attitude towards fishing by many of our anglers, a change which, I might add, is reflected in your magazine.

Nowadays angling seems to be treated as some kind of scientific experiment. One has only to read the articles and look at the advertisements to learn of 'super, dynamic rods, styled for the seventies', 'fish where the action is', and 'catch more fish with such and such lines' – all quotations from the July issue. I do not blame *Trout and Salmon*; it is merely a medium through which people express themselves.

C. R. Pearce's article even told us when to fish and advised us to take staggered meal breaks between times of take. It would seem that angling is being transformed into some kind of money-making campaign, with everyone jumping on the bandwagon.

How long was it when we last saw the true angler, unadorned with shooting-head lines or all the fancy tackle for the 'angler of the seventies'? The rivers and fish have not changed, so why should we? People may answer by saying that population and disease have killed so many fish that new methods are required to catch them.

Izaak Walton once described angling as a 'virtue of humility which has a calmness of spirit and a world of other blessings attending upon it'. Now it is a rat-race with most anglers racing each other to try to catch the most fish in the shortest time possible.

Cannot we enjoy the few quiet hours spent alone, lazily flicking a fly across a run and stopping for a break when we feel like it and not when the sun is at a certain height and your shadow is at its longest? Surely you do not measure the enjoyment of the day by the quantity of the catch.

Let us stop and reconsider what angling really is in the truest sense of the word.

Chapter five

COPING WITH DISASTER

🙠 *A fishing day is not something to be taken lightly. It should never even be contemplated when worries are gambolling around in your head like spring lambs, for the first cast is certain to put the fly into a just-out-of-reach branch; reliable rods will break; strong leaders fail and fish will be lost for the silliest reasons.*
🙠 *But what of those days when, for no fault of your own, disaster decides to come along too?*

WHAT A WONDERFUL DAY!

by MIKE PETERS, *December 1985*

'WHAT A wonderful day!' As I sped along the country lanes the spring sunshine was warming its way through the early-morning mist. Daffodils were nodding in the gentle breeze and a myriad birds were playing amorous games in the hedgerows.

'Good morning, daffodils,' I called, and each gave a friendly nod in reply. 'Wonderful morning, birds.' 'Wonderful,' they dawn-chorused.

Fish were already dimpling the surface of the reservoir as I unpacked the car. A large flask of steaming-hot coffee, a huge packet of tasty sandwiches, a box of exquisitely tied creations, the product of many long winter evenings spent at the fly-tying bench. Then came a coil of bright-blue rope and ten feet of chain attached to an anchor guaranteed to hold a floating oil-rig in a North Sea gale. I set up my new carbon rod and laid it gently on the dew-covered grass. Half a bottle of brandy, in case of emergency, completed the essentials.

The Colonel's Volvo crunched across the car-park gravel. 'Wonderful day,' he said. 'I was about to say the same thing myself,' I replied.

A quick visit to the fishing lodge for a day ticket from the friendly bailiff, and I was off.

At the first mighty pull on the oars the coffee flask tottered on the edge of the stern seat. I rushed to grab it. The musical tinkling of a thousand pieces of Thermos was joined by an awesome crunch as I stepped on the top joint of the new rod.

'Back already?' asked the friendly bailiff at the lodge. 'I don't suppose you could let me have a small nail and some of that quick-setting glue? I've trodden on my new rod,' I said.

A hundred yards out fish were rising all round me. I silently shipped the oars and lowered the anchor and chain carefully over the side. The bright-blue rope snaked into the clear water . . . and disappeared. There's an old Chinese saying: 'Man who anchors in deep water with short rope must be off his noddle. Especially if he doesn't tie the end of the rope to the boat.'

I took a swig at the emergency brandy. A fish rose ten yards from the boat and I plopped a Pheasant Tail Nymph right on his nose. 'Not such a bad day, after all,' I thought as I reached for the landing-net. I could have sworn I'd packed that net. The fish departed. I emptied the emergency bottle. Another fish rose, the line whistled out and stopped in mid-air.

'Back again?' said the friendly bailiff. 'Could you get this fly out of my ear?' I enquired.

Back at the jetty none of the half-dozen fishermen unloading their first limit bags of the day noticed the bleeding ear.

'Settle down; don't panic,' I said to myself and took stock of the situation. With no anchor and no net the sensible thing would be to fish from the bank, for at least if I hooked something I could always try to beach it. I decided to row right across the reservoir and try some gentle nymphing from the shelter of the far bank. It was a good mile of rowing against the breeze but well worth the effort. Third time lucky, and off I paddled again. Twenty minutes of hard rowing and only halfway across, the brandy was beginning to work its way through my system so, obeying the call of nature in the time-honoured angling tradition, I filled the bailer. I am still not sure how it happened – perhaps it was a sudden change in the wind, maybe it was the emergency brandy, but somehow the contents of the bailer ended up in the lunchbox full of tasty sandwiches. I rowed on.

The Colonel was netting a huge trout from his well-anchored boat as I passed. 'Wonderful day,' he bellowed. 'How are you doing?' 'Not bad,' I lied. The blood was now dripping down my neck.

As I jumped ashore I knew in mid-leap that I had done it again. Before I could turn round, the boat had slipped out of reach and was now bobbing merrily through a shoal of rising fish back to the lodge. I stood there for a full minute – helpless, fishless, anchorless, netless, hungry, thirsty, still bleeding . . . and now boatless. I walked the two miles back to the lodge, stopping only to kick the heads off a clump of moronic nodding daffodils.

'Not you again,' said the friendly bailiff. 'I've lost the boat,' I said.

The *Marie Celeste* drifted gently into the bank. I collected what was left of my gear, hurled the empty emergency bottle at a rising fish and glowered back to the car-park. The Colonel, shovelling half a ton of trout into the Volvo, turned and smiled.

'Wonderful day! How did you get on?'

'Bugger off!' I said, and slammed the boot, neatly slicing the remains of my new rod half.

≈ *Charles Carfrae is sure that the sight of a magpie was an ill omen.*

FISHLESS DAYS WHEN A MAGPIE FLIES TO THE LEFT

by CHARLES CARFRAE, *October 1969*

SINGLE MAGPIES are traditionally regarded as fowls of ill omen – 'one for sorrow', as the old rhyme begins. For many years I convinced myself that any view of a single magpie on a fishing day was, if not fatal, at least gravely prejudicial to sport.

It was not until a decade ago that a competent authority assured me that the really deadly magpie was always the one seen flying from right to left; a bird flying from left to right could almost be disregarded. This is a more comforting doctrine, halving as it does one's chances of ill luck should a solitary magpie be encountered. It works remarkably well, if that is the word; or did until very recently.

There are a few simple rules. One must, for instance, see the bird oneself. If a child sitting in the car should yell, 'Daddy, there's a magpie!' it is important immediately to fix one's eyes firmly on the road just ahead. And quite often magpies will begin by flying to

right or to left and then disconcertingly change course through 180 degrees. They seem more prone to indecision than other birds.

When this happens, it is the direction in which the bird is last seen flying which counts. Thus right-flying birds should never be watched out of sight; left-flying birds invariably, in case they grant one a last-minute reprieve by reversing direction. Do not believe, by the way, those who maintain that to raise one's hat, spit or otherwise salute a magpie will avert its evil. Such straw-clutching gestures are futile as well as undignified.

The sight of a 'bad' magpie does not necessarily prevent me from fishing on a day that seems otherwise suitable. Generally, I still go but in a defeatist spirit, more to confirm that nothing will come of it than to catch fish. It has to be admitted that once on the river one often forgets about the magpie and, at times, one hasn't known whom or what to blame for lack of success until the bird is recalled to memory and failure at once accounted for.

Over and over again have I proved to my own satisfaction the malign influence of this pied nest-robber.

During the third week of May this year, however, a puzzling thing happened which I am still not certain how to interpret. The previous night I had been out trying for a sea trout on the River Dart, near my house, and though failing to catch one had felt two or three pulls, definitely those of peal.

They were the first encountered since the end of April. At least something was there and if the weather was kind that evening there seemed a very fair chance of opening the season's overdue account.

In the course of the afternoon a magpie flew from right to left directly in front of the car. Discouraged, indeed really upset, I made a point of returning home via a lane near which was a magpie's nest, hoping against hope to catch a glimpse of the pair together. Such a sighting, of course, would not only have wiped the slate clean but have been definitely advantageous.

Needless to say, what I actually saw, all too plainly, was not two magpies but one, again flying to the left. This was altogether too much. The fates had now made it crystal clear that no useful purpose would be served by a visit to the river that night. Sadly I resigned myself.

At tea time I told my family of this double omen and mentioned that I had no intention of fishing. They were most unsympathetic. I was roundly attacked; my 'superstitions', as they called them, laughed to scorn. Much was said concerning magpies, wits and lack of them, primitive attitudes of mind and so forth. Besides, they pointed out, the larder was nearly empty. Thoroughly piqued by this storm of ridicule, I shifted ground, though not attitude, and announced that to keep the peace I would go out after all, solely to demonstrate how wrong they were and how right I was.

The night was clear and cold with a young moon behind the trees – not very promising. Within three-quarters of an hour the water would begin to 'smoke' and then the chances of a first would be minimal, no matter how many magpies had or had not disclosed themselves earlier.

In the first five minutes I hooked and landed a peal, the first of the season. It was a small one for May, not much above a pound-and-a-half. If it hadn't been for those wretched birds, I told myself, it would have been a three-pounder. Still, in the circumstances, it was something.

I fished on, but thoughts continued to run more on magpies than trout. Should the unexpected occur and a second fish seize the fly – a black and white one, incidentally – misfortune of some sort would surely intervene.

Ten minutes later a second sea trout did take hold. It was a much stronger and heavier fish than the first. Obviously it would come unstuck, or the line would be snagged, the cast broken or the reel would jam, so I remained perfectly calm, almost detached, as a man should when confronted with inevitable disaster outside his control. But the minutes passed and the peal was still on, growing stronger and stronger, weaving at speed all over the river and pulling hard for the bushes on the bank.

When the backing started running through the rings, thoughts of magpies were pushed away and all attention devoted to the matter in hand, for this was an exceptionally powerful and active fish. Peal over four pounds, though strong, determined and dour, had in my experience seldom run really fast or far – yet this one could hardly weigh less than five, by the feel of it.

At last the pace began to slow and those magpies returned to haunt my thoughts. It seemed impossible that this gallant peal should even be brought to net. But it was, and at the first attempt, some 20 minutes after being hooked.

One look at the fish and I was inclined to raise my estimate. In fact, it weighed nearly eight-and-a-half pounds, my heaviest since 1964 and second heaviest ever.

Next morning at breakfast, my family, welcoming the generous amount of ammunition thus provided, began again to enjoy exercising their wit at my expense. Now was the moment, they said, to drop these preposterous superstitions, the hollowness of which had been so dramatically exposed. In future I should allow myself to be guided by logic and common-sense alone.

But however reasonable these words – and one is bound to admit grains of sense in them – it is hard for me to accept any suggestion that the validity of such cherished beliefs has been exploded. Magpies have proved to be reliable guides for too long to be discarded out of hand, as it were. At the same time, clearly some re-thinking was called for.

Having now considered this incident from all angles, I believe there may be a plausible explanation. Abandoning, with some reluctance, a theory that the black and white fly on which the fish was taken has, by a species of Sympathetic Magic, power to exorcise the malice of a black and white bird, I now lean towards a simpler possibility, one mathematically based. Just as two minuses make a plus, could not *two* left-flying magpies seen on the same day neutralise each other's baneful influence? Could they not, indeed, produce an influence positively benign?

It will be interesting to learn in due course whether or not this explanation is the correct one.

George Shelton casts a practised eye over an aspect of angling many treat too lightly.

THE ART OF FALLING IN
by GEORGE SHELTON, February 1974

ALL GREAT fishing writers have their own strong points. Hugh Falkus is the eminent sage on sea trout fishing at night, Frank Sawyer is a mighty man with a nymph, and Dick Walker – is there anything he can't do?

My friends will tell you, on the slightest pretext, that I know nowt about owt. They're wrong, of course. There is one facet of fishing on which I am the world's supreme expert: the art of falling in.

I can proudly say that falling in is an art I have studied all my life, starting, if my mother is to be believed, in early childhood when my first few tottering steps as a bellowing infant deposited me firmly in an attractive pool on the Dovey, thereby ruining my father's fishing for the day. As childood passed to adulthood, so did my expertise at falling in increase, and I now feel sufficiently expert to share my secrets with the world at large.

The art of falling in can be summarised briefly under the following headings: Forwards; backwards; sideways; and headlong.

The angler will do well to remember that in falling forwards any element of clumsiness should be avoided. The best tactics are to wade downstream, preferably singing or whistling cheerfully at the same time, while contemplating hopefully on the day's fishing to come. The right foot should be placed firmly beneath an underwater tree root, or alternatively the left foot placed on top of a hole in the river bed not less than 7 feet deep, and the fall forwards should be executed quickly and gracefully. It is considered bad form to endeavour to retrieve any cap or other headgear thereby deposited into the river, and a total loss of all tackle carried is obligatory.

Any angler wishing to become proficient at falling backwards would do well to study Buster Keaton or other similar films. Wading upstream or downstream will suffice, provided that the left heel is placed firmly upon the underwater equivalent of a banana skin.

Remember that at the point at which the left leg becomes totally extended, every seeming effort should be made to maintain balance with the right leg, while both arms should be stretched upright. A loud cry of 'Aargh-h-h!' is optional, but the head and lower portions of the body must be immersed firmly, ensuring that no dry articles of clothing remain. The expert will prefer to delay removing any particles of weed or other incumbrances until the bank is reached, but the beginner may find that it helps to remove floating logs which have become embedded in the person.

Any angler who has become proficient at falling in forwards and backwards should have no difficulty in mastering the sideways skill, although slightly different tactics must be adopted. I find it best to reach a reasonable point towards the centre of the river and spend several minutes unsuccessfully endeavouring to catch fish, saving the thrill of the actual manoeuvre until an attempt is made to retreat to the bank. With any luck, the angler will find that immediately adjoining the river bank there is a trough in the river bed, at the edge of which there is a large stone upon which the right foot can be placed. If sufficient pressure is exercised at this point, the stone will move, thereby throwing the whole body in a graceful arc into the deeper water immediately adjoining the bank. Some experts consider it appropriate that the head should be struck a smart blow upon an adjoining tree branch, but if this is to be done, any endeavour to use the branch as a means of escape from the water should be firmly avoided.

It may surprise some anglers to know that exercise of falling headlong is not carried out, in its initial stages, in the river. I find that the most satisfactory approach is to walk towards an attractive salmon pool on any river. On reaching the river bank, the angler should place both feet firmly upon a part of the bank which is suitably undercut by the current, and should then gaze hopefully into the river.

After a few seconds, the bank will almost certainly collapse, and the angler may then in a graceful swan dive enter any particular part of the pool he prefers. Some anglers have been known to execute a jack-knife dive or sideways somersault, but the truly competent angler will avoid any such flashy tactics and will content himself with the satisfying splash which ensues. Following this means of entry, I have often found it enjoyable to allow the current to wash me down several miles of rocky river, before any endeavour is made to seek the sanctuary of dry land.

I hope these few words will have helped any aspiring anglers wishing to master this difficult but rewarding feature of the noble art of angling, but remember that as with anything else, practice makes perfect. I've practised. Often.

DANGER AHEAD!

by GEORGE SHELTON, *June 1985*

WHY IS it that every time I decide to go on a salmon-fishing trip, my old friend Disaster decides to join me?

Why is it that while my fishing friends stroll serenely along an idyllic river bank, I blunder wildly about, tripping over tree trunks, tearing my clothing on barbed wire strands and catching my hair in overhanging brambles?

Why is it that everyone I know wades safely and elegantly along tumbling streams, while I tumble inelegantly and decidedly unsafely among boulder strewn torrents?

'Carry a wading stick,' cry my acquaintances. 'Can't go wrong.' I did, twice. The first time I tripped over it and went headlong; the second time I jabbed my waders instead of the river bottom tearing a nasty hole in the boot and causing vast quantities of water to gush up my trouser leg. It was a mercy the cut on my foot didn't go septic.

What about the time when, heaving huge quantities of tackle along a narrow path atop a steep bank above the Welsh Dee, I stumbled over a tree root, falling precipitately and painfully some 50 feet into the torrent below? Did I receive assistance and sympathy from a fishing acquaintance who was with me on that occasion? No. 'Did you enjoy your trip?' was his only query.

I often wonder how many other salmon anglers have met with an irate stallion and, deciding that discretion was the better part of valour, determined to wade the stream to avoid a volley of flashing hooves, only to find (a) that the stream was too deep to wade, (b) that the current was too strong to swim across, (c) that the bank was too steep to climb back up.

At the precise moment before what should be my hour of triumph, my good friend Disaster feels a pressing obligation to link arms inextricably with me. Like the time last September when, fishing the Cumberland Esk, I had at last established solid contact with a good-looking grilse, and it was only at the last moment that, bending down to slip the net triumphantly under my fish, I lost my footing. I didn't so much mind losing the fish, but I felt that it was perhaps unfair that I had to spend the next hour diving to the bottom of a deep pool in an endeavour (unsuccessful as it proved) to retrieve the tackle bag which fell in the river along with me.

Only once did I feel that I had come to grips with Disaster. I must be the only man in living fishing history who has gone trolling on Loch Tay, only to have his outboard motor fall overboard when in the middle of that beautiful expanse of water. It was some time later, when my boat had been blown on to an island in the Loch, that I began to appreciate the presence of my angling companion, a petite and attractive brunette who,

as receptionist at the hotel at which I was staying, had foolishly agreed to accompany me on that fishing trip. During the hours we were stranded a warm and cordial relationship developed, and I felt that at long last I had succeeded in converting misfortune into glory.

But Disaster was equal to the occasion. The receptionist sustained a nasty attack of bronchitis, due no doubt to her exposure to the elements and me, and during her prolonged period of convalescence, she formed a lasting attachment with her medical adviser which ultimately resulted in her nuptials.

Why does it always happen to me?

THE FISH-LOSER
by LOGIE-BRUCE LOCKHART, *August 1976*

PERHAPS IT was a form of masochism born of incipient senility, but I had come to believe that I actually enjoy losing fish.

When very small, I made a spec-

tacular start on my fish-losing career. The senior members of the family were fishing in Loch Mudle from the safe comfort of a boat; I had been dismissed to the burn.

Suddenly a swirl like a seal at

play sent my heart plunging through my stomach. I struck wildly, and a great fish steamed down the swollen burn with small boy in pursuit. At the age of eight I had no clear standard of comparison, but I knew this was no ordinary burn sea trout. With helpless desperation I hung on while the salmon did what it liked.

Fortunately, there were no trees along the bank, no waterfalls or rapids, and I was able to prevent him taking out all the line by running after him. How that fish didn't break me I shall never know; but after what seemed an eternity, it lay below me, tired and almost motionless, within reach of my net. The burn was deep, and the heather hung far out over the bank. The net was tiny, little more than a toy. It was all I could do to reach the giant fish at full stretch without falling through the heather into 6 feet of water.

He was too big for the net, but I did get his tail end in, and for a moment he was balanced in mid air on his way to the bank. But his unexpected weight, once out of the water, was too much for me. The net wobbled, he gave a last flop, and I saw – and even heard – the gut snap just above the fly.

He lay there stunned for a second, and I could see the gleam of the Mallard and Silver in his upper jaw. Without waiting to think, splash!, I threw down rod and net and jumped straight on top of him. The water was well out of my depth, but that didn't matter, because I felt him in my arms for a fraction of a second before he escaped with a wriggle and a flap. That feeling will be with me to my dying day. As I kicked my way to the surface I saw a great wave as he sped through the shallows at the head of the pool, and away . . .

No-one but a born fisherman can understand the agony of that moment. I wept, and for years afterwards the pain returned whenever I thought of it. There had been no witnesses; the memory had to remain an unshared secret.

Over the years, I have lost a great many more fish. Habit has dulled the pain. Grown-ups don't weep. 'I accept the universe!' said some gushing lady to Thomas Carlyle. 'Gad! You'd better!' was his sardonic reply. These words have inspired me to look back at all the fish I've lost in a new way. How much happier a place the world must be for all those prize trout still at large! One remembers all the fish one loses, not many of those one catches. How rich in such memories I have become! While others point to desiccated specimens of such and such a weight, caught in such and such a place on a given date, growing dusty in glass cases on the unlit side of the front hall, mine lurk alive and still growing, monstrous shadowy forms for ever haunting the deep waters of my vivid memory.

Now, like many middle-aged fishermen, I've philosophised my way to an almost oriental patient at-one-ness with the will of the wind and the waters. I take my 14-year-old son down to the Tweed, and although my heart still beats wildly to see the primeval emotions flitting across his face as failure and success follow one another in their eternally unjust and erratic way, I have to recognise that my role is now that of the elder statesman, counselling patience and calm in every adversity. I've fished that water for 30 years, I've hooked and lost salmon on my trout rod. It has nothing worse in store, no new horror to sear my battle-scarred soul.

On the Saturday of the Melrose seven-a-sides, which I should have been watching, I went down to Lord Haig's stretch with my son, Bede. It is lovely water with a stately salmon pool below a wooded bank spattered with primroses. Up and downstream, the broad Tweed curves its way at the bottom of a 300 foot valley with sides which defy access. How beautiful the April waters on this sparkling day, and how misleading. The wading is difficult and treacherous at the Gate Heugh above 400 yards of tumbling trout runs.

In low water the depth varies from 1½–3 feet, with a narrow channel for the mainstream some 3 feet deeper: an ideal succession of half-pools and half-rapids. Given a heavy shower, the river rises rapidly by a further dangerous 2 feet. The bottom consists of a blend of large slippery boulders and shelving rocks, which can plunge one over the top of one's waders into the powerful current at any time. We fished our way up this formidable stretch with toil and tribulation. Few trout were showing, although we had seen an 11 lb salmon landed. I had two small trout and a grayling, and Bede, cold and wet, after two blank and unlucky days, was on the point of giving up in despair.

At the top of the Gate Heugh is a big flat rock: casting upstream from it, I have caught many a good trout, including my best-ever Tweed brown trout of 1 lb 14 oz. Cold and tired, I had just concluded that no more trout would be rising, for it was past three o'clock. Nevertheless, the rock offered comparative comfort, and I continued for a few moments, and was encouraged by rising and missing a good fish. There was a promising-looking eddy a little further out, so I ventured out from the rock into the deeper water, and, on a long line, rose and this time hooked another.

To my surprise it tore my line out upstream in the irresistible way which announces something really substantial. Instead of stopping after the first surge, it went on. I held on nervously as my little 8-foot rod bent alarmingly, and remembered that it was last year's nylon, and 4 lb breaking strain at that. What sort of a hold had my tiny Greenwell got? The fish leaped, silhouetted against the dancing, dazzling sunlit ripples. It was big, but I couldn't see it clearly. It looked too dark for a grilse or a sea trout.

There followed a grim battle as the fish swung, boring deep, round me in a semi-circle. I tried to recover line, and it came to within a few feet. I fumbled at my net, but my best efforts to hold it against the current failed, and it took out more line, until it was far below me, and I wondered whether I could ever stop it. For a long time there was deadlock, but eventually I got some line back and saw him come up to the surface with a great back fin. Clearly he was a brown trout, but I could not guess the size except to say that he was certainly over 4 lb, and the hardest-fighting trout I had ever felt.

I brought him almost within netting range again, but he was plainly just resting, for he swirled to the top, jumped again, making my rod rattle, and made off downstream like a marlin. By this time, Bede, who had seen the fight from far below, was struggling up to see the fun. Despairing of ever forcing the fish up against the current, and not daring to make for the bank, because the perilous wading might make me stumble and fall, I remained uneasily perched on top of a vast submarine boulder, praying I should not lose my balance. Slowly I coaxed him round to the inshore side of me, hoping that Bede,

20 yards below me, might be able to net him in the quieter and shallower waters.

I had always believed there were giant trout in the Gate Heugh, and now I would be able to prove it. I briefly visualised whether this one would look better in a glass case in the entrance hall or the drawing room. But now the devil must have entered into him, for suddenly he was away again. His strength took me aback, the rod bent to a croquet hoop as the fish made straight for Bede, who wisely resisted having a dab with the net as the line actually brushed against his waders.

I nearly lost my foothold, got my balance again, and tried to slow the fish, only to be countered by a final burst of power – and he was away! The fly had gone with him and the line flapped loose. All philosophy forgotten, I swore and bellowed, and even thrashed the river with my impotent and fly-less cast, like John Cleese thrashing his car for stalling. In my fury I actually jumped up and down like a naughty child, staggered, slipped over the top of my waders, and wrenched my arm in my attempt to recover. All the accumulated misery of every fish ever lost came back multiplied a hundred-fold as I cursed the river, the sport and the futility of life.

With a final bellow of pain and anger, I looked towards my son for sympathy.

He was roaring with laughter.

WOMEN IN THE WILLOWS
by IAN HENDERSON, *March 1991*

SALMON FISHING is a constant joy. Even the long dark days of the close season can be lightened by happy memories of the golden days that have gone before. Except, of course, that there weren't any last season, which was a dead loss. My one little salmon, which was probably only a sea trout anyway, didn't leave a lot of scope for reminiscence. Memories of 1990 are a mite hazier than usual.

You know how the salmon-fisher always starts: 'The line had just gone slack when I felt a kind of double knock as though I was snagged on a rock.' All the best salmon seem to knock before entering. This one always turns out to be a teen-pound fresh-run sea-liced macho fish. Well, in my case in 1990, all I can say is that I *did* get snagged on a rock. Many rocks. I also got snagged on bushes, trees, fertiliser bags, waders and once, though I hesitate to admit it, on a girl on horseback.

There are other memories. The memories of all the rumours that sustain the angler during the season: 'The river-mouth is just black with fish waiting for the water to rise'. When the water rose, then fish invariably ran right through, for the next rumour, inevitably, was: 'They're taking fish up Corrie-way' (Corrie-way being ten miles upriver). The one constant factor concerning rumours is that they *are* constant; the same ones seep through each year. The only original rumour I can recall off-hand was two years ago when Bill Robertson told me he had seen a

man take a 'bar of silver' with 'sea-lice still on it'. I think Bill had got just a wee bit carried away there and had run two rumours together in his excitement. That was no bad thing, though, for last season we needed all the rumours we could get.

Memory goes far back. I remember when I was a lad in Borgue in the south-west of Scotland — and that's far back. The rumour had reached us that 'the herling are running' and that was the one rumour we were waiting for. We called them herling or rather 'hirlin'. Other folk call them sewin or finnock or what have you. They are the young of the sea trout, anyhow, and they shoal up and down the river-mouths in summer just for the hell of it. We used to catch them in the Skyreburn, near Gatehouse, with brandling worms on a Stewart tackle — in numbers.

This particular memory is of an old boy who always appeared with the herling. He sat on a ledge of rock at the tail-end of a pool just above a steep run of broken water. He never moved. Except to take herling off his hook. We would roam the riverbank, up and down, crossing and re-crossing, seeking the elusive herling. He sat tight.

We had the odd fish and he had a barrow-load. I can see him still – better than I could then, actually – for I used to think he was catching them the same way we were. Now I know better. The old sod was foul-hooking them. Not a shadow of a doubt. All my life I had treasured the memory of this archetypal countryman in total empathy with Nature, versed in the ways of the wild and fully conversant with the migratory routines of *Salmo trutta minor*. Only recently did it dawn on me that the old crook was rip- ping them from the spot where they rested after fighting their way up the fall: the old sinner.

Last season's memories are somewhat different if no less poignant. There was that evening when I went fishing on the strength of a rumour that the Wil- lows Pool was holding fish. The Willows Pool is the only pool in our beat that can hold fish. It is a long, deep run fed by a fairly steep cascade that hits the far bank on the curve to slide slow and dark down a long ravine over gravel. If there are no fish in the Willows, there are no fish in the beat. That evening the sun was bright, the river was low but the rumour was strong.

When I drove down, the gate was open, indicating no stock in the field, so I took the car right down to the river. There is a high embankment at the Willows and I kitted up on the field side and sa- voured the last few moments of excited anticipation. Sunlight shafting through the trees, bees droning through the flowers. Warmth, light, per- fume, peace and joy. Oh to be a salmon an- gler when the Willows holds fish! I could hear the happy cries of children from the farm on the other side of the river and I echoed them in my heart.

With the rod up and a lightly dressed Dunkeld on a size six hook, I donned thigh boots and fishing jacket, settled the deer- stalker on the back of my head and eased myself over the bund to con- front the quarry. I saw them as soon as I cleared the top of the rise. Three of them. One shooting downstream in the main current under the far bank and two swim-ming leisurely up in the slack water below me. The one heading down had long blonde hair, one of the two heading up had short blonde air, while the third had on a little red swimming cap with her hair tucked inside. The one on the far side was doing the crawl, flat out with the current: the two nearest me were doing a relaxed breast stroke. And I mean breast stroke. All three were wearing bikinis.

What does one do? They flashed sunbeam smiles at me and climbed out to ask if I minded their having a swim before picnicking? Who could? – even with the nearest salmon now cowering, terrified, behind a rock 15 miles up Corrie? They had three bicycles propped against a bush and a cloth set out with flasks and sandwich boxes. I stood there in my all-weather out-fit like a fugitive Eskimo. (I can't fish without wearing my multi-pocketed wax jacket with the furry lining. I have things I need in the pockets.) There I stood with my waders burning hot to the touch and sweat coursing down my back. Some of it caused by the sun. The

girls laughed and joked as they shook pearls of water out of their hair and stroked warmth back into long, firm limbs. Theirs were the happy cries I had heard when I got out of the car. The children from the farm were all indoors watching Teenage Mutant Ninja Hero Turtles on video.

Fishing the Willows then was about as far out of the question as blaming the girls for spoiling it would have been. I settled for ac-cepting a cup of coffee from the taller of the two blondes and a chat with the three of them while they picnicked.

Squatting there in my olive-green storm-proofed waxed wear with these naiads sporting around me in the sunshine as steam rose from my hat, I felt a new dimen-sion to my salmon angling. I felt a proper pillock.

The lasting memory of that day, and indeed of the whole of the 1990 season, was of the merry, tinkling, silvery-bright laughter of my wife when she met me at the door with her customary 'No fish, sweetie-pie?' and I had to tell her.

That still hurts, today.

Chapter six

A QUESTION OF MANNERS

⋙ *Newcomers to game fishing can be forgiven for stepping in front of a salmon pool, casting across your line when boat fishing or standing on the skyline when you're just about to make the telling cast.*

⋙ *The remedy, except for the dyed-in-the-wool, the fish-at-all-costs man prepared to ruin every other angler's day, is showing a good example. But should we be content just to mutter and let the interloper get away with it?*

COURTESY ON THE RIVER

by G. P. R. BALFOUR-KINNEAR, *February 1956*

MOST FISHERMEN are sportsmen and good felllows who think of the interests of others, but there are some whose behaviour is reprehensible either from ignorance, thoughtlessness or selfishness. The motorist has a code for good manners on the roads, so why not have, and try to enforce, a recognised code for civility on the rivers?

One of the most common crimes is to step in and fish in front of somebody else. This is obviously as unpardonable as jumping a bus queue, and should not be tolerated. If every fisherman exercised his rights and refused to allow such behaviour it would not happen so frequently.

I am not suggesting that it should be necessary to indulge in slogging matches in order to enforce good manners on the waterside. If, however, every fisherman made a point of objecting, when his rights were infringed, and pointed out the offender to others, public opinion would soon have the desired effect.

I remember seeing one fisherman protect his rights in what was perhaps a rather drastic but none the less effective manner. He had been at the tail end of a queue and had awaited his turn to fish a short lie. He had no sooner begun to fish when another fisher arrived and stepped in front of him. The man who had the right of the pool merely made a false cast on one side of this intruder's head, and then on the other side. Afterwards he mentioned casually that it was surprising how few men would stand up to a salmon fly whizzing past their ears!

Another bad offence is to begin to fish on the other side of a pool ahead of somebody fishing on this side, so that the newcomer's line will be first over the fish. I once saw a keeper on the other side do this. The man fishing on this side, and who had the right of the pool, having got there first, politely suggested that he was being crowded. The keeper, however, merely gave a surly reply and continued to fish. Our friend let out extra line and cast over the keeper's line. Having hooked this he pulled it in and re-moved the fly. In the circumstances, I am inclined to think that this was warranted, especially as the fly was posted back to the keeper.

All such incidents are, however, regrettable and mar the peace and pleasure of the day; but when there are those who deliberately flout the rules such incidents may be unavoidable if the code of the river is to be upheld for the benefit of all concerned.

Should you happen to arrive at a pool simultaneously with someone on the other side you each, of course, have an equal right to fish it, but, as that would be impracticable, a happy solution is to toss for who goes first.

Should the fisherman on the other side of the river hook the bottom, and be unable to recover his tackle, offer to clear it for him. He may do the same for you some day. If you hook his line and pull it in, so that you may take it in your hand, you are in no way risking the loss of your own tackle.

Always be careful to shut gates and see that they are properly fastened. If making a fire be sure that it is in a safe place, is not spoiling the amenity, and that it is well stamped out before you go away. Do not leave lunch paper, orange peel or cigarette cartons to litter the bank. Push them down a rabbit hole or under a big stone. Don't throw bottles into the river or break them. A rabbit hole is also a good place for them. Or, best of all, carry your litter home with you.

If you are fishing for salmon, and the man on the other side hooks one while you are fishing the same pool, you must stop fishing. If you continued to fish, and also hooked a salmon, your lines would be almost certain to cross, and one of the fish would be lost. The man who hooks the first salmon has the right of the fairway, but, because the rods on the other side of the pool have to stop fishing, it is his duty to land his fish as quickly as he can.

When you come to what you consider to be the best part of a pool, and others are awaiting their turn to fish it, do not linger there but take an honest step between each cast. To anchor yourself in a good place is merely to waste your own time, as the fish there have already refused your lure, and you are also spoiling the chances of the other fishermen as well as holding them back.

All that we have to do is to follow the code ourselves, and to explain as nicely as possible to any who may infringe it what it is that they are doing wrong, so that they may follow our example for the common good.

COURTESY IN ANGLING
by RICHARD CONNELL, *June 1962*

KNOWING WHERE and when to cut in to fish when others are already employed can present a difficulty for even the experienced. And great resentment will be incurred by the angler who fails to conduct himself properly in this respect.

Generally it is best to adopt the queue system. Quietly settle yourself at the starting point in the pool being fished and wait until the stretch has had time to settle before starting. On a large water this may not take long; on a small busy water I have waited for up to an hour for a good stretch to settle after rough treatment. In salmon fishing on a large pool you may start in when the first rod is over half-way down.

On very long pools it is permissible

to start well below a rod, fishing down: the criterion for distance being that conversation should be impossible. You must then fish down. Never, never fish up a relatively short stretch towards an established, descending rod. *Vice versa*, of course, also applies. If a rod has just started down a long pool you may fish up from the tail to about the pool middle. With dry fly already on the way up on such a pool wet fly can start down but will come out a reasonable distance before meeting. The rule is that last to start stops fishing first a fair distance before the meeting point.

These rules apply to a busy water. Where there is plenty of space, never break into a pool being fished. Find your own stretch. Small pools must never be broken into.

A river has got to be very wide before independent fishing on each bank is permissible. A good cast from each bank should leave a fair gap of water between in the middle. Narrow pools and single runs should be conceded to a rod already started on the far bank.

The Tweed from below Galashiels is a good example of a river usually fishable simultaneously from both banks.

The dry fly fisher waiting at the tail of a small pool to fish up is often troubled by a wet fly starting down, often after he has patiently rested the water. *Vice versa* less often also occurs. If you wish to fish such a stretch and a rod is established anywhere on it but not fishing, ask first if he intends to fish.

Arriving to fish the bank of a large loch with other rods dispersed you may start in anywhere provided you are at least shouting distance away from the other fishers and have not had to disturb anglers in getting there. Where a relatively short shore is being fished apply the queue system. Two anglers on a lengthy shore may employ by mutual agreement the 'leap frog' method. A starts at the top and, keeping well back, B walks downshore an agreed distance and starts. A fishes down to B's start, comes out and, keeping well back, walks down past B before starting again. This ensures that both get a fair share of undisturbed water. The 'keeping back' bit must be well done.

Wading is the bane of all busy fishing waters. Its use often ruins 75 per cent of the stream for fishing and on a small river this figure is likely to reach 100 per cent.

Water of a foot to 3 feet which, given a chance, would provide the best fishing, is spoiled by the tyro who erroneously imagines that all the fish must be in the great dark swirl on the far bank. The trouble is that when one rod has been seen to wade down a pool the next feels that, to have any chance, he must wade that little bit deeper. Wading not only ruins the chances of sport, it destroys countless larvae, snails and trout food crushed and torn from security.

Envisage the scene. Three waders in the course of a morning have blundered through an excellent stretch of streamy water to fish a deep hole on the far side. They vanish elsewhere and ten minutes later a proficient angler appears. He is almost certainly going to fish the promising-looking shallow run which he is unaware will take a long period of rest to settle and so he follows in the wake of the spoilers, puzzled, fishless and convinced that the trout stocks are dwindling.

If you are going to fish in company, wear at most thigh waders and restrict their use to a mini-mum. The majority of stretches ruined by wading could easily be covered by fishing from one side and then the other. On small rivers waders are only required to change banks. Deep waders are the equipment of those who have their own fishing, are engaged on vast waters such as the Tay or lower Tweed or are fishing badly overgrown rivers where bank fishing is impossible. Too often they are the toy of the angler who prides himself more on his equipment than his technique. Keep in mind that six inches of water or more flowing over your boots usually means that you are standing in what should be excellent fishing water.

Many anglers, when they get into a boat seem to go mad and some of the conduct I have witnessed on well-known lochs, apart from considerations of courtesy, has been ludicrous. There may be collisions or fishers in one boat getting their casts entangled with those in another. On one painful occasion after a collision, while the occupants of two boats threatened each other with their rods, they both lost oars. Such incidents are not without humour for the beholder. To become involved in such unpleasantness, however, can spoil the flavour of a whole day's fishing.

There are two courtesies to observe when boat fishing; that accorded to other boats and the consideration of companions in the boat with you. A boat works in drifts and, on a small loch or in a bay, these may be only a few hundred yards in length. If you must fish such a drift already engaged, apply the queue system. Never cut in, in front of another boat. Where open water is involved over long distances you may start well ahead of another boat parallel to it but well out of its direct path. If you have to cut across the fishing water at right angles it must be done well ahead of the descending boat and accomplished quickly and quietly. Should you require to return against the drift you must pull well away to the side and from the fishing water before turning up.

The common practice in rough conditions of seeking to row easily in the lees and calmer waters is selfish and to be condemned when others are fishing. Under such conditions these are the only places

where fishing will be possible. I encountered one specimen who actually grounded his boat trying to pass between mine and the shore of an island in whose lee I was fishing. He had rowed right down my drift. Such conduct is inexcusable until the rough becomes dangerous.

If another boat is seen to be catching fish and you are not it is not an excuse to edge closer and closer. Trout do not feed in long rectangular strips 12 to 14 feet wide.

Two or three people within the confines of a boat can be a trial to each other if a courteous code is not observed and eccentric conduct avoided, a fact well known to club secretaries who have to group members on outings. To insist upon standing fishing while the others sit, is a major crime. Not only does this disturb fish, the angler with flailing arm being a monument visible for many yards around, it is also dangerous, as the whole equilibrium is upset.

A proper division of the water into two or three sections must be made and poaching in the preserves of a neighbour avoided no matter how attractively the fish rise therein and the numbers he catches. If you are doing nothing and he is courteous he will, after a while, ask you to change places with him. This, however, seldom effects a change in the balance of sport. With three rods fishing each should take a fair turn at the middle. Learn to cast in rhythm with the others to avoid the irritation of tangles.

Never cast lengthwise for any reason. Your hooks will probably rake the boat at head level and eye-sights are damaged or ruined all too often by this thoughtless conduct. A lashing hook is a menace to be kept away from companions. Do not insist upon thrashing the water with a great length of line when your companion is using a normal length. Avoid bumping or rattling noisily with your feet. Don't sway the boat with an exaggerated movement every time you cast. Your companion and the fish will take exception. Take your turn at any tasks involved – rowing, baling and so on. Don't nag for the drifts to be changed every ten minutes or so to suit your own ideas.

We live in the age of the vandal – the inferior who craves superiority and must prove it by leaving his mark. Unable to satisfy his basic craving for notice by the produc-tion of great works of art or any other intelligent effort, he descends to the simplest method of all – destruction. It is with an angry horror that I have watched the spread of vandalism to fishing waters. Fences and gates broken up for firewood or fun, notice boards disfigured and broken, dry-stone dykes which have stood for ages, tumbled and strewn, boats and boat-houses damaged, trees snapped off, torn up and disfigured. There are people who fish now guilty of such crimes.

Anglers are absolutely dependent upon the goodwill of proprietors of property and no precaution is too little or too great to take if it will ensure that the countryside and other amenities are left in as pleasing a state as we found them. We cannot expect to fish otherwise.

Litter leaving is a thoughtless, selfish discourtesy. The abandonment of glass near a waterside in any shape or form is criminal. A broken piece constitutes a permanent menace and it is usually children who suffer.

What can be done to improve angling courtesy and halt the back-sliding? The experienced angler of integrity must guard against apathy and a deterioration of his own standards. He should never become discouraged and must offer the example which may eventually be followed by those less skilled but nevertheless enthusiastic and keen to become proper anglers.

The chronic discourteous ones and the criminal types can only be dealt with by proprietors of fishings, associations, club secretaries and all with authority over fishings. Strict rules on procedure and etiquette ruthlessly supported are the only hope of preserving the peaceful, pleasant nature of angling and they must, as well as applying rules, limit the numbers fishing to a proportion where a courteous code will work.

The authorities concerned have a duty to the sport to realise the situation and act before it deteriorates too far.

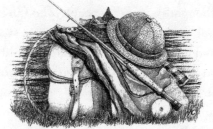

Chapter seven

PIONEERS AND DISCIPLES

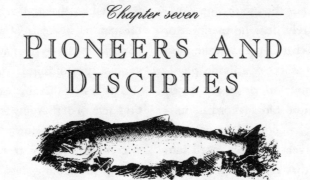

🐟 *How many flies from the many thousands tied over the centuries by anglers searching for that ever-elusive infallible fly are still with us?*

🐟 *If the fail-me-never fly was ever invented, it should be banned and the dressing burned. For what a dull business fly fishing would be. Wrapping fur and feather around a hook to concoct an acceptable imitation or impression of a natural insect or food item is, in truth, a more fascinating pastime than fishing itself.*

🐟 *There have always been flies of fashion and fancy whose quick silver fame is as ephemeral as the insects they are intended to mimic. Few flies are genuinely new, most being variations in varying degrees on an old and trusted theme, and any attempt to claim a variation as the original has always been guaranteed to set the fur and feather flying.*

🐟 *Those fly dressers whose names are remembered were not merely the creators of highly successful patterns, but pioneers in the vital realms of giving a fly life, or translucence. Rarely has shape, form or even colour alone been sufficient to make a pattern different enough for the result to be acclaimed as a truly classic fly.*

IT'S WHAT A FLY DOES THAT COUNTS
by GEOFFREY BUCKNALL, *November 1978*

WHILE I would not wish to offend anyone's sensitivities, I must confess that few new inventions of fly-patterns impress me. The reason is simple. A great many novel patterns are described, but nearly always the inventor is hypnotised by colour, or the use of a new material. Rarely does he mention or consider what is, perhaps, the most important aspect of a fly: its physical behaviour on, or in, the water. It's the same old Halfordian mistake that has dogged us for decades; fly-tyers are sidetracked into thinking that the way in which a pattern looks to us in the air is the way in which it will appear to a trout in the water.

Of course the first thing a fly-tyer should consider is the way in which a trout recognises its food. Much experimental work has already been done on this, and the general conclusion is that up to its fourth year at any rate, unless its vision is impaired by eye fluke or other disease, the trout recognises its food by its activity.

The word 'activity' here is important because it must not be confused with mobility by itself. Obviously, the 'spent gnat' is not mobile, but the death of a Mayfly may be thought of as a sad form of activity, repetitive enough at a given time to set up a pattern of preoccupied feeding. In passing, the fact that old, or semi-blind trout, scavenging does not affect

the premise that the behaviour of the natural insect is of paramount concern to the fly-tyer with an inventive turn of mind.

The reason that the 'exact imitation' school of fly-tying fell into disrepute, even before the less-discerning rainbow trout became widespread in our waters, was not so much its dogmatism as its emphasis on size and colour at the expense of form. It is axiomatic that if a trout recognises food by behaviour patterns, then this behaviour has to be implanted both in the structure of the artificial fly and the way in which it is fished. I have concluded that perfection is neither achievable nor necessary in this, because the trout's response to food is a conditioned reflex. The fly, and its presentation have only to be good enough to trigger that instinctive response.

Reasoning processes do not exist in trout, and one of the just criticisms of an excessive 'put-and-take' stocking policy is that natural wariness and feeding responses are conditioned out of the trout, irrespective of their age and size. Doubtlessly such qualities eventually return to the fish, given sufficient dispersal space and time. Reservoirs have such space and time; small fisheries may not possess them unless fishing and stocking policy is carefully managed.

This brings me back to the fly and its physical structure. In imitative fly fishing the feeding behaviour of the fish must influence tactics and these are served, in their turn, by the way in which the fly is fashioned. An example comes from my own Footballer nymph which was deliberately designed to cut through the surface film quickly. The Footballer is cast accurately to intercept a cruising trout, seen to be taking the buzzer pupa when it is at its most vulnerable stage, that is, when it is hanging below the surface film before hatching into the adult fly.

That is why I gave the fly a plain abdomen, thorax, and head, and left out materials to copy breathing tubes, emerging legs and wings. Any extra tufts of hackle or silk would possibly have interfered with the speedy piercing of the surface film by the fly.

Some years after the Footballer's invention, a well-known fly fisherman remarked to me that he was surprised I had not 'modernised' the Footballer by adding these appendages. Obviously he thought that I was concerned with the purely imitative aspect of the fly; he did not realise that I had designed it to suit my interceptive tactic.

That is one example of the structure of a fly being related to the feeding behaviour of the fish. If the Footballer is cast accurately enough to a trout already preoccupied with the buzzer pupa, it is sufficient for such a trout to 'expect' to find a certain mode of activity in that place at that time. The pin-point cast is intended to allow insufficient time for the trout's feeding response to be other than immediate and instinctive.

Richard Walker's sedge pattern, which he made for skimming the water at Grafham, is another pattern which, although imperfect in imitative terms, is eminently successful in a behavioural context.

In both of those examples a visual attack is being made upon the trout. When surface – or near-surface – activity is absent, the angler must imagine what is happening underwater. Consider, for example, how trout feed on corixa, the water boatman. This denizen of the water-margins stays mostly on the bottom, but occasionally scuttles to the surface to renew its air supply. In waters where it is prolific it is a popular food-item of trout, and, as my post-mortems show, it can cause preoccupied feeding.

The angler may discover this by spooning his first fish, or, more likely, he may guess or know from experience that in a certain place at a certain time corixa-feeding will be taking place.

I prefer to fish a weighted corixa on a long leader from a floating line. After casting, I wait a fair length of time for the fly to reach the bottom. Then I begin a slow, steady retrieve to give the impression of lift-off from the lake floor.

It's fairly easy to make a corixa serve this need. The hook is lapped with fuse-wire, plumping it out in the middle. Then dub a lightish-brown hair over to get that dirty-fawn colour of the body. The shell-like shiny back is dark brown nylon raffia, varnished, with a few fibres of pheasant tail on either side of the body as paddles. This pattern has been very killing for me over the years, and it is an adaptation of a slightly more complicated dressing by C. F. Walker.

It is clearly possible to relate example after example of the importance of fly-structure. The fascinating question is why colour and size have dominated fly-design in recent years, bringing a proliferation of new patterns with ingenious names. The two reasons are the widespread preference by anglers for rainbow trout, and the necessity for small fisheries stocked on a put-and-take basis.

Fly fishing has many fascinating paradoxes, one of which is that imitative flies are a great simplification of technique. Newly-introduced rainbows, still conditioned to pellet-feeding, roam their strange environment, feeding at random as hunger drives them. They will take the careful imitation as easily as they will an exotic monstrosity.

The only truly deceptive creature in this encounter is the angler himself.

I don't criticise these fisheries; we need them all. But, the best opportunity for the attack on trout feeding with preoccupation comes on the large reservoir where fish have both time and space in which to develop natural responses to natural food. Fish can be selective and true tactical fly fishing comes into its own. I don't believe in the 'instant conversion' of newly-introduced rainbows to wary creatures of the wild. It is an illusion.

In fly-tying terms, this means that it is not enough to sit down at the vice with a coloured plate of a certain insect before you, then to select certain materials to simulate it. The earlier, vital questions to be asked are: How should this fly behave in, or on the water? What structure must I build into the fly and what fishing technique must I apply, to obtain that behaviour-pattern?

In the case of my Footballer, I improved its performance by detracting from its imitative possibilities. Most of the big advances in fly technique have come from such an approach. One has but to think of the low-water salmon fly as a classical example. They stand out from the deluge of new inventions which are merely variations of colour and shape, most of which cannot stand the test of time.

This seems a harsh judgement, but I do apply it to my own tying. Over the years, in books and articles, I would have found it easy enough to invent dozens of short-lived patterns. As it is, I decided early to claim originality only for flies designed to meet a genuine structural need, and so I put my name to very few inventions.

I like to think that such patterns as the Footballer and the Beastie lure will go on killing fish for many a year yet. Those two typify my philosophy because they featured a special structure to serve a special tactic.

❧ *Fly dressers are not slow off the mark to herald a new pattern as being genuinely new. But, more often than not, the revolutionary fly will be little more than a re-vamp, using more modern materials, of another first tied many years before. Even to assume such a loose time-scale is dangerous in itself as most flies are just re-introductions of what can often be quite ancient patterns.*

❧ *The truly classic patterns are those which were designed to be fished in very specific circumstances by fisher fly dressers who caught fish or tied flies not simply for enjoyment, but because it was how they earned a living.*

THE FOLK TRADITION OF FLY-TYING

by C. R. PEARCE, November 1970

FLY-TYING IS a practical art. Its products have to catch fish. This must have guided the hands and eyes of its practitioners from the beginning, though some flies may seem more of fancy than of function. Yet many of them catch fish, either because fish can be daft enough for anything (which is happily sometimes true) or because even fancy flies may accidentally embody sound principles of design.

Trial-and-error is the scientific method of a traditional phase, and survival depends on success. Many successful modern flies are little more than simplifications or elaborations of old recipes. Thus is tradition justified. Nevertheless, a sophisticated and quite ruthless scientific development is even now superseding the centuries-old traditional practices.

Perhaps we should distinguish two kinds of tradition, both of which have contributed to the development of angling methods, namely the folk tradition and the literary one. I doubt if anyone has bothered to separate them sufficiently.

Fly-tyers of the past were mostly rural craftsmen with a conservative respect for tradition and a real, if limited, interest in the facts of nature and fish behaviour. They seldom read books. They adjusted to local conditions, and the methods they evolved (for development, however slow, did take place over the centuries) were appropriate to their own areas.

W. H. Lawrie, in his recent books, has described the different fly-styles of different regions. For instance, the very distinctive Scottish styles associated with the Tweed, Clyde, and Tummel areas. England, too, produced its own variety. Inevitably, methods of fishing differed according to differences in the fishing waters themselves, and these methods are often not successfully transplantable. Localised styles in artificial flies were mainly products of the folk tradition.

But angling has a long rich literary tradition, not the least of its pleasures, and literature has its own, often separate line of development. In the early literature plagiarism was rife and one frequently suspects writers of being indifferent to, or even ignorant of, local practices which must sometimes have been more varied and sensitive than what was printed in their books. From *The Boke of St Albans* to *The Practical Angler* almost the same dozen drab flies were described in five centuries of print. We cannot doubt they were in fact used by practical as well as literary anglers. But their susceptibility to subtle changes of detail to suit different waters seemed to escape notice by the writers. Thus the two traditions tended to separate and proceed in parallel instead of reinforcing each other.

Eventually, however, the folk tradition asserted itself. Some nineteenth-century angling writers, more familiar with the bench than the desk, brought into the literature a refreshing sense of reality. In them the folk tradition at last became articulate. I am thinking of men like John Younger, the St Boswells' cobbler. Other contemporaries, like Thomas Tod Stoddart and W. C. Stewart, were at home in both traditions. In their day, flies, like contemporary furniture, were being elaborated by ingenious inventors beyond functional limits, at least as far as native practices defined them. Folk tradition was being swamped and might have been extinguished had it not fought back.

Awa wi yer tinsey sae braw!
Our troots winna thole it ava,
sang Stoddart:
Wee dour-looking huiks are the thing,
Moose body and laverock wing.

The very title of Stewart's classic, *The Practical Angler*, is a protest against the literary tradition. Within its pages he names his influences: 'the best professional anglers of the day. . . . We have gained more from half an hour's conversation with such than from all the books we ever read up on the subject, and their number is not small; most works upon angling being rather amusing than instructive'. He scorned 'fine-spun theories'. Of course, he didn't put an end to them. Both theory and the protest against it seem destined to accompany the sport of fishing for ever.

But exponents of the folk tradition, however practical they might strive to be, could occasionally give rein to fancy. I cannot resist the pleasure of quoting again from Stoddart. In his *Angler's Companion*, this time in prose, he once more knocks the gaudy trend in fly-tying, waxing sarcastic about the variety of coloured materials considered necessary. Isn't there something almost uncanny about this mock prophecy which seems to anticipate by more than a century the use of fluorescent materials? 'Nay, were it possible, by some adaptation of phosphorus, to cause hooks to reveal their trimmings in the dark, no doubt a nocturnal assortment would become possessed ... of all the powers of diablerie and witchcraft'. But don't get me wrong; I am not claiming fluorescence as part of the folk tradition. It belongs to the scientific development of fishing methods that succeeded the folk tradition and may even supersede it.

In a very obvious sense this scientific period of fishing history belongs to the literary rather than to the folk tradition. Its agents were the educated types writing for a social elite, until the 1870 Education Acts greatly increased their readership. Since then, though big words, like entomology and ichthyology, don't catch trout, they have helped to improve fishing methods and augment the total quantity of fishing pleasure.

This later development has already gone through several phases of its own.

Nevertheless, a good case can be made out for the view that science has not yet done much more than improve on the old. Nearly everything of lasting value was already embedded in the folk contribution, even nymph and dry-fly fishing. John Younger, an obscure Tweed-side shoemaker, was the precursor of Skues by nearly a century (though Skues himself might have named Stewart instead); and Stoddart and Stewart all but invented dry-fly fishing before it began on the English chalk-streams. 'All but,' you may say, is 'not quite'; but it supports my case that these things already existed in germ within the folk tradition, which is much richer than was thought and may still contain a few undisclosed secrets, as I shall presently show.

Angling's scientific age, through which we are still passing, has many achievements to its credit, though some have suffered partial eclipse by the successes that followed. Halford and the earlier exponents of the principle of exact imitation are being deservedly rehabilitated today. Did they not focus our eyes on actual insects instead of on traditional or fanciful recipes? Halford has been criticised because he wasn't born a trout or with a trout's vision. But by making us interested in the appearance and identity of water insects, he brought anglers back to the sources that originally inspired the anonymous founders of the folk tradition and laid a basis for subsequent development.

Today, it almost seems, everything necessary is known about the life-histories of the commoner water flies. We keep reading new studies about the rarer or more 'difficult' insects; but the average angler is well grounded on his rudiments, and when he goes in for higher education it is not always necessary for success but rather a means of satisfying an aroused interest. For more practical purposes he still follows tradition (scientifically enriched, of course). He may refer to Harris or Goddard, using their keys and coloured photographs to help him identify the fly on the water. He buys at the tackle shop the latest creations by Lane or Walker or Sawyer or Bucknall or Clegg; or else he gets their recipes for his own tying.

In fact, it is difficult to escape tradition. Even the few, the very few even today, who try to match the size, form, shade, and translucency of their tyings with the characters of the natural insects, even when they improve on Halford by using a mirror in a bowl of water and wetting their materials before selection, are not far from the great man who accelerated the rate, but did not greatly change the direction in which tradition was going.

The mention of translucency just now recalls J. W. Dunne, angler and philosopher, who sought to transcend the limits of substance and time. Both experiments are now rather out of fashion. In trying to evaporate the solidity of the body of an artificial fly by whitening the hook-shank and using Cellulite instead of silk, his object was to get the effect of life. The body of the living fly, he claimed, was suffused in light, but the light went out in death. Trout are predators, attracted by living food. Translucency is an indicator of life. It's a good old argument, long-embedded in the tradition. Dunne's successors who use hair and dubbings to get similar effects have come round full circle to the traditional starting point. Mouse, mole, rabbit, hare, and other furs have always been used for the very same purpose.

The appearance or suggestion of life is one of the secrets I promised to exemplify in the tradition. I quote again from W. C. Stewart as the heir of the folk tradition, one of the first articulate voices speaking for the anonymous originators of the British way of angling. One of his objectives was to make his spiders look alive. Shape and neatness were more important, he thought, than colour, provided the four common drab colours of natural insects were used. But, above all, liveliness was essential.

He repeats this again and again as a basic conviction. The trout must be 'deceived by an appearance of life'. If the fly is 'made of sufficiently soft materials, the water agitates the feathers and gives them a life-like appearance, which has a wonderful effect and is of itself a sufficient reason for trout preferring them....' The hackles, hen rather than cock, should be from common native birds: 'Their superiority consists in their much greater resemblance to the legs of an insect, and their extreme soft-

ness.... The least motion will agitate and impart a singularly life-like appearance to it, whereas it would have no effect upon a cock hackle' (remember, he advocated upstream rather than downstream fishing).

Thus Stewart sought to build liveliness into his flies by his method of construction. The great G. E. M. Skues, founder of modern nymph fishing, acknowledged himself Stewart's disciple in his methods of putting 'kick' into his creations. No doubt scientific experiment will take over the problem from where these men left it. Perhaps artificials will be made to behave of themselves by the exploitation of the re-coil tendencies of certain synthetic materials. The technique of the 'induced take' and the re-discovery of the 'dropperless cast' (first described in print by Stoddart) are interesting contemporary attacks on this important problem.

Assuredly, the scientific revolution, in which we live, and which affects angling as well as everything else, will continue to transform methods. The folk tradition, which, as I have tried to show, is very rich, may eventually be swamped and extinguished. But before that happens, perhaps as a kind of insurance against it happening, it is good to look back on the aims and methods of the past and to give them due credit.

◆ *The truly innovative thinking behind the flies created by a small group of pioneer fly dressers whose patterns influenced much of what is done on today's trout waters, both running and still, formed a fascinating series in the early seventies.*

◆ *Some of the revolutionary flies were tied by entomologists with a detailed eye on the natural insect and its behaviour; others by river keepers in tune with the many mysteries that unfolded with the passing of the riverside seasons. A few were tied by mathematicians and philosophers whose quest to find an artificial representation followed a very different path.*

FAMOUS FLY DRESSERS
by DONALD OVERFIELD, *January 1971*

1. G. E. M. SKUES
January 1971

A Newfoundlander by birth, Skues caught his first chalk-stream trout in the summer of 1875. A disciple of Halford, he was a dry-fly man only for many years until, when fishing the Itchen, the trout refused his floating offering. His thoughts turned to underwater life and how it could be represented. Without this road to Damascus decision, would we still be firmly under the spell of Halfordmania?

Skues has been considered by many to have been the inventor of nymph fishing. That he did not in fact invent this form of angling does not in any way alter the importance of his place in fly fishing history. What he did do was to bring a measure of sanity on to the chalk-streams of this country, which, during the late nineteenth and early part of the twentieth century, were in the grip of Halfordmania, a condition far more severe in the disciples of Halford than in the great man himself.

Skues was born in Newfoundland in 1858, coming to England with his family in 1861. Two years later his parents sailed for India, leaving the young G.E.M. in the care of grandparents in Somerset. He proved to be a bright lad, winning a scholarship to Winchester when he was 14. It was here that he caught his first trout, during the summer of 1875, taken from the Old Barge beat of the River Itchen, a water he was destined to fish for more than 56 years and which he described so well in his later books.

On leaving Winchester at the age of 20, he was articled to a firm of solicitors, eventually becoming a partner in the firm when he was 37. Unlike Halford, who had, it seems, unlimited time and money to devote to his researches, Skues was always hard-pressed to find enough time to put his many ideas to the test, being an active partner in his profession up to the age of 82.

In his early fly fishing years he, like so many others, was under the spell of Halford and the dry fly. A day on the Itchen in 1892 caused him to reflect on the wisdom of using only the floater. No matter what he offered the trout that day, his dry flies were ignored. It was the sinking of a poorly dressed Dark Olive which brought results and sowed the seeds that were to germinate in later years into true upstream nymphing as a respectable and most efficient means of taking trout.

His early writings on the subject brought much abuse via the correspondence columns of that time. What many failed to realise was that he was putting order and system into what had been an accepted form of angling, particularly in the North, for many years – namely the use of the upstream wet fly. Unlike many of his attackers, he was never dogmatic, usually prefacing his comments with such terms as, 'it is only my personal belief', a trait rare in angling writers both then and now!

His attitude to fly dressing was refreshing. He certainly did not consider all that had gone before to be of no use, but he did think that in the case of the artificial nymph there was room for improvement in the dressings. Though not a trained entomologist, he was a sharp-eyed observer, and he realised that the style of tying the nymph was wide open for experimentation loosely based on the exact representation theory. His early dressings were certainly aimed at true representation, but he later developed what could best be described as the caricature style.

As most fly dressers do, he experimented with many new materials and, again like most thoughtful dressers, he came to the conclusion that silk, fur and feather could not be bettered. Rarely did he use quill for bodies, having realised at an early stage the value of furs to represent the translucency of the natural – seals' fur for the bodies of his spinners, softer fur such as mole and water-rat for the nymphs, and heron and condor herl for the floaters.

For all his forward thinking, he seems to have had one mental block – his refusal to dress the wings of a dun as seen in nature, pressed close together in the vertical plane. He insisted on dressing his artificials in the purist tradition with double split wings, possibly in the belief that they landed more gently on the water.

Throughout his life he carried on a voluminous correspondence with fellow fly dressers all over the world. Many can testify to his generosity and, in later life, the ease with which he could be nettled! As I write this I have before me a letter recently arrived from America

from Karl Otto von Keinbusch, a near contemporary of Skues. Keinbusch corresponded for some time with him and in one letter he gave Skues the dressing of the Rat-faced Macdougal. This brought back the stinging reply that only the Yankees could give a fly such an outlandish name. Keinbusch replied, 'What about the Bloody Butcher?' Skues did not reply for some little time!

One of my treasures is a nymph tied by Skues. It is his dressing of the Iron Blue nymph, and though tied quite late in his life – he tied flies up to his eighty-seventh year – it is a perfect example of what a nymph should look like.

The exquisitely tapered body is of mole's fur spun on to crimson silk, the silk exposed for two turns at the tail end. The whisks are three short, white, soft hackle fibres and the legs are represented by no more than two turns of a hackle from a jackdaw, very short in the fibre. The nymph has a delicacy and economy of materials about it, so different from some of the commercially tied horrors of today.

Apart from his skills at the fly-tying bench, and by the stream, he was also a gifted writer, his contribution to the literature of angling being considerable.

His first book, *Minor Tactics of the Chalk-stream*, was published in 1910, followed in 1921 by what must rank as one of the milestones in fly fishing literature, *The Way of a Trout with a Fly*. In 1932 was published *Sidelines, Sidelights and Reflections*, and in 1939 *Nymph Fishing for Chalk-stream Trout*. Two further books were published after his death, *Silk, Fur and Feather* and *Itchen Memories*.

Skues was for many years a member of the Fly-fishers' Club in London, but his modesty would seem to have stopped him accept-ing the presidency of that club, an honour he richly deserved.

He was fortunate in that he enjoyed a long and interesting life. Just four days before his death he was busy writing to his many friends on fly dressing matters. He died only one week away from his ninety-first birthday, during August, 1949.

He can be best summed up as a man who was skilled in his craft, be it fly dressing or at the waterside, a keen observer with an open and receptive mind, and a man not given to dogmatic statements in his writings. All these are attributes rarely found in one man.

🜁 *It is logical that any fly should include in its name its colour and form or most important material, hence patterns like the Mallard and Claret, Snipe and Purple and so on. More modern patterns, and particularly those transient nine-day-wonders, sport more fanciful names often linked with their promise of great execution. The Dark Marauder, Rasputin and Ace of Spades spring immediately to mind.*

🜁 *Around the turn of the century, fly dressers had a far more memorable way of naming the fruits of their vices. A pinch of wool plucked from a sensitive part of a ram was an important ingredient in the fly sent up by a Devon fly-tyer for inspection by Skues, who, mindful of the niceties of his age, gave it its never-to-be-forgotten name.*

2. R. S. AUSTIN

August 1971

It is possible for a man to be a highly competent fly dresser, well-known within his immediate area, dressing flies to suit his native rivers and yet remain relatively unknown outside his parish boundaries. But it needs only one fly of proven worth to be devised at his bench to ensure him a place in the long history of angling. For R. S. Austin that fly was the Tups Indispensable.

Towards the turn of the nineteenth century Austin lived at Tiverton, in Devon, where he combined the business of being a hair dresser with that of a professional fly-tyer. Before settling in Tiverton he had spent many years in the Army, attaining the rank of sergeant-major in the Royal Artillery and serving in the Crimean War.

During the summer of 1900 G. E. M. Skues was engaged in correspondence with Austin on matters relating to fly dressing, and in the course of their letter writing Austin sent to Skues a sample of a fly tied on a Limerick hook, stating that he, Austin, had taken a number of large trout, more than 2 lb, from the mouth of the River Loman with the fly. Skues returned the fly and asked what the body materials were. Austin replied, sending him both the dressing and a quantity of the body dubbing.

Skues proved the value of the fly dressed with the body material sent to him when he rose 18 trout on the River Wandle in one day's fishing towards the end of the 1900 season, repeated the performance on a day in April, 1901, by taking seven brace of trout from the Itchen.

Skues had suggested to Austin that this successful fly should be christened and put forward the name Tup's Indispensable, being a veiled reference to the location on the animal from which the main dubbing ingredient was obtained. Austin was non-committal about it, but a report in *The Field* describing Skues' excellent day on the Itchen, in which he referred to the fly as the Tup's Indispensable, sealed its fate, and it has been known by that name ever since. Austin, in turn, was deluged with requests for this pattern.

In later years Austin set down his favourite dressings, though these were not printed commercially. Among them is his dressing for the Red Spinner. This he gives as follows . . . 'This is a hackled fly tied with yellow silk on a No. 00 hook. It is made with a body sparsely dressed, of a mixture of white ram's wool and lemon coloured spaniel's fur in equal parts, and a little fur from a hare's poll, and sufficient red mohair to give the mixture a pinkish shade. It is hackled with a yellow spangled lightish blue cock's hackle and has whisks of the same colour'.

This, basically, is the dressing of the Tup's Indispensable, although it omits the distinguishing feature of two or three turns of yellow silk at the tail end of the body. That this feature is an integral part of the Tup's is shown in a letter from Austin to Skues wherein he states ... 'the small yellow tip is conspicuous in the natural fly and I have regarded it as a very desirable feature in the imitation'.

From this we can be sure that Austin was most certainly endeavouring to represent a recognisable species but does the description 'Red Spinner' identify it? The term can cover a number of the olives, but it would not seem to be a close representation of the large dark olive. The medium olive female spinner does have two yellowish segments at the rear of the body, although the remainder var-

ies from a yellow-olive-brown to a reddish-brown. The female small dark olive spinner again shows the last body segments as being yellow, but the rest of the body is dark brown to reddish-brown – hardly the colour of the dubbing mix for the Tup's Indispensable. Could it be that Austin had named the fly in error, and that it was not intended to represent one of the red spinners?

Courtney Williams in his book, *A Dictionary of Trout Flies*, considers that the artificial described could represent the male pale watery spinner. The body of that fly is of a creamy translucence with an olive sheen, but the last three segments are of an orange-brown colour, certainly not yellow, a point Austin is most insistent upon.

I have spent a considerable time trying to form a conclusive opinion as to what Austin was getting at. The term red spinner can, I think, be discounted in line with Courtney Williams' suggestion, but his impression that Austin was trying to imitate the male pale watery spinner is also subject to doubt.

My opinion, for what it is worth, is that the Tup's Indispensable comes nearest to the female yellow May spinner, at least so far as the body coloration is concerned, but to be dogmatic would be the height of stupidity. The fact that it is frequently taken when a variety of olives or pale wateries are on the water only adds confusion, but that it is a first-class fly is beyond dispute.

A sample of the original dubbing material was kept between glass slides at the Fly-fishers' Club in London for many years, having been presented to the club by Skues. This dubbing differs slightly from the Red Spinner dressing set down by Austin in that it also included a small quantity of cream seal's fur. However, this is a minor point, and it can be assumed that the Red Spinner dressing of Austin, plus the addition of the turns of yellow silk at the tail, will produce the Tup's Indispensable.

Following Skues' publicity of this fly in *The Field*, Austin was hard put to keep up with the orders that poured in to him. Many anglers wished to know what the materials were which made up the dubbing, but Austin kept this a close secret, sharing it only with Skues and C. A. Hassam, a most expert fly-tyer and friend of Skues. Many tried to determine the individual materials by separating the dubbing; but this proved to be no easy task when all they had to go on was a collection of fibres divorced from their bulk source. This difficulty no doubt explains many of the most awful flies masquerading as Tup's over the years.

Austin requested that Skues and Hassam should keep his secret, and this they did until long after Austin's death in 1911. The fly continued to be tied commercially by Miss Austin, the daughter of R.S., and it was not until she retired from business in 1936, or thereabouts, that permission was given for Skues to reveal the true dressing of the Tup's Indispensable. This he did through the medium of the summer edition of the Fly-fishers' Club *Journal* in 1936.

❧ Unlike his fellow countrymen, Theodore Gordon was not content to confine his fishing in the Pennsylvania streams to offering the wet fly in the standard down-and-across technique.
❧ An ardent disciple of the English Halfordian dry-fly-only school, Gordon developed a race of flies to imitate his own country's naturals and he can truly be called the pioneer of 'matching the hatch' in America.

3. THEODORE GORDON
February 1971

Theodore Gordon has been called the Halford of America, and not without good reason. He was the first angler in that country to try to systemise the dressing of artificials in relation to the natural fly on the water, and he seems to have been one of the first to appreciate the advantages, in certain circumstances, of up-stream dry-fly angling.

Before the early part of the twentieth century, American anglers had been content to fish the downstream wet fly, though some no doubt did cast upstream for variation. There may even have been one or two anglers who gave thought to the dry fly, but I think it is fair to say that Gordon, through his writings in angling magazines of the period, gave dry-fly angling the impetus to make it a recognised technique in that country.

He was born in Pittsburgh, Pennsylvania, in 1854. As a young man he spent much of his time fishing the streams and rivers around his home. His hero at that time would seem to have been Francis Francis, whose book, *A Book of Angling*, he considered as his piscatorial bible. He can have gained little knowledge of the dry fly from that particular volume, Francis devoting only two paragraphs to the subject. It was not until he was 36 and making his way as a successful Wall Street financier that the techniques of the dry fly came to his notice.

A book which he had ordered from England finally arrived towards the end of 1889. That book was F. M. Halford's *Dry Fly Fishing in Theory and Practice*. Gordon became absorbed in what Halford postulated, and a trans-Atlantic correspondence started. On February 22, 1890, Gordon received a packet from Halford containing 48 patterns of the dry fly. He lost no time in putting them to the test on the rivers and streams of the Catskill mountain area which were now his angling haunts. His experiences soon revealed to him that while one or two of Halford's patterns bore some similarity to the natural flies, the remainder were far removed from the local ephemeroptera. He set out to adapt Halford's theories and patterns to suit the prevailing conditions and fly life.

At that time no book on entomology relating to American fly-life had been published. In fact the first, to my knowledge, was Preston Jennings' volume, *A Book of Trout Flies*, and this was not published until the mid-'thirties, many years after Gordon's death. And of course American fly-life differs considerably from one side of the country to the other, to a far greater extent than is the case here.

It is to the detriment of fly-dressing literature that Gordon never published the results of his studies in book form. But he did write articles for the angling magazines, and he did carry on correspondence with many fly-dressers in this country, Skues and Marston being but two. These letters, and the articles, were gathered together and edited by John MacDonald, and were finally published in 1947 under the title *The Complete Fisherman: The Notes of Theodore Gordon.*

From these collected writings we can deduce that Gordon was a most observant and thoughtful angler. His fishing journeys took him to many rivers up and down the eastern seaboard, where he was forever noting the variations in the fly-life. His main concern, though, were the ephemeroptera of the Catskill mountains, and he was the pioneer in his country of 'matching the hatch'.

He departed from the Halford disciples' doctrine of rigid imitation in that he dressed his patterns more in keeping with the impressionist school, believing that one basic dressing with certain changes of shade could be made to represent not only one species of fly at different times of the year, but that this one fly could imitate a number of naturals.

His most famous fly must surely be the Quill Gordon, the hook size can vary between 10 and 14. The body is wound from light stripped peacock quill for the summer fly and a darker shade of quill for the spring months. The hackle ranges from blue dun in spring to pale honey dun in summer. Tail whisks should be three fibres from the summer duck feather, the wings from the same feather, rolled. Gordon invariably rolled his wings. In spite of his obvious regard for Halford, he never felt disposed to give his flies split wings, believing the rolled wing to be more realistic. Some present-day dressings of this fly stipulate a gold wire rib, but I do not think Gordon used this doubtful refinement.

In 1905, when he was 41, Gordon became a professional fly-dresser, and from that time he was never far away from his Catskill streams. What prompted him to start tying flies for a living can only be guessed at, but one suspects that his personal world of high finance may well have crashed about his ears – and Wall Street is no place for an overnight pauper. Details of his activities at that period are vague and we may never know the reasons for this change in his life. Whatever the cause, he could now spend his time doing what was uppermost in his mind – evolving patterns to suit the naturals of the Catskills.

He was to enjoy 19 years engaged in this study, writing his articles and keeping up a flood of letters with anglers in this country.

In 1915 he died from tuberculosis, which had been creeping up on him over a number of years. He was 61. Rumour had it that he had been working on a book setting out all his dressings with the corresponding natural flies, but no manuscript was ever discovered.

It was not until 1947 and the publication of his edited articles and letters that anglers began to sit up and take notice that here was an American, unheard of for many years, who had contributed something of real value to the history of fly fishing. His memory was finally honoured by the formation of the Theodore Gordon Flyfishers' Club in New York in 1962. This excellent organisation has been in the forefront of the drive against pollution and it is continually trying to educate anglers in the matter of trout conservancy. The club has issued thousands of posters to be shown at the streamside which carry the message, 'Limit Your Kill, Don't Kill Your Limit'. Gordon would have approved of that.

All modern fly fishers owe a debt of gratitude to Alfred Ronalds, for it was he who brought order out of chaos by relating the angler's name for the flies of his day to the families of natural insects they had been tied to represent.

It is perhaps not so widely known that Ronalds, in his classic Flyfishers' Entomology, *actually pre-dated the generally accepted date of the flowering of the dry fly by some fifty years.*

4. ALFRED RONALDS

November 1971

Though my angling library is not of the size, or value, to bring bibliophiles beating a path to my door, brandishing cheque books, I do nevertheless have a certain number of books with which I would be extremely loath to part, and high on that list is a mint copy of the fifth edition of Alfred Ronalds' *The Flyfishers' Entomology*.

This book, so ably written by this fly-tying entomologist, was an immediate success when first published in 1836 and was to remain so, running into eleven editions, the last one being in 1921, all of them now avidly sought by the angling book collector.

What was the appeal of the book? There had been other books relating to the matching of the artificial to the natural fly, but these paled into insignificance when compared to Ronalds' superb work. He was one of the first to

bring order and system into the complex subject, sorting out each insect and classifying it in relation to the recognised Latin nomenclature, so providing a sound basis for identification at a time when other writers were inclined to invent their own system and naming of the natural fly, to the confusion of everyone. That Ronalds was not entirely accurate is of small import, and some of the anomalies of the earlier editions were put right in the fifth edition, edited by Barnard Smith. What is important is the fact that Ronalds set the pattern for subsequent books.

Apart from its obvious attempt at scientific accuracy, one of the most appealing aspects of *The Flyfishers' Entomology* is the superb hand-coloured copper-plate illustrations showing the natural fly alongside the appropriate artificial – a method of illustration which has considerable value and one which, surprisingly, Halford did not emulate. Indeed, Halford gave illustrations only of the artificials, and it was left to his nephew, Martin Mosely, to produce a small volume showing the natural flies, which is best read in conjunction with Halford's work.

I am quite willing to go on record as stating that not one book on trout flies and their imitations has ever been published, either before or after Ronalds, that can hold a candle to his outstanding illustrations. Each plate is a work of art, and I believe I am correct when I say that it was Ronalds himself who engraved the plates. Later editions, in particular the 1921 Sheringham edition, are but pale imitations of the earlier copies. So much for modern printing techniques, though one must admit that hand-coloured illustrations would put the cost of a similar modern work beyond the pockets of all but a few.

Most of the ground-work that culminated in *The Flyfishers' Entomology* was carried out on the rivers and streams of Staffordshire, where Ronalds lived. He was no idle observer of the ways of the trout and its feeding habits, and he went to considerable trouble and expense to build himself a substantial brick observatory set on the banks of the River Blyth, near Uttoxeter. From this vantage-point he spent many hours observing at close range the natural fly-life of that stream, and the manner in which the trout reacted to the natural insects under varying conditions.

Early in his book Ronalds endears himself to those who would believe that it is logical to dress the artificials with materials close to the natural fly in shade and colour. Having given his opinion regarding the sense of taste of the trout, and having arrived at the conclusion that this sense is inferior to that of the human animal, he goes on to say '. . . but it furnishes no plea to the quacks and bunglers, who, inventing or espousing a new theory, whereby to hide their want of skill or spare their pains, would kill all fish with one fly, as some doctors would cure all diseases with one pill'. I like that!

Ronalds' instructions for the dressing of the artificial trout fly runs to about four pages, the bulk of the volume being concerned with describing the dressings and materials, 47 artificials being fully set out and illustrated. However, the relatively small number of pages devoted to the mechanics of tying a fly provide a lucid example.

All the flies described and illustrated in this book are typical of the wet flies of the period if we exclude the three palmer dressings which Ronalds devised as being representative of three types of caterpillar, but I am of the same opinion as Sheringham, who edited the last edition, that Ronalds came within an ace of describing dry-fly angling when he wrote: 'When a fish has just risen at a natural object, it is well for the fisherman to try to throw into the curl occasioned by the rise, and left as a mark for him; but should the undulations have nearly died away before he can throw to the spot, then he should throw (as nearly as he can judge) a yard or two above it, and allow the flies to float down to the supposed place of the fish.'

Sheringham in a footnote to the last edition says '. . . really it is the dry fly in everything but oil' –

meaning, of course, the flotant. Had Ronalds, at the time he penned those words, realised the significance of the floating dun, then he would have pre-dated the generally accepted date of the flowering of the dry-fly by some 50 years.

Eight years after his book was published, Ronalds left his native Staffordshire and moved to North Wales, where no doubt he fished, but of his activities there are no records. He was to remain there only for a brief four years before once more removing, in 1848, this time to Australia.

To Ronalds we owe a twofold debt: He brought order into fly-dressing by relating the angler's names for flies of the day to the recognised entomological system, and he gave to fly fishing and fly-tying one of the most beautiful books ever published.

While undoubtedly being one of the most controversial figures in fly fishing history, it seems that Halford was not quite the stiff-necked purist that he was reputed to be, the 'upstream dry fly at any costs' reputation being earned for him by more blinkered followers.

ᴥ *The man himself, while contributing much to the growing art of the dry fly, was never so dogmatic and even said that the coarse fisher was just as much a sportsman as the most rigid dry-fly angler, sentiments greatly at odds with his generally accepted reputation.*

5. FREDERICK HALFORD
April 1971

The name of Halford is still capable of causing some anglers to search their minds for the most derogatory and disparaging comments that they can lay tongue to. A gentle questioning of such folk will usually unearth the fact that they have scant knowledge of his books or the man himself, and that their critical judgment is based on handed down folklore. I would doubt whether any angling fly-dresser has been misquoted so often as Frederick M. Halford.

What are the facts of the case? He was born in the Midlands in 1844 and came early to the craft of angling. Adjoining the family home there was a pond in which lived roach and perch. Angling for these creatures sowed the seed that was to flower into the systematic dry-fly code of his later years and make Halford one of the most controversial figures in fishing history.

When he was seven the Halford menage moved to London and the young lad was very soon fishing the Serpentine and Long Pool. In time he came to know the Thames very well from Henley to Twickenham. It was not until the age of 23 that he seriously considered fly fishing as a sporting means of taking trout. A family friend offered him a few days on the Wandle for the 1868 season; and this offer he was quick to take up to further his knowledge of angling.

He set about obtaining the requisite tackle – a rod of 11 feet, the butt and intermediates of hickory and the top joint of cane. He was persuaded to purchase the time-honoured plaited silk and hair line, but he had not been fishing for many months when he quickly saw the real advantages of the then new dressed silk line.

On the matter of flies, his book, *An Angler's Autobiography*, contains a passage which strikes a familiar chord in most of us when we look back on our early days. He is referring to the shop assistant from whom he bought his first selection. '. . . with the affectation of superior knowledge which some of these worthies will adopt, he proceeded to fill the book [*fly book*] with a multitude of what he called standard flies . . . but all far too large for the river in question.'

It was on the Wandle that Halford fell for the charm and complexity of fly fishing, a style of angling which was to make him a legend in his own time. His dry-fly theories spread far beyond the boundaries of the chalk-streams in the South which were to become his regular haunt, collecting on the way many disciples who proved to be far more rigid in their application of the dry-fly code than the *guru* ever intended them to be. These stiff-necked anglers were to be responsible for many of the myths which surrounded the name of Halford.

He was fortunate in being able to retire from business at the age of 45. At this time he had a rod on the Itchen. Four years later he was on the Test, a member of the Houghton Club, and in 1893 he rented a beat on the Kennet at Ramsbury. From 1897 until 1904 he rented various waters on the upper Test and on the Itchen near to Winchester. In 1905 he returned to the more celebrated areas of the Test.

During these years he formulated and systemised the dry-fly code. Previously this had been a very hit-and-miss affair. But he had the time, and the intelligence, to study the entomology of the Test and finally to arrive at a series of dressings which would, in his mind, represent the naturals to be found on that river. A study in such depth had not been carried out before.

If any charge can be levelled at Halford, with any hope of it sticking, it is that he persisted in preaching the advantage of exact representation. Laudable in itself, he nevertheless viewed the fly from the wrong attitude. All his dressings may well have been 'exact' in the eyes of the dresser, but he overlooked one major point – and that was what the fly looked like when seen by the trout, from underneath. We must assume that he was conversant with the translucence of the natural fly's body and the effect of transmitted light on the creature.

It is easy for us, with hindsight, to say, 'What a silly mistake', though this would seem to be one of the very few mistakes he did make. No doubt his flies dressed with their quill or silk bodies would function quite effectively when seen in reflected light. He was aware of the translucent effect of furs and dubbing, but we must remember that during the early part of his fly fishing career the practice of assisting a dry fly to float with the aid of paraffin had not been used to any great extent and, to my knowledge, amadou had not arrived on the scene.

Apart from the question of the body materials, he would seem to have been right on other aspects of the dry fly. He went to great lengths to latch the precise colour of the legs, whisks and wings, and paid considerable attention to size. Today's fly-dressers could do worse than to study all his books.

Floating Flies and How to Dress Them, published in 1886, was the first of a series of books which were to revolutionise fly fishing and cause deep division in the angling ranks. Three years later came *Dry Fly Fishing in Theory and Practice*, to be followed in 1895 by *Making a Fishery*, in which he set down his experiences of trying to improve his beat on the Kennet. 1897 gave us *Dry Fly Entomology*, while 1910 saw *Modern Development of the Dry Fly*. His last book, *The Dry Fly Man's Handbook*, came out only one year before his death in 1914.

A careful study of these books will reveal a fly-dresser and angler far removed from the image painted by some of his critics. We have been told that he abhorred wet-fly fishing. He is on record as saying: '. . . convinced that to be a first-rate performer with the wet fly required considerable natural aptitude and a prolonged study of the subject.' We hear that he considered any form of fishing, other than dry fly, to be beneath consideration, but in 1891 he wrote: 'The bottom-fishers are as true a sportsmen as the most severe dry-fly purist'. Does that sound like an angling snob?

Those who have not read his books are oft-times insistent that he said one should cast only upstream. But that is not so. He saw no reason why one should not cast downstream, but added that one's chance with the dry-fly would be remote – which is logical when one considers the drag factor. The comment most frequently trotted out is how he discarded the Gold-ribbed Hare's Ear fly because he did not know what it represented. He did discard it, it is true, but one must remember that he was formulating a precise system of classification in which there was no room for guess-work. Each artificial had to be a representation of an identifiable natural fly, and within these confines it would be logical to throw out the G.R.H.E.

The fact that in his later years he became rather pedantic, and that some of his theories on entomology have been proved wrong, does not detract one jot or tittle from Halford's contribution to the craft of fly fishing. Through his patient research he gave to angling literature a series of books which will always command respect. Would that there were more like him.

≈ *While history will record certain flies and methods as being the brainchild of a particular angler, the truth is that some, if not all, were being used for many years before being offered into the public eye.*
≈ *Yorkshire's Alex Mackintosh was clearly one of those sadly forgotten pioneers whose ideas formed at least the germ of what was to earn another a secure place in fly fishing history. Nearly two hundred years ago, Mackintosh was certainly aware of the importance of achieving translucence in the artificial and was most exacting as to the materials used and even when and where they were gathered. How many of today's fly dressers would go to the trouble of seeking 'brown hair from the flank of a brindled calf collected in the Spring'?*

6. ALEX MACKINTOSH
September 1971

The chalk-streams of the East Riding of Yorkshire have produced remarkably little in the way of angling literature over the years compared to that which has come from the much-vaunted waters of the Test valley in Hampshire. The northern streams, with their source deep in the chalk strata of the Wolds, are the equal of any to be found in the South Country, be it from the standpoint of water purity, the quality and quantity of trout, the fly-life, and not least the beauty of the surrounding countryside. The Driffield Beck, the

Foston waters and the Costa can hold their own against all-comers.

Occasional references to the streams are to be found in only a few books. Halford records fishing the area when writing his auto-biography, as does J. W. Hills in his book, *My Sporting Life*. C. F. Walker, in *Angler's Odyssey*, de-votes a whole chapter to the north-ern streams, while H. R. Francis tells of interesting days on both the Foston and the Driffield water dur-ing the mid-1800s in his contribu-tion to the Badminton Library series, *Fishing, Salmon and Trout*.

Though the streams of the East Riding have yet to produce literary anglers after the style of Plunket Greene, Skues and Halford, at least one local fisherman considered it worthwhile to set down his methods and techniques for taking fish from the Driffield water. That man was Alexander Mackintosh, and his book, *The Driffield Angler*, was first published in 1806.

Mackintosh was, as one would suspect, a Scot and not a native of the Yorkshire Wolds. However, towards the close of the eighteenth century he was living in the small market town of Driffield where he divided his time between the run-ning of the Red Lion Hotel, situ-ated in Middle Street North, hard by the fine old parish church, and fishing the stream which is within brisk walking distance of the town.

Mackintosh must surely have been a popular personality with the local sportsmen of that time, his es-tablishment providing the head-quarters for the Middleton East Hunt and the gathering place for anglers, many of whom came from many miles away to stay at the Red Lion while enjoying their days fishing on the Driffield Beck.

In those times the Driffield Ang-ling Club, now one of the premier clubs in the country, was not in existence. The formation of that au-gust body did not come about until 1833, and before that date Mackin-tosh tells us that . . . 'permission to fish will not be difficult to obtain for gentlemen and fair sportsmen'. No doubt he acted as go-between for the riparian owners and his guests who wished to fish the stream.

Mackintosh established a well-founded reputation as a skilful an-gler and fly-tyer, his chapter on fly-dressing in *The Driffield Angler* being of considerable interest and worthy of study in that many of the dressings would seem to be the result of careful observation of the natural fly, and not just repetitions of previous patterns. His knowledge of entomology was limited. Nevertheless, flies tied to his patterns would still take trout today.

I am fortunate in being able to cast a fly on water which still has a decent hatch of Mayfly, and I can testify to the efficacy of Mackintosh's dressing of the Green Drake. He gives it thus: 'The wings, the grey-spotted feather of a mallard dyed yellow; the body, a little fine wool from the ram's testicles, which is a beautiful dusty yellow, and ribbed with copper-coloured silk, with a dark bittern's hackle for legs and two hairs from the fitchet's tail for the tail, or forks, and a bit of the brown peacock's harl from the tail feather for the head. This is a large fly.'

This dressing, modified only in respect of the feathers which are now on protected birds, though retaining as near as possible the colours of the originals, proved very good medicine for the trout of this age, particularly so when fished flush with the surface in the manner of the spinner. I feel sure that the dusty yellow ram's wool body contributed much to the success of the fly.

Mackintosh's dressing must be one of the earliest references to the use of ram's wool from that particular part of the animal, pre-dating that other famous fly to use a similar body material, the Tup's Indispensable, by some 94 years.

All but two of his dressings specify a dubbed body, the odd men out being the Black Silver Hackle, which uses black ostrich herl, and the Grizzle Hackle, which calls for the fibres from the pheasant tail.

An examination of his stock of dubbing materials would no doubt surprise many of the younger fly-dressers of today, who may imagine that exotic materials have come into use only over the last few years. We find that he uses 'the roots of camel hair, sable fur, bear's hair, black and gold hog's wool, brown hair from the flank of a brindled calf collected in the spring, dark red and black spaniel's fur, black water dog's fur, mohair, the down of the fox-cub' and many more materials which, when carefully blended, give a far better representation of the translucent body of the natural fly than all the silks and stripped peacock herls.

That Mackintosh's book was received with enthusiasm there can be little doubt, because four years after the original publication, in 1806, a second edition became available to which he added instructions for shooting, hunting and deer stalking. This was followed 11 years later by yet a third edition. Despite the number of copies which must have been on the market in the early part of the nineteenth century, few seem to have survived, and now *The Driffield Angler* is a collector's item, those which find their way on to the market commanding a fair price.

Despite the success of his book, the old angler, fly-tyer and innkeeper would seem to have had considerable difficulty in hanging on to any profits accruing from the sale of his work, because eight years after the third edition was published he died in the Driffield workhouse, a sad end for a most accomplished fly-dresser and angler.

   Throughout his long career as a professional fly dresser, Roger Woolley never used a vice, maintaining that personal contact between materials and hook was essential to the tying of a neat and secure fly.
   Woolley was particularly fond of what became known as the Glanrhos style of tying in which a single hackle was used to form both wings and legs. He was one of very few professionals to be praised by G. E. M. Skues for his imitations of the natural nymphs.

7. ROGER WOOLLEY
December 1971

Roger Woolley was one of that rare breed of professional fly-dressers who took a most enthusiastic interest in the fly-life of the rivers and streams, devising a considerable number of patterns in line with his observations of the natural fly in all its forms. Not for him the run-of-the-mill production-line techniques, tying flies to other dressers' receipts, though he would, of course, tie any fly to a particular pattern to order.

Woolley spent all his life within close distance of his beloved River Dove. He was born in the year 1877 at 13 Burton Street, Tutbury, Derbyshire, and even as a child he could always be found by the river. This is not unusual, for small boys are drawn to running water, but where young Woolley differed from others was that he was not there to throw stones and splash in the shallows, but, armed with notebook and pencil, to make sketches and notes of what he saw. He seems to have had a natural bent towards entomology, coupled, of course, with a desire to take trout. In this latter endeavour he was helped by his father, a keen angler and a first-class game shot.

Though he was greatly interested in the relationship between the natural fly and the trout, it would seem that he did not tie artificial flies during those early years, and it was not until he was nineteen, in 1896, that the activity that was to dominate his long life came to the fore. In that year he went to Ireland, having taken the post of coachman to a wealthy family, with whom he remained for two years. During that time he met an Irish fly-dresser – alas, history does not name him – and became absorbed with the intricacies of fur and feather.

On his return to England in 1898 he set up in business as a hairdresser-cum-fly-tyer at 5 Marston Road, Hatton, Derbyshire, a few miles from his birthplace. Within a short time fly-dressing became his major source of income. His reputation for the dressing of a neat, secure fly became known locally and then, as with most good craftsmen, the word soon got around and orders came in from places many miles removed from his Derbyshire streams.

Throughout his long career Woolley never used a fly-tying vice. He maintained that to tie a good fly needed the personal contact of fingers to hook and materials, so that the tension of silk and feather could be judged to a fine degree. Of his favourite materials for the bodies of artificials, he, like many other good dressers, came down heavily on the side of seal's fur, because of its translucency and liveliness. His personal preference for winging was for hackle-fibre or hackle-point wings.

He was particularly fond of the winging method first made known by the late Graham Clarke and known as the Glanrhos style of fly. This method involves the use of one hackle to do service both as the wing and the legs. Following the tying in of the whisks and the body, a hackle is prepared in the usual manner by stripping off the flue and stroking the fibres to stand at right-angles to the stalk, except for the tip of the hackle, which is to do service as a single wing.

This hackle tip is tied on to the hook-shank in the vertical plane, the length being judged to give about the height of the natural wing. The remaining hackle is then wound around the hook-shank in the normal manner. The only drawback to this method is that the use of one hackle limits the dressing to that of a natural fly where the wings and legs are of a corresponding colour. Of course, the method can be used for both the wet and dry fly.

If Woolley had a personal preference among the types of artificial, it seems that the nymph must have come high on the list. He corresponded with G. E. M. Skues on this subject over a considerable period and received the accolade of the great man's approval when Skues wrote in *Nymph Fishing for Chalk-stream Trout* that 'tackle dealers in general, wholesale or retail, with few exceptions (of whom Mr Roger Woolley, of Hatton, Derby, and Mr T. J. Hanna, of Stonard Street, Moneymore, Co. Derry, are bright examples) make little effort at genuine representa-

tions of the natural nymph.' The time spent studying the natural fly-life of the river had obviously not been wasted.

Not only did Woolley achieve a well-deserved reputation for his trout flies, but his flies dressed particularly for the grayling were also noted. In *Modern Trout-Fly Dressing*, published in 1932, he lists no fewer than 30 flies specifically for grayling fishing, many of his own devising. When Woolley's book was in its rough draft form he submitted it to Skues, who gave it his unqualified approval. Today, it remains one of the most comprehensive books on fly-tying ever published. If it has a fault, it lies in the poor quality of the illustrations, not so much from the artistic aspect as from the reproduction techniques used. A second edition was published in 1939.

Woolley was also responsible for another book, published in 1938. Called *Fly-fishers' Flies* it sets out the flies, with adequate descriptions, that one is likely to meet with while fishing. Both books are now collectors' items and hard to find.

The demand for Woolley's flies increased and to help him he taught his daughters, of whom there were four, to tie the artificial. Though these flies were not tied by Roger Woolley, he insisted that each fly be examined by him before despatch, and being rightly proud of his own reputation, he would ruthlessly throw out any fly that did not come up to his own personal high standard. He did, of course, continue to dress flies to special order.

Roger Woolley died in his eighty-second year in 1959, still in the little town of Tutbury where he started to dress flies 61 long years before.

❧ Dunne had already designed and flown the first British military aeroplane before channelling his mathematician's mind on to the elusive challenge of tying a dry fly with a translucent body. He succeeded, and his meticulously constructed flies did work, but only when the sun shone. Nevertheless, Dunne's theories brought other and equally fertile minds to bear on the problem and many modern flies bear witness to his genius.

8. J. W. DUNNE
March 1971

In 1924 a book was published which caused many fly-dressers to re-think on their attitude to the question of fly representation. This book was called *Sunshine and the Dry Fly*, and it was written by John William Dunne.

He was principally a mathematician and philosopher who devoted only a brief period of his life to the intricacies of artificial trout-fly design. Born in the latter part of the nineteenth century, he quickly established himself as a pioneer of aircraft design. He was responsible for the first British military aeroplane, built in 1907 under conditions of great secrecy at Blair Atholl. He not only designed the machine, but also flew it.

He is possibly better-known outside the sphere of angling than within it, his books on philosophy and mathematics having had wide acclaim. His volume *An Experiment With Time*, published in 1927, has long been the cause of much discussion, and many hold that his theories cannot be disproved to-day. His sole contribution to the fly fishing world has also caused many to sit and ponder.

In his book he offered the results of his experiments carried out when trying to devise that elusive thing, the translucent body of the dry fly. One quickly realises that Dunne fully understood the problems facing him in trying to achieve his object. The natural fly, when viewed by the trout, is usually seen via transmitted light through the body, and on this aspect he concentrated his efforts.

After considerable experiment he hit upon the idea of painting the shank of the hook with white enamel to obtain the effect of diffusing the reflection. He had tried earlier experiments using silver tinsel wrapped round the hook, but such a covering gave only a thin bright reflection at its high point along the shank, not the overall effect he was seeking. Round the white-painted surface he wound artificial silk to form the body shape (this material is not to be confused with natural silk) and the fly was then completed in the normal manner. When it was soaked in medicinal paraffin and the fly held up to a bright sky, the manner in which a trout would view it, the body became translucent and the solid hard core of the hook shank, because of the diffusing effect of the white enamel, was not apparent. The artificial retained this effect for a long period before needing a further application of paraffin.

During the time he was preparing his book he was experimenting with strands of artificial silks called 'Esplend'or'. Before publication date he contacted the makers of the silks and suggested that it might be a good idea to market a range specifically for fly-tying. This was done and the strands of silk were sold under the trade name of 'Cellulite'.

Dunne went to great lengths to get the exact shade to match the body of the natural fly. The silk manufacturers had supplied him with a sample card of 136 different shades, but he could not find the precise colours he required, and therefore he had to blend the fibres from various strands to achieve his objective. He tells us that it took five weeks of solid endeavour to get the correct body shade of the Blue-winged Olive.

His written instructions for the body of the female is akin to a mathematical formula: $3(298A) + 1(298) + \frac{3}{4}(287)$. What all this means is three lengths from shade number 298A are blended with one length from 298. To this is added three-quarters of the diameter from a length of number 287. Throughout the book he never refers to actual colours or shades. This applies to the hackles as well as the body materials.

He was at great pains to specify the colour and characteristics of the hackles to be used, but then confounded his reader by giving these colours and other details by means of code numbers. It would seem that if one wished to tie Dunne's patterns one had to buy the specially selected hackles from Messeena's, of Leamington Spa, who sold them made up into packets. This firm, of course, is now part of the Veniard concern.

Dunne's dressing of the Dark Mayfly (female) calls for six turns of 'P' behind six turns of 'H2' behind six turns of 'G2'. The code 'P' signifies a palest blue dun saddle hackle, 3 inches long; 'H2' is a pale ginger grizzle cock hackle 3 inches long; and 'G2' represents a grizzled blue dun saddle hackle with very stiff fibres, these having slight brown markings. This hackle is then dyed a greeny yellow. This must surely be the ultimate in precise descriptions of dressing materials.

Dunne's flies do not seem to have been very popular with the rank-and-file of amateur tyers, possibly because of the complications in dressing them. Another likely reason is that the artificial silk dressing of the body was extremely fragile and the teeth of trout could play havoc with the fly. I doubt if a Dunne dressing would stand up to more than one trout. The silk also lacked buoyancy. His dressings, while of considerable academic interest, could be effective only when viewed in strong sunlight, i.e. under conditions of strong transmitted light. On a grey day, the like of which we usually encounter, then they cease to be effective and become no better or worse than any other form of dressing. Be that as it may, Dunne brought fresh thought to bear on the matter and opened the door for future experimenters.

While his translucent body may not have been a roaring success, he did come up with some ideas which I have found to be most effective. One of these is the use of hackle fibres dyed bottle-green and fiery red-wine colour for the wings of the Black Gnat. A mixed bunch of fibres, about 20 of the green and 10 of the red, mixed together and tied sloping back over the body seems to be most effective. It gives a fair representation of the iridescence of the natural wing. He also dispensed with the hackle tip idea for the wings of spinners, preferring to use bunches of hackle fibres tied at right-angles to the hook shank. He makes no claim to having invented the latter method.

It is fly fishing's loss that Dunne did not continue his experiments in an endeavour to reproduce a body which did not have to rely on bright sunlight to achieve translucency. It would seem that having partially proved his point he gave up further work on this subject and went back to his philosophical thoughts and mathematical problems, for *Sunshine and the Dry Fly* was the only angling book to come from his pen.

He died, aged 73, shortly after the last war, at Banbury.

🐟 *William Lunn's pioneering work on the River Test would have been quite enough to make sure of his place in angling history. Add the founding of a dynasty of expert keepers and the creation of a race of highly efficient patterns, and his contribution to fly fishing becomes even more remarkable.*

9. WILLIAM LUNN
October 1971

The River Test in Hampshire, and in particular the excellent waters of the Houghton Club, has known many distinguished and famous fly-fishers down the years, but few can have left such a permanent mark on the area as did Lunn. I doubt if any other man could claim to have founded a dynasty of expert water-keepers as he did, the third generation of his line now being in control of the Houghton Club beats. To think of the Houghton is to think of the Lunns.

William James Lunn was born in London on January 2, 1862. When he was four years old his father was drowned at sea and he was consequently taken by his mother to live at Newport, Essex, where his grandfather was the manager of a brick works. At the age of 12 he ran away from home and took employment on a farm, where he stayed two years before becoming a keeper's assistant on the High Ashurst estate in Surrey. Here he rapidly rose to be the head-keeper. When he was 20 he left High Ashurst to become head-keeper to Sir Arthur Clay at Burrows Lea.

When he was 24 Herbert Norman, then secretary of the Houghton Club, suggested that Lunn should join him on the Test in the post of personal attendant, and so he came to that famous water. Norman's choice was a good one, and I doubt if the club ever had reason to regret it. Within a year, Lunn was in complete charge of the beats of that club, following the retirement of the old keeper, Faithful, a position he was to hold until he retired at the age of 70 in 1932, when he handed over to his son, Alfred.

Lunn came to the Houghton during a time of change in the techniques of fly fishing. Blow-line angling with the live Mayfly still lingered, but the craft of the dry-fly was coming to the fore, and Lunn was to know and be the friend of many of the great men whose names spell out the evolution of that form of angling.

Settling down in his home at Sheepbridge Shallow, he began to improve and maintain the fishery. He was responsible for innovations which are now to be seen on many waters, the use of fly-boards to allow eggs to hatch on the underside free from the depredations of the caddis being one of them. Lunn's interest in and the study of the natural fly-life of the Test is well known, his observations having been well documented in that excellent book, *River Keeper*, by J. W. Hills, published in 1934.

It is curious that despite his obvious interest in all aspects of river life, 29 years were to elapse before Lunn turned his hand to fly-tying, at the suggestion of E. J. Power, in an attempt to translate what he had learned from the natural fly into fur and feather.

Whether Lunn decided at the outset of his fly-dressing activities to use only those materials which were readily available we do not know, but an investigation of his documented dressings show a singular lack of the exotic. Not for him the 'Third-feather-of-the-primary-range-taken-from-the-left-wing-of-the-lesser-Tunisian-mud-splodger-gathered-only-on-the-second-Sunday-after-Epiphany' type of thing. All his materials were those readily available from the fowl-pen or the river bank.

Within a matter of months of taking up fly-dressing, Lunn had evolved the fly that was to make his name in fly fishing history – Lunn's Particular. This fly was first offered to the trout early in the 1917 season as a representation of an olive spinner. It proved successful and gained a reputation, somewhat hard to substantiate, of being able to attract shy fish. One thing we do know is that the fly is a fair pattern for a number of the olive spinners. This fly was followed by another 39 dressings of his own devising, of which the Houghton Ruby, Yellow Boy and Lunn's Caperer are possibly the best-known and most used today.

Lunn had a refreshing approach to fly-dressing and his knowledge of the natural insects and the ways of the trout quickly brought him to the conclusion that the Halford style of dressing, which still held considerable sway, with its insistence on attempting to dress an exact replica of the natural as seen by the angler, rather than the fly-fisher visualising the artificial from the point of view of the trout, was the wrong way to go about it. One could call Lunn's style of dressing impressionistic rather than imitative.

A major point of departure from the Halford style concerned the winging of the artificial. The Halford chalk-stream series were usually winged with solid feather-fibre, many having double wings. Lunn winged only 11 of his 40 patterns, and of those 11 five were for the sedge or caperer dressing, not the duns. All his spinners were dressed with hackle-point wings tied on flat at right angles to the hook-shank.

If criticism can be levelled at Lunn as a fly-dresser, it falls into two categories. First, many of his dressings bear names which give no indication as to their natural counterpart. He was not alone in this fault. Many lists of flies show artificials named after individuals – so-and-so's Fancy, what's-his-name's Infallible – not a very scientific approach to the subject. J. W. Hills, in *River Keeper*, goes some way to unravelling the problem, but the origin of some of Lunn's flies remains a mystery.

Second, the bodies of his artificials are mainly formed from opaque materials, such as hackle stalks and stripped quill, 25 of them falling within this category. Bodies dressed so must present to the trout a dark, hard silhouette, lacking any of the translucency of the natural fly. However, Lunn's flies undoubtedly took trout on the Houghton water, and they continue to do so to this day on rivers far removed from the Test Valley.

Now the Houghton beats are in the equally capable hands of William Lunn's grandson, Mick Lunn. To talk with him over a glass of ale in the Grosvenor Hotel at Stockbridge, headquarters of the club, is to be made aware of a sense of continuity and history, for 85 years of accumulated knowledge and experience handed down over three generations rest with him. Few anglers can lay claim to such a great tradition.

❧ Frank Sawyer was a quiet countryman, a gifted teacher and acknowledged master of the nymph. There can be little argument that the pattern that bears his name is not only one of the most used flies anywhere in the world, but it also spurred many fly fishers into trying the classic style with which the nymph is so inextricably linked.

SAWYER REMEMBERED
by BARRY LLOYD, *August 1985*

ON A WARM June day two summers ago I was nearing the end of the 200-mile journey as I motored down the quiet Test valley. Signs to Leckford, Whitchurch and Chilbolton evoked memories of fishing days gone by, and then the wide main street of Stockbridge came into sight. Faded red-brick cottages with lichen-covered tiles lined the road, and there was the famous bulge of the portico of the Grosvenor Hotel, home of the Houghton Club with its enormous stuffed trout and Landseer paintings.

On I drove through twisting country lanes with the hedgerows a riot of colour from the wild fuchsias and honeysuckle, while hazel bushes soaked up the sun to bring forth their fruit. Fresh, green crops were pushing up through fertile red-brown soil speckled with white pebbles from the chalk.

Small copses stood like sentinels on the hilltops, and the raucous calls of pheasants seemed to echo off the 'cotton-wool' clouds in an azure sky. I slipped past roadside cottages with their thatched roofs, pastel-shaded walls and tidy vegetable gardens, and sometimes a more imposing home came into view down beech-lined drives.

Finally, I turned into the small village of Netheravon and caught a glimpse of the cool waters of the Avon, glistening in the sunlight as they pushed between the white flowers of the ranunculus. Along a narrow, pebble-covered track beside the lush water-meadows a solitary chestnut cast a welcome shade over a group of Guernsey cows. Then a square, grey-stoned tower came into view and there by the lychgate, nestling beneath the churchyard yew tree, a group of people stood quietly talking. I heard snatches of conversation

prefaced by: 'Do you remember when Frank . . . ?' For in this so English of settings I had come to the memorial service for a man who had seemed truly a part of that countryside . . . Frank Sawyer.

Perhaps it was a measure of the man himself that the assembled people came from all walks of life: generals and privates; rich and famous; unknowns and ordinary country folk; knights of the realm and farm labourers; fishermen and shooting men; representatives of nationwide associations and a little neighbouring fishing club. They were a real cross-section of the countryside and those who earned their living in it or appreciated its pleasures. But all had as a common factor a high regard and respect for one man and his knowledge, and his ability to pass it on.

I will leave it to those better-equipped than I to assess the contribution which Frank Sawyer made to our understanding of the countryside and its creatures. No doubt a biography will one day appear and he will take his place alongside Halford, Skues and Hills. What I can say is that, despite the fame which came his way, he remained essentially a modest man. This was exemplified to me by the tribute he paid Skues for the information gained from him; yet his friends firmly maintain that Skues learned far more from Frank.

After the service, I slipped away from the church and walked through the cool shade of the wood to the river. There I sat on a hummock of grass on the sunlit banking and gazed upstream to where the overhanging branches of the trees shaded the waters of Choulston Shallows, one of Frank's favourite parts of the river, and one which had been his last view as he passed peacefully away.

I could well understand his love of that stretch. Butterflies fluttered among the wild dog-roses and Mayfly spinners danced in the shafts of sunlight filtering through the leaves. A pair of swallows hunted for duns just beginning to come off the waters, and here and there a small trout shared in the hunt.

I turned to look downstream to the pool on the corner. This was where Frank had taken me to fish for grayling one October day, the first time I had met him. I was transported back in time. The green leaves of summer gave way to the golden hues of autumn. Once again I heard the bellow of a sergeant-major drilling recruits, the rumble and grind of passing tanks, and the clatter from olive-green helicopters. I remember thinking that if this was the peace and quiet of a chalk-stream, then give me the Welsh mountains; for I had forgotten that Frank was the keeper of the Combined Services' Club.

Soon he guided me to an interesting stretch of river away from the cacophony, where peace descended once more. Then, on that never-to-be forgotten pool, the mysteries of nymph fishing were unfolded, each and every aspect explained and demonstrated with the facility of a true expert.

Though I had some years' experience of salmon fishing, dry-fly fishing, and the intricacies of North-country wet-fly fishing, my efforts were inept in the extreme. But never once did he belittle them, and slowly, through his infinite patience and that merry twinkle in his eyes, I did indeed begin to grasp the technique.

After that I had the privilege of fishing with Frank on several occasions, and we often laughed at my bumbling ineptitude on that day. We also had some discussions on entomology, and he would listen with polite interest when I described variation in the habits of nymphs on North-country rivers, familiar to me, more alien to him.

Perhaps what I remember best about Frank, apart from his quiet sense of humour and country-style gentlemanly manners, was his ability to stimulate me to learn for myself more about the different aspects of fishing. He had little patience with those who wanted to be spoon-fed, or, indeed, with those who just wanted to pump him for knowledge for their own ends. One of his greatest contributions to fly fishing was to point many beginners in the right direction, intervening only if a gentle nudge were needed to keep them on the right path. It was truly the sign of a great teacher, and this pupil, at least, will always be grateful for the knowledge gained from the master of the nymph.

Now regarded as a sheet-anchor pattern in a hatch of large spring olives, the Imperial went through many changes before the fly we now know was born.

AN ENGLISHMAN ON THE TEIFI
by MOC MORGAN, May 1981

ONE HUNDRED and twenty-four years ago an angling book that was to revolutionise the sport of angling was published. Its central theme could be summarised in this extract: 'The greatest error of fly-fishing as usually practised is that the angler fishes downstream whereas he should fish up'.

The book was *The Practical Angler*, by W. C. Stewart. Stewart was an angler of few flies. All his patterns were lightly-dressed and they caught many trout in the rivers of his native Scotland.

Although the book was to influence anglers probably more than did any other book of its time, Stewart's preaching did not make many converts in Wales. The wet-fly-downstream method remained in vogue throughout the decades, and is indeed widely practised today. It has been described as a 'chuck-and-chance' method, but I doubt if the originator of that description ever saw a great wet-fly angler operating. Had he done so I'm sure his description would have been kinder.

In Wales there was a time when our rivers ran high for a few days after a flood. That was in the days before rivers were raped and pillaged by the drainage operators. Now we have flash rivers which take only a few hours to run clear after a flood. In those olden days the wet-fly anglers would be out a day or two after the flood and in the stout-coloured water they would catch a lot of fish.

One wet-fly angler I knew in the immediate post-war years fished with a soft split cane 10 foot rod and an old worn silk line. His cast would be some 9 feet long with three flies: A Pheasant Tail on the point, Snipe and Purple on the middle dropper, and a Partridge and Red on the bob. The flies would sweep downstream across the river like a giant windscreen wiper and would take fish with uncanny regularity.

It all looked so simple until you tried to do it yourself. This down-stream wet-fly master was one Dai George. An accident had left him with a rather mutilated body. His right hand lacked two fingers, and the left one three. His right leg was also somewhat damaged and to all these handicaps could be added Parkinson's disease, which ensured that the tip of his rod was always quivering like a reed in a storm. Despite all the drawbacks, Dai was a great catcher of fish and had the gift of making everybody around him laugh.

The Teifi, which below Tregaron runs regal and full-blossomed, is a great place to be in March and April, months which offer the best of the downstream wet-fly fishing.

The early days of the 1963 fishing season were probably the coldest on record. The pools on the Teifi were skirted with ice that had been there since Boxing Day. Into this setting came a distinguished angler, the late Oliver Kite. It was not a fitting setting for a fly fisher treading once again the sweet young grass of a new season, but Oliver Kite would walk the banks of the Teifi and select from the fish that moved to the large spring olives that hatched daily about one o'clock.

It was then that the Imperial fly was devised as a copy of the male of the large spring olive. The great angler would bring back a brace or two daily and these were displayed on the old chest in the hall of the Talbot Hotel. All the local anglers visited the Talbot nightly and Oliver Kite's fish brought in more custom than a topless barmaid would have done!

Those of us who met him and were able to tie his magical dry fly, realised the potential of the dry fly even in the early days of March. It would be wrong to think that the Imperial pattern came immediately; truth told, Oliver Kite modified his first version considerably.

The first effort was tied with green silk and had a ginger hackle. I have no doubt that Oliver Kite was the greatest angler I was privileged to meet, but his fly-tying was not in the same class. He, like Stewart, did not believe in overdressing flies. Today's accepted dressing is:

Silk: Purple.
Tail and hackle: Blue dun.

Body: Heron herl, doubled and redoubled to make a bulky thorax.

Oliver Kite fished the Teifi just below the old market town of Tregaron. A bridge crosses the river at Pont Llanio, and it was there that he took his fish. For many years the local anglers wondered why the trout below Pont Llanio held hundreds of big trout and anglers often used to try to get their flies on it around mid-day when the flies started hatching in March and April or late in the evening in June and July, the sedge time. The 'secret' was the nearby milk factory and its waste-pipe!

Last year my catches for March and April slightly favoured the dry fly. Then came the wet fly upstream, and least successful was the downstream wet fly. It is a pity there is no longer an angler of the quality of Dai George to do justice to the downstream method and show that it still has a place in the modern angling scene.

& Keen as ever to maintain originality of a fly's dressing, fly-tying historian Donald Overfield was very quick off the mark to correct the statement that the Imperial was to be thought of as merely a general purpose fly and that its body, a key factor in its make-up, should sport an ostrich herl body.

KITE'S IMPERIAL
letter from DONALD OVERFIELD, June 1970.

STEPHEN LEE should check his facts before committing them to print, particularly with regard to Kite's Imperial. It was never intended to sport an ostrich-herl body, at least not by its originator, and he should know. I have before me as I write some examples of the fly given to me by Oliver Kite shortly before his death and most certainly the body is heron herl, a fact confirmed in his letters to me. Mr Lee will also find that the modern authoritative books on fly tying give the same dressing.

Mr Lee is also quite wrong in his assumptions that the Imperial was devised as a general-purpose fly. It was not. Kite first dressed this fly in 1962 as a 'straightforward imitation of the large olive'. The original model was a male dun taken from the River Teifi in Wales. Following seasons proved to Kite that the fly was useful as a general representation and he used it accordingly

but, I repeat, it was not designed with that purpose in view.

For the benefit of readers who wish to tie the Imperial correctly, here is Kite's original dressing: Hook – early spring, No. 1: from May onwards, No. 0. Tying silk – purple. Hackle – honey dun (Kite did use light ginger on many occasions). Whisks – greyish brown in spring, honey dun later in the season. Body – four undyed primary heron herls, doubled and re-doubled to form the thorax, ribbed with fine gold wire.

I admire Mr Lee's confidence in stating that 'the success of the Gold-Ribbed Hare's Ear is not hard to explain'. Its success has certainly puzzled a lot of thoughtful anglers for many years. In its original, and true, form it did not sport wings and a bushy hackle and was usually fished wet or just in the surface film. The general opinion has been that it is taken for a nymph or an emergent dun and this I would go along with. What the present bastardised creation represents I do not know, and if through observation and research Mr Lee has discovered sound evidence to support his theory that the trout take it for the Medium Olive dun, I, for one, would be most interested to read of his findings.

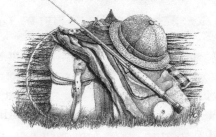

—————— *Chapter eight* ——————

THE GREAT LURE DEBATE

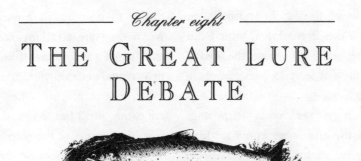

- *To some, even the mention of the word lure is to invite being branded as a less than skilled fly fisher. Such distinctions will always be made in any sport by groups with opposing views.*
- *If a lure is thoughtfully designed and fished so as to imitate or create an impression of a living creature, does it automatically fall into the same category as a flashy attractor, and are they simply fancies to be pulled back at breakneck speeds by the supposedly less able?*
- *For certain, they do bring early success for the newcomer who may or may not graduate to complete an all-round repertoire.*
- *Dick Walker tackled the lure question head-on and stirred up the hornets' nest that is still buzzing today.*
- *'What is a lure?' 'How should they be fished?' and 'Why do trout take them?' were among the bullets fired in the direction of anyone prepared to listen.*

ENIGMAS OF THE LURE
by RICHARD WALKER, *June 1975*

THE DICTIONARY definition of the term 'lure' is not of much help in an angling context, but to define it in our sense is rather difficult. However, to most anglers, a lure is a device which makes no attempt to imitate any kind of insect; which is usually from 1⅓ inches to as much as 4 inches long; which has a 'wing' of hair or feather making a relatively small angle with the shank or shanks of the hook or hooks on which it is dressed; and which can be expected to arouse the disapproval of at least 25 per cent of fly fishers.

That is somewhat surprising, since the lure as we know it today is by no means new. Multi-hook lures were in use at Blagdon about 70 years ago, and were probably employed for sea-trout fishing a good deal earlier than that.

Why do trout take lures?

I suggest that there may be three motives: hunger, curiosity, and aggression. It is important to distinguish these, because lures of different types are involved.

Not only trout, but also pike and perch attack lures, and it is significant that those lures that attract perch and pike best, are those that attempt to imitate small fish. The best lure I know of for catching perch is called the Hanningfield Lure. It incorporates features intended to suggest those of small perch or rudd: a speckled feather wing to suggest a scaly back; white hair underwing with silver-ribbed body, to imitate the sides and belly; orange throat hackle and tail, to imitate fins; and a fish shape when drawn through the water.

This pattern is not generally ef-fective for trout; it does well only when they are attacking concentrations of small coarse fish. One may speculate from this, and from other evidence, that when trout are eating small fish, a lure that incorporates some of the recognition features of small fish is the best choice; but when the trout are eating insects, daphnia, or snails, a fish-imitating lure is by no means necessarily the best kind to offer them.

At this point the reader may ask why use a lure when the fish are eating insects? Why not use an imitation of the insect species they are eating? I can only reply, why, indeed? The fact is that we now have a section of trout-fishers who constantly seek the short cut: they have no wish to involve themselves in the intellectual exercise of identifying the diet of the trout at a particular time, and fishing, perhaps even devising, an imitation of that diet. They have found that they can avoid any need to do so by using a lure of some kind and pulling it fast through the area in which the trout are feeding. My role here is to report rather than to recommend, and I have therefore to say that it would seem that the best sort of lure to use in such circumstances is one in which there are relatively few points of resemblance to small fish, but rather a general impression that is likely to attract most attention.

Among the ingredients that help in this are hot-orange hair, hackles or marabou, black, yellow and white materials, including fluorescent ones; and relatively fast movement. It seems possible that such lures, which include patterns such as the Whisky Fly, Chief Needabeh, Black Lure, Sweeney Todd, Yellow Peril and others, excite trout to attack them because their intrusion into a feeding territory is resented, or else they stimulate curiosity on the part of the trout.

We often find trout following such lures without taking them, or, sometimes, plucking at them without being hooked. Since trout can swim much faster than any angler can retrieve a lure, such behaviour is surely evidence that the trout are either trying to drive away an intruder, or else are curious about the lure and wish to know what it feels like as well as what it looks like. A firm take in such circum-

stances is more likely to be due to the trout carrying aggression or curiosity to an extreme, rather than a desire to eat the lure. It may also be significant that a trout that has followed a lure, and has perhaps plucked at it, will seldom show interest if the same lure is offered to it a second time. This is perhaps evidence of curiosity rather than aggression.

For this reason, continuing to fish the same lure in the same area for long periods without success is unwise. All the trout within casting range will probably have examined the lure and lost interest in it during the first 10 or 15 minutes, and only a fish moving into the area and seeing the lure for the first time is likely to take. It therefore pays to change either the lure or one's place of fishing if no results are obtained within a quarter or an hour or so.

How should lures be constructed? This question brings us back to the trout's motivation. When the trout takes the lure for a little fish he means to eat, he attacks the head end, swimming parallel to the lure and turning quickly across its path. A single hook suffices, and the trout is usually firmly hooked in the scissors.

This will also happen when aggression or curiosity lead the trout to take a firm hold; but if not, then the chances of hooking a trout are increased if a hook is located at the rear of the lure, in a tandem arrangement of two or three hooks. Incidentally, perch attack a lure — or a real fish — quite differently from trout. They snap at the tail of their quarry, so if you want to catch a perch, put a hook right at the back of your lure and embellish it with hair or feather to imitate a tail quite positively.

How should lures be fished? Where trout are attacking concentrations of coarse-fish, use a fish-imitating lure and fish it slowly, trying different combinations of slow, steady pulls, little jerks and long pauses.

If you fish attention-attracting lures rather than fish-imitating ones, far more often than not a steady fast retrieve proves most effective; no pauses, no slowing-down or speeding-up. It so often happens that a trout takes a lure when an angler is reeling in his line, often after he has made cast after cast in the same area, that I am forced to conclude that the retrieve at constant speed has special attraction. Much the same applies when lures are trailed behind a moving boat, or where the same effect is obtained without flouting anti-trailing rules, by the use of lee-boards or special rudders.

Retrieving by reeling in involves loss of time, since a good deal of line has to be pulled off the reel and worked out after each retrieve. That can be avoided by tucking the rod under the arm and using both hands to pull line through the butt ring, using a hand-over-hand motion to keep the lure moving at a constant speed. A smart tug with the hand will hook most of the taking fish.

This pre-supposes that the trout cannot be seen. Where they can, or where at least a bow wave made by a following trout is visible, it sometimes pays to stop the retrieve quite suddenly, pause and start again equally suddenly, when the trout will often be found hooked.

It is also wise to remember that when using a fast-sinking line, a lure is being pulled by the sinking line even though the angler is not retrieving. Takes quite often come at this time, and unless the angler is alert to their possibility, many will be missed. When this happens it is a clear hint to allow less sinking time; to start the retrieve sooner after casting, because the trout aren't as deep as you thought!

There is a great deal of debate about the ethics of lure-fishing. I should be sorry to see any restrictions placed on it in large water-supply reservoirs and other sheets of water of comparable size, where there is no evidence that its use leads to too high a catch rate. When trout are eating fry, or when they are obviously not feeding on insects, the use of an appropriate lure may catch a fish or two and save an angler, who may have travelled a long way, from a blank day. In these conditions, using a lure is perfectly reasonable.

I am, however, sorry for those anglers who have no ideas beyond casting out a lure as far as possible and stripping it in as fast as they can, regardless of what the trout are doing. They don't know how much pleasure they are missing. That they often catch a lot of fish is undeniable, but they never learn what fly fishing is really about.

• *Enter into the fray two of the most respected names in fly fishing, Brian Clarke and John Goddard, who brought their wealth of experience and their innovative minds to bear.*
• *Between them, they dispelled for ever the theory that lure fishing was a mindless pastime indulged in by those who could not grasp the supposed intricacies of the dry fly and the nymph.*

SO, IS IT CURIOSITY THAT KILLS THE TROUT?

by BRIAN CLARKE, *April 1974*

I THINK it possible to convince most open-minded men that there are powerful reasons for attributing the success of lures to any supposed likeness to minnows or fry.

The task now is to find another reason for the fact that lures do, as we all know, lead to the downfall of vast numbers of trout; and it is obvious that if their success cannot be attributed to a likeness to small fish, then we must seek elsewhere the reasons for their effectiveness. And there are, it seems to me, three principal areas we must examine, if we refuse to attribute to trout, motivations that we do not ourselves experience. These possibilities are: that trout, notwithstanding the fact that they do not take lures for small fish, may nevertheless accept them as some other form of food; that trout that attack lures are motivated by aggression; and that trout intercept lures because they are motivated by one or other of the shades of curiosity.

In discussing these possibilities, it is necessary to appreciate that nowhere am I attributing great intelligence to the trout, or thought processes. Where possible courses of action are discussed, it is only in the context of possible motivations attributed to trout by others. It is also necessary to remember that we are not dealing in this article with statistics, clinically compiled. We are discussing a balance of probabilities, and seeking to identify the

most likely reason for trout getting caught on lures, in all the circumstances.

Against that background, then, let us take the possible motivation of food, first. To argue that trout take lures because they think lures are a form of food, is a positive statement of belief which, by its very certainty, excludes qualification or doubt.

Where is the evidence to sustain a position as firm as this? We know what food is available to trout in the underwater environment in which they live, because we can see it. Likewise, we know what trout in the main select from this natural larder because we can perform autopsies on them. Where is there anything in either of these – whether in what we know they do eat, or in what they have available to them if they wish – that looks and behaves like most (or, indeed, any) of the lures that habitually catch trout? And if we say 'Well, perhaps they don't take them for creatures they know as food, but as an alternative or new source of food,' then we are in the area of hypothesis and speculation which to most observers would be inconsistent with a positive belief that lures are taken as food. The best that can be said on this score is that fish may sometimes explore lures to see if they are edible, which is a different matter altogether, and one to which I will return later.

Conceivably, it could also be argued that trout take anything that moves, in the belief that it is food: but again, this cannot be so. First of all, lures very often fail to catch fish, even though they very obviously move; and secondly, if lures do catch fish, it is a common experience to find that it is a particular kind of lure which is accepted, to the exclusion of all or most others. And if trout are being selective in the lures they take, then movement alone cannot be a sufficient motivation: there is, clearly, an additional factor at work, which promotes the fish's reaction.

Let us agree that no doubt some fish, sometimes, take lures because they think they are eating food: but not enough of them, it seems reasonable to suggest, to account for all or even most trout which lures catch.

The second possible motivation is aggression. Why should a trout react aggressively towards a lure? There seem, again, only a handful of main-line possibilities: because the fish itself feels under physical threat (in which case the underlying motivation would be fear); a reaction provoked by some inbuilt territorial instinct; and an instinctive, belligerent response to anything that is unknown or unfamiliar. Again, let us look at them one by one.

≈ *Fear.* While anything, of course, is possible, it does not seem that this is acceptable as a common reason for trout getting caught on lures. The reasons for this include the fact that: lures are physically much smaller than the creatures allegedly terrified by them, and, indeed, are similar in size to creatures which occasionally trout eat, and habitually live happily among; lures do not deviate from a straight line when retrieved, and presumably alarmed trout would therefore not feel 'cornered' by them (the classical circumstance in which frightened creatures attack); a lure in the vicinity of a trout must at least as often be moving away from the fish as towards it; and if afraid, why would not the trout simply bolt away from the threatening object, rather than directly towards it?

≈ *Territorial instinct*: To suggest

that this motivation is the key, is to suggest that the vast majority of trout (which do, of course, get caught on lures) possess a territorial instinct. Most trout which are fished for in stillwater, and get caught on lures, are rainbows. The great bulk of the available evidence suggests that rainbows have little or no territorial instinct, even on comparatively small waters where space, presumably, is at some kind of premium. This alone is enough to place a question-mark over this candidate for motivation. However, on the big reservoirs, where rainbows again predominate, many lures that get attacked, are attacked by shoaling rainbows; and these shoals are highly mobile. Individual fish in highly mobile packs could scarcely be said to have much claim to territory of their own.

It is just possible that some would suggest that the reason shoaling rainbows attack lures is from some sense of competition within the territory of the pack, as in 'If I don't get it, one of the others will'. I can only answer that in my own experience, and that of my friends, neither rainbows nor browns have shown an eagerness to queue up and jump on the hook, even when the water has been thick with them. Sometimes it has happened, of course, but it has been very much the exception. If it is an aggressively competitive instinct that moves a trout to attack a lure, it is a curiously occasional apology for what one could reasonably expect to be a continuing instant-response mechanism among fish that find themselves in groups.

❧ *An instinctive, belligerent response to anything unknown or unfamiliar.* Many of the same objections apply here. While it is possible that the occasional fish gets caught as a result of some suicidal tantrum, the word instinct again implies a latent capacity, continually present, and simply needing an appropriate stimulus to trigger it off. Whatever else can be said of trout, it is not that this belligerence is constantly present, and is triggered off when a lure comes by. We know for a fact that trout refuse far more lures (or anything else) than they accept; and this instinctive aggression must therefore be under a great deal of control (which means it cannot be a blindly belligerent response), or it must be only occasionally present (which again weakens the concept of an ongoing blind response to anything unfamiliar).

A third possibility, that it is not just the lure itself that triggers off this latent capacity for responsive aggression, but a whole accumulation of factors in the environment (e.g. fluctuations in water temperature, atmospheric pressure, oxygenation and so on) as the lure is offered is, of course, on the cards to a small degree. But often, once more, the type of lure itself must be an additional factor in the 'environment shift', because, as we have already seen, one lure will frequently be successful under a given set of conditions, while others are meticulously ignored. And we still have to account for a myriad of day-to-day incidents, ranging from 'short-rising' to the constant, half-hearted plucking of lures in retrieve, which do not happily square with a general presumption of blind belligerence as a factor contributing to the downfall of the majority of trout.

So far we have looked at hunger and aggression, two commonly-mooted, and largely black-and-white, possible motivations for trout taking lures. Individually, no doubt they will account for a few fish; but certainly that is as far as I would be prepared to go. And, what is more, they are 'messy' theories in that, as the argument – or at least the balance of probabilities – encircles each general point, we are forced to impute to the trout ever more sophisticated thought processes, and ever more hypothetical motivations, in order to sustain our position – ranging from, on the one hand, 'All right, they don't take them for food they recognise, but they may think they're some other kind of food, anyway,' to, on the other hand, 'Perhaps it's some kind of aggressive, competitive instinct that makes them bite'.

What I am concerned with here is not to account for one, or two, or a few fish being caught, but to find an acceptable reason why the vast majority of trout might get caught. And as we cannot know anything for certain – at least, that is, until someone produces a particularly articulate trout which is willing to spill the beans – the best we can do is to look at all the available information, and draw the most reasonable conclusion from it.

So far, we have looked at the motivation of hunger, and found it wanting; and we have examined aggression, and expressed our doubts. All of which leaves us with curiosity. Where, then, does an examination of that lead us?

It leads us, in short, to my belief that the most important common denominator in the success of lures is the curiosity of trout; and that the great majority of trout get themselves caught not because they want to eat a lure, or because they want to attack it, but because they are investigating it.

Let us see how this stands up in the light of our day-to-day experience, and what we can reasonably deduce from it.

If a trout is to carry out an investigation of a lure, it seems to me that there are only two levels upon which it can operate: it can investigate by observation; and (a more advanced measure) it can investigate by feel. Space prevents me detailing every possible activity which we experience in our day-to-day fishing, which is consistent with the curiosity theory without

requiring all kinds of extraneous additional assumptions to shore them up; and I will confine myself, therefore, to two kinds of phenomena which we have already mentioned, which are common, and which can be accounted for in the first instance by the notion of a trout observing a lure, and in the second by a trout feeling a lure. I will add to it a statement which accounts, also, for the trout we eventually do catch, which is still consistent with the theory of a fish investigating a lure rather than consuming or attempting to savage it.

As has already been said, we are all familiar with the problem of short-rising trout. I do not believe that short-rising trout are rising in the accepted sense of the term, or that in some way they 'miss' the fly. I believe that a so-called short-rising trout has decided it is worth coming up to a lure in order to observe it, and then, suddenly, at some point in the retrieve, decides it does not like what it sees. The reason we fail to hook a short-rising trout is because it had never attempted, nor had arrived at any intention, of touching the fly. The so-called 'rise' is not a rise at all, but a surface boil caused by displacement of the water, as the fish turns abruptly away. 'Short-rises' occur when we are fishing deep, too: the reason we do not know about them is simply because the thrust of water caused by the quickly-turning fish, is dissipated before it reaches the surface. When there is no boil from a fish high in the water, either it did not bother to investigate the fly, or it turned away too slowly to cause a disturbance.

If a fish has not been deterred by the appearance of a fly or lure, the manner in which it moves or anything else, it proceeds to the second level of investigation open to it – that of 'feeling' the lure. And how else is a trout to feel or sample anything, other than by taking it into its mouth? Which brings us to the second illustration. All of us, again, are familiar with a trout following a travelling lure – and particularly one being recovered by the constant retrieve. There is a continuing, maddening, tap-tapping on the end of the line, which seems to go on interminably until, finally, the fish does, or does not, get itself caught. What this trout is doing is mouthing the long streamer-ends of the wings, getting a feel for them, sampling them, and occasionally building up its confidence as it investigates an interesting phenomenon.

And what of the trout that get caught? Well here, perhaps, is the crunch. When anglers talk of lures and trout, they build in their predispositions. They talk of trout 'taking' a lure, or 'attacking' a lure, which implies a powerful, preconceived motivation for the trout taking a lure into its mouth – to consume it, or to savage it. But we really know none of this. All we know for certain is that trout get caught on lures, and that when they are caught, it is because they take the lure into their mouths.

I suggest that trout that get caught on lures do not do so because they purposefully intend to eat the lures, or because they aggressively savage them. I suggest that the trout has little conscious motivation, other than to probe in the only way open to it, something interesting and unfamiliar. There is no fundamental difference between a fish sampling, say, a stone or a twig, and a fish sampling a lure. In the course of a lifetime, a trout must take many things into its mouth which eventually it decides it does not want. When it reaches that conclusion, it spits them out again.

There is no reason to suppose

that a fish that gets caught on a lure has been behaving in a way that is untypical of its behaviour with twigs and stones. It is simply sampling the lure a little too fulsomely, reaching beyond the barb, while the angler is retrieving his line. The hook gains a slight purchase; the fish starts, giving the hook a firmer purchase still; the angler feels the drag or the fish's reaction to the hook point, and instinctively tightens. In far less time than it takes to tell, the trout is hooked, without ever getting the opportunity to spit out the lure, as it would have done in the normal course of events.

There is, of course, the occasional full-blooded smash take, as there are occasional examples of everything else. But occasional examples do not make cases, and in the main I am as certain as it is possible to be that the key to the success of lures is curiosity and investigation on the part of the trout.

The theory is totally consistent with the only thing we know for certain – that, at some point, the trout takes the lure into its mouth: and it can account for a very great number of the day-to-day phenomena which each of us sees at the waterside. It is, I suggest, a far more acceptable conclusion than one that says that trout accept lures because they want to eat them, or because they see lures as something to be destroyed or frightened off. These other theories imply a specific motivation to the trout, from the moment it sees and approaches the lure. I do not, as I have said, think that trout approach lures with the intention of eating them, or doing anything else. I think trout approach lures with some kind of numbed purposelessness – they simply go to have a look. Once they have begun to investigate, and their confidence has been built up, they may indeed attempt to swallow the lure: but that intention would come after the approach and the action which leads to them getting caught – the taking of the lures into their mouths.

Where, then, does all this leave us? In a purely subjective sense, there are great satisfactions to knowing – or at least to thinking we know – as much about the fish we pursue as possible. And for that reason alone, I hope this analysis will lead to discussion. But there are practical applications, too.

In the first instance, within the limitations of the number of fish in the original experiment upon which autopsies were performed, we can reasonably say that trout do not take lures for small fish. By looking at the other possible reasons trout may take lures, we can say that: it is unlikely that trout take lures because they think that lures are some other form of food; it is unlikely that trout attack lures from simple aggression; and that trout are probably motivated by a largely unconscious desire to investigate only, when they get caught. We can also say that if trout do not take lures for small fish, and 95 per cent of trout prefer not to eat small fish (last month), then we should, in the main, abandon any effort to suggest both the appearance of real small fish, and our efforts to retrieve lure and flasher patterns in the manner in which we know small fish move.

On the other hand, if we can reasonably believe that most trout take lures into their mouths in order to investigate them – sometimes, no doubt, eventually concluding that the lures have food potential; sometimes, no doubt, from a rather aggressive disposition; but in the main simply because they are motivated by curiosity – then we have a far more sensible area on which to concentrate our inventive and imaginative skills. It is true that we will still be subject to shifts in environmental factors and other imponderables which affect the behaviour of trout: but so are we with the other motivations, and at least we will have an apparently rational position to start from.

In terms of lure design, I certainly do not consider myself competent to go further. The only comment I think I can make is to say that if curiosity is the motivation which sends trout chasing after lures, then a possible starting point may be sheer visibility, on the basis that the more trout that see a lure, the more trout will have the opportunity of exercising their curiosity towards it. And the more trout we can persuade to do that, the more trout we eventually may catch.

WHY TROUT TAKE LURES

by JOHN GODDARD, *June 1974*

IN HIS excellent analysis of why trout take lures Brian Clarke quite rightly pointed out initially that over the years it has been generally accepted that most lures were intended to represent small fish, fry or sticklebacks on which trout are reputed to feed avidly at all times. Up to a point I confirm his findings in this respect, as over the years, during my own research, particularly with autopsies, I have seldom found small fish in the stomach contents, except on certain waters at specific times of the year.

But while I agree that trout do not accept lures as food in the form of fry throughout most of the summer, I must also point out that on those waters where fry do abound, many trout, particularly the larger browns, do settle down to feed upon them exclusively, usually during the late summer when the fry start to shoal in the margins or when they emerge from the sanctuary of the weedbeds in shallow water.

I can quote many instances at such times when I have caught trout that have been so full of fry that they have been literally spew-ing them out of their mouths as they have been netted. In fact, on several stillwaters that I fish for two or three weeks during late July or early August it is all but impossible to catch trout at all unless one is prepared to mount an imitation of a stickleback or a perch fry. According to Brian, autopsies carried out over a period of two years by him and several friends does not confirm this, but, in fairness, the reason for this is probably due to the absence of this phenomenon on the waters they fish.

The other theories advanced are that trout are motivated to take lures out of fear, aggression, curiosity, or as some other form of food. In his final analysis Brian seems to favour curiosity, and while he puts forward several excellent theories to substantiate his conclusions, I am afraid I do not altogether agree. In my humble opinion I think we have to look at this situation from a far broader spectrum.

I feel that up to a point we can discount the fear aspect, and aggression, except possibly just before pairing and mating, or on those few stillwaters where trout, even rainbows, stake out territorial rights to a certain area of water. As for curiosity, I agree Brian has a good case in some respects, as from my own observations I am sure he is right that some trout do follow a lure to investigate it, and then often take it into their mouths to feel or taste this strange invader. On the other hand, I am sure many anglers will have had experiences similar to my own when using a lure, when trout, and in some cases the same trout, will follow a lure almost to the rod tip time and time again, but consistently refuse it. Conversely, I have on occasions mounted a different lure, and every trout that I have covered has immediately accepted it without hesitation. In the latter case I am sure it is accepted as a form of food.

Because of all this I am inclined to think that trout accept lures for a number of reasons, depending on a variety of factors appertaining at the time – weather, water temperature, depth of water, time of day, as well as the other reasons put forward. In addition, I suggest one other factor which I think Brian has overlooked, and which I am sure is equally valid. This is the automatic reflex action which all

trout seem to possess. How many times have we all experienced the surprise take of a trout as our fly has landed in the water, or other occasions when a lure cast behind and to one side of a trout that can be clearly seen is immediately snapped up by the trout as soon as it appears in his window?

Finally, I definitely disagree with Brian's reasons for dismissing the motivation of trout to take lures as some other form of food. I am sure that at times certain patterns of lure are taken as a form of food if the trout is hungry and if the lure loosely represents a form of food on which it has recently been feeding. 'Where,' asks Brian, 'is there anything in either of these natural larders – whether in what we know they do eat, or in what they have available to them if they wish – that looks and behaves like most (or, indeed, any) of the lures that habitually catch trout?' Well, I would put forward the following examples.

❧ *The Worm Fly:* This is one of the earlier and most popular lures, and, as I suggested in my book *Trout Flies of Stillwater*, this is quite a good representation of either an alder fly larva, or certain of the darker species of sedge pupa.

๛ *The Black Lure:* A very popular and often effective lure, it is, I am sure, taken at times for some of the large dark-coloured leeches that are common on many stillwaters.

๛ *The Baby Doll:* This – in fact, many basically white-coloured lures – is undoubtedly taken for one of the many of the larger pale-coloured species of sedge pupa.

๛ *The Teal and Green:* Typical of green-bodied lures that are probably taken for some of the larger green-coloured damosel nymphs.

I could quote many other examples, but up to comparatively recently I have always been puzzled as to why many large lures with predominant green, blue or red dressings should often prove effective, as I could think of no true form of aquatic life that even loosely approached such colours and sizes. But last season I discovered, by pure chance, the probable answer even to this mystery.

On a calm, warm summer day in July last season, my colleague, Cliff Henry and myself decided to spend a complete day on our local reservoir catching and photographing damosel nymphs in order to establish the reason for the wide range of colours in which they are found. Taking a boat and resisting the strong temptation to take our rods as well as our cameras, we proceeded to a quiet bay where we had previously spotted a lot of these particular nymphs. We anchored the boat close to the branches of a submerged tree that were sticking up out of the water, as we reasoned that any nymphs in the area would be sure to make for these branches as they always transform into the adult winged form via emergent vegetation.

Sure enough, we found several nymphs drying out on the branches in preparation for the final moult, and these we duly removed and photographed. We then settled down to observe the arrival of further specimens, while at the same time idly watching masses of the large adult blue-bodied winged males and green-bodied females gyrating around the branches. My reverie was suddenly interrupted by Cliff saying: 'You won't believe this but I am sure I just saw a winged adult emerge from beneath the surface!' I was just about to make a sarcastic reply, when to our absolute amazement we both clearly observed a repeat performance, literally under our noses. Determined to find the reason for this phenomenon, we both settled down patiently to a searching appraisal of the situation.

It was shortly after this that we both noticed a lot of winged adults were mating in the air and copulating tail to tail. The blue-bodied male seemed to be the predominant partner, supporting the female, who had her wings partially closed. After a short interval a pair alighted on one of the branches and the male, still supporting the female, proceeded to crawl backwards down the branch until the female at his tail was pushed underwater. As soon as she was fully submerged, they parted, and she continued on her own to crawl underwater down the branch to a depth of 3–4 feet until she found some weed where she commenced to oviposit.

Fortunately, the water was very clear and we were able to note her actions closely, but even now, in retrospect, it seems incredible that she remained underwater, moving from weed patch to weed patch, quite rapidly, for more than 25 minutes. At the end of this time she was many feet away from where she originally descended and, having completed her task, she then swam, or rather struggled, to the surface. All this time the male had been slowly circling over the area where they parted company, but as soon as she emerged above the surface he darted down and joined her again, when they flew off. During the ensuing few hours we observed many other pairs do a repeat performance, some females remaining underwater for more than 40 minutes.

Over the years, many authorities have reported finding adult winged damosel flies in the stomach contents of trout they have caught, and to the best of my knowledge it has always been generally accepted that trout have obtained these by leaping out of the water and intercepting low-flying specimens.

Due to this chance observation, it now seems beyond reasonable doubt that during the mating period of these flies in July and August, trout will feed upon these underwater where this occurs. As many of these adults are upwards of 2 inches long, this could account in some instances for trout readily accepting what are normally considered extremely large lures.

While the most common damosel flies are blue- or green- bodied, there are other species with red and other body colours, so this could well provide room for much experiment. We have dressed some artificials to represent these adults underwater, and we are now eagerly awaiting a chance to try them.

TROUT AND THE MOUTH TEST
letter from GEOFFREY MORTIMER, *March 1962*

I THINK that all the recent discussion and controversy as to why a trout takes a creation such as a Whisky Fly, when it bears no resemblance to any aquatic insect or fish has been looked at from a too-human aspect. After all, why shouldn't a trout take an object moving through the water if that object appears to have life and especially if its movement resembles that of a food item upon which the trout may infrequently feed? I argue that its form and colour are immaterial to a certain extent, and its movement is much more important, as this symbolises life.

There is no need, I think, for the trout to have ever seen the 'fly' before, so long as the fly, or whatever you may wish to call it, appears to have life. Then I see no reason why it shouldn't take it. After all, a trout has to take its first dragonfly nymph, cranefly, or moth at some time in its life, let alone crayfish and small frogs, having never seen one before. Why shouldn't it adopt the same attitude towards 'Christmas decorations'.

The fact that the 'fly' has brilliance and flash most probably only makes the trout more curious about it and whether it is edible. If you were a trout, especially a stock trout, wouldn't you take it and see? Suppose that angler with the pipe missed you on the strike, would a strange metallic feeling in your mouth deter you from taking another equally strange moving object? Remember, you're a trout, similar to your neighbour; unlike those peculiar humans!

Chapter nine

FLY DRESSING – FACT, FICTION AND FANTASY

🐾 *Does a good grounding in entomology put more fish in the basket, or is a little knowledge, or none at all, a big disadvantage and do we really need to mimic every minute detail and colour to be successful?*

🐾 *Countless generations of fertile minds have explored, debated and failed to reach a conclusion acceptable to all. Probably the only logical answer is to wait until we can find that unlikely creature, the talking trout. Until that improbable day, we can only continue to experiment and theorise.*

ENTOMOLOGY – IS IT A LOT OF NONSENSE?

by DERMOT WILSON, *September 1960*

THERE ARE two types of dry fly fisherman. The first is the one who says that science and entomology and all that sort of thing are a lot of nonsense, and don't help to catch fish. The second rather enjoys dabbling in entomology.

In a way, the second is the unluckier of the two. He tends to get laughed at, not only by the first type, but by all the rest of the world – who imagine him pottering around with his magnifying glass, mouthing Latin names.

But he *will* catch more fish than the 'entomology is a lot of nonsense' school. Or he usually will. One thing is certain – he will always enjoy his fishing a great deal more. Entomology – or fly-spot-ting – is rather like train spotting or bird watching. It is a pleasure in itself. It really doubles the pleasure of fishing.

And fly spotting can be very important to one's basket. Often fish seem to be prepared to take almost any fly. But on other occasions there may be a short hatch of those certain flies which trout sometimes prefer to anything else. Unless one recognises the fly and imitates it quickly, great opportunities may be lost.

Not all flies fall in this category, but I have found that the Black Gnat is a good example. When a swarm of Black Gnats falls on the water, frequently trout will take nothing else. Delay tying on a Black Gnat and the rise may finish, leaving one cursing oneself for a fool.

The Iron Blue is another fly like this. The trouble is that hatches of Iron Blue usually seem to take place a little later in the day than hatches of Medium Olive and Pale Watery. The hatches often overlap.

As a result, one may start off fishing the rise quite happily with, say, a Hare's Ear. The fish feeding on Medium Olives will take it. But suddenly they lose interest. A careful look may reveal that this is be-cause the Iron Blues have started hatching. If one is too blind a fly spotter to notice this, one will stop catching fish.

In the evening, the same applies to the Blue-winged Olive. Until it hatches, fish may feed on spinner. When it hatches, it may only last five or ten minutes. It is most important to change one's fly quickly.

On my river – a chalk stream – I have found that these are the occasions on which quick fly recognition is most vital. There are other occasions when it is less vital. But it never does any harm!

Perhaps it is even more essential to be able to tell whether trout are feeding on the surface, or whether they are feeding beneath it. If they are feeding on it, are they feeding to spinner or dun? It can make a big difference.

And how about amateur autopsies? I mean the idea made famous by Skues, of 'marrow scooping' a trout to find out what it has been feeding on. This is always interesting, and can sometimes be valuable.

All one needs is a marrow scoop and a small white enamel bowl. The trouble is that marrow scoops are appallingly expensive. It took me some time to find out that the handle of any ordinary desert spoon is almost as efficient.

Before I found this out – in fact the first time I ever embarked on marrow scooping – I managed to make a prize idiot of myself for a whole weekend. This is how it happened. I had just read Skues on marrow scooping, and was anxious to try it out.

My first difficulty was that I had not the faintest idea of what a marrow scoop was. How was I to know that it was an obsolete item of silverware? I only knew that Skues had used one. I thought it had something to do with vegetable marrows, and was probably used in the kitchen. I thought it might be stocked by ironmongers.

So I went to several ironmongers. I asked them if they had any marrow scoops. Being no more anxious than I was to display ignorance, they all said cautiously, 'Hum – well, what did you want it for?' This was a difficult question. I could only blush and stammer: 'Well, for examining the contents of trouts' stomachs.' They all thought I was mad.

Eventually, however, I did find a marrow scoop at a silversmith's. I also bought a small white enamel bowl, so that I was thoroughly equipped a-la-Skues. All this meant that I missed the rise on the Saturday. I caught nothing, and could not use the marrow scoop.

The next day I was due to fish a very good stretch of water. I met my host and explained to him that in the interests of science, I intended to marrow scoop any fish I caught. He was duly impressed, and agreed that it would be very interesting.

After a while I caught a trout, and hurried up the bank to find my host. 'Now,' I said, 'we'll see what the trout are feeding on.' I filled the bowl with water, and got to work with the marrow scoop. 'I expect,' I said, 'that we'll find some Black Gnats, and quite a few Ephemerid nymphs.'

After the marrow scoop had been pulled out of the trout's mouth, we dipped it in the bowl. Then we bent over the bowl, peering to see whether my scientific forecast was correct. We looked, and looked again. There was no doubt about the result. The contents of that trout's stomach consisted of – one plain indiarubber band!

Despite the humiliations, I am not really ashamed of trying to be an amateur entomologist.

❧ Is the fly dresser's ultimate dream one of creating a fly so accurate that even the canniest trout would fail to tell the difference between it and the real thing?

❧ The warning of the dangerous waters being steered when attempting to imitate the works of the Creator is a timely one for all who sit at the fly vice.

❧ Even so, few fly dressers can resist the temptation, and from their efforts sometimes comes a fly that works, not because a clever marriage of dextrous fingers and the keenest eye managed to imitate exactly the natural insect, but because of the inclusion of all the right trigger elements.

❧ Taking this theory to its natural conclusion, some thinking fly dressers like Dick Walker put forward the case for deliberate exaggeration of colour and shape.

NO MORE EXACT IMITATION!
by RICHARD WALKER, *March 1972*

THE OTHER day I realised, somewhat ruefully, that I had been tying trout flies for more than 40 years, having started doing so at a tender age for the sole reason that I hadn't the money to buy them.

Looking back over those years, I find that I seem to have spent them in a series of delusions, my consolation being that these delusions have been shared by a good many others, some of them great and famous men.

Of these various delusions, the one I laboured under longest, and have only quite recently discarded, was that if it were only possible to tie an artificial fly that no trout could distinguish from the real thing, then that would be perfection.

Let me qualify that. I believed that the perfect artificial should resemble its natural prototype in every respect – size, shape, colour, translucence and behaviour.

I no longer believe this.

Two things brought about my change of heart. One was on account of the research carried out by Dr Dietrich Magnus, of Darmstadt. The other was the realisation that if insects were ideally suited to attract trout, those that live in the water or emerge from it would soon be extinct. It is much more likely that in at least some respects, aquatic insects have evolved in a way that avoids the attention of trout and other predators.

Dr Dietrich Magnus was neither investigating the behaviour of trout, nor that of aquatic insects. What he wanted to discover was the means by which the females of a species of butterfly, the silver-washed fritillary, attract the males.

The method he adopted was to construct a rotating beam, turning in a horizontal plane, at each end of which was attached a model butterfly, the wings of which could be flapped at varying speeds. At one end of the beam was a model that, as far as could be contrived, resembled a real female. It was the same size, it was of the same colour, and its wings flapped at the same time. This was the control.

At the other end of the beam, Dr Magnus tried various models that differed from the real thing. The whole apparatus was contained in a cage in which large numbers of male silver-washed fritillaries were confined, so that Dr Magnus could observe their reactions to his model females.

He found that the real thing — or rather, the closest copy he could make of it — was by no means the most attractive. To cut a long story short, the male fritillaries were unanimous in their preference for a lady four times natural size, flapping her wings 10 times faster than the real one can, and with a greatly simplified pattern of orange and red markings.

The inference is — and it seems to me a fair one — that the female silver-washed fritillary's appearance and behaviour have evolved in a compromise between attraction to the male and camouflage to protect her from predators. It is of no use to the female fritillary to be immensely attractive to the males if that draws the attention of, for example, a hungry thrush.

It seems to me probable that similar considerations apply to many insects, probably to the majority. They are to some extent camouflaged to avoid the attention of predators; and if this is so, then it is likely that by exaggerating, in our artificial flies, certain characteristics of the natural insects, we can make them even more attractive than a perfect imitation would be.

What are the characteristics that we can with advantage exaggerate?

I think that they must be some of the characteristics by which the trout recognise insects of that species. Dr Magnus's male fritillaries, while preferring a simplified pattern of orange and black, were not interested in any other combination of colours.

So the problem would seem to be that of choosing which characteristics to exaggerate, and to exaggerate them to a sufficient extent, without destroying their effect as points of recognition by the trout. The most obvious way to exaggerate is in respect of colour. An interesting example was given in *Trout and Salmon* last November when Mr C. R. Pearce drew attention to the efficacy of Commander C. F. Walker's dressing for the nymph of the claret, dun, *Leptophlebia vespertina*.

As Mr Pearce pointed out, even in this dressing, which is an attempt at exact imitation, the claret typing silk shows clearly through the dubbing when the thing is wet. It appears much more claret than the natural nymph, in which I, personally, have never observed the least sign of claret, though some is perceptible in the dun stage.

Another example can be found in that North Country favourite,

Snipe and Purple, which is taken when the iron blue is on – and sometimes when it isn't. No iron blue, at any stage, has as bright a purple body as the Snipe and Purple; but there is a hint of purple in the real insect. The exaggeration of this is clearly attractive to the trout.

I have no doubt that experienced fly-fishers can think of many more examples. So can I; but perhaps I have said enough about them to make the point. I find that when I review my experiences down the years, and read what others have written, I find example after example where exaggeration in fly-dressing has proved effective.

I am sure those same experienced readers can remember occasions when a particular pattern, often a fancy one, caught fish when no other succeeded. It is common to hear or read something like this: 'The fish were obviously feeding, but I tried pattern after pattern without success, until at last I tied on, in desperation, Blogg's Benefit. Though it bore no relation to any natural insect, it proved to be exactly what the trout wanted. Fish after fish . . .' And so on.

Well, it is true that Blogg's Benefit didn't look a bit like a real insect, to the angler. It didn't look like a real insect to the trout, but, purely by chance, it included in its appearance, in exaggerated form, some of the features by which the trout recognised the insects they were eating. They found it even more attractive than the real thing.

I think it probable that on those rare days when the angler hooks fish after fish, he is always using a fly that is more attractive to the trout than the real insects they are eating. Very often indeed, the angler's artificial is among dozens, even hundreds, of real insects. The odds against its being taken, if the trout could not distinguish it from the real insects, would be quite long.

In a fly tied to imitate a particular kind of insect, there is certain to be simplification, which is a form of exaggeration. Very often the colours of the materials are brighter, or more concentrated. I suggest that quite often this accidental exaggeration can be an asset rather than a liability. It might not be carrying the argument too far to suggest that if that were not in fact the case we should catch far fewer fish.

If accidental exaggeration can make an artificial fly more attractive than a real one, then is it not likely that well-thought-out, deliberate exaggeration, based on an accurate assessment of the characteristics of the natural by which trout recognise it, would be more effective still?

🐟 *But do fish see those exaggerated colours and acceptance trigger-points in the same way that persuaded the angler to pick the fly from his box?*

DO FISH FAVOUR CERTAIN COLOURS?
by F. T. K. BULLMORE, *May 1970*

AN OLD gillie friend with whom I used to fish that queen · of all salmon rivers, the Irish Erne, was always firm in the belief that all fish are colour blind. To him it did not matter in the least whether you tied on a Yellow Torrish or a

Black Doctor. When I used to argue this point he always insisted that it was 'the way a fly swims through the water and not the colour that makes the fish reach for it'. There is, of course, a lot in this conception. Movement in any sub-surface fly is most important, but I am a long way from being convinced that fish are unable to differentiate one colour from another, and long may I remain so, for colour blind trout would be very boring creatures to tie flies for.

The exact imitation purist goes to endless trouble to acquire just the exact shade of colour in his hackles that he thinks will best imitate the fly on the water. To him, his creations are no doubt indistinguishable from the real thing, but the trout below may for some unaccountable reason, think otherwise. We have, of course, well-known patterns of artificial flies that have proved their ability to deceive fish into thinking they are real duns or spinners. There are, however, so many 'exact imitations' which are refused that we can reach only two conclusions – that fish are colour blind or that colour, viewed below the surface of the stream, and seen through a fish's eye, must look very different

from what it does to a human being, looking down on the surface of the water.

As an example, nothing could possibly look less like anything likely to be met on a Hampshire chalk stream than that very popular fly of this part of the world, the Orange Quill. With its brilliant orange hackle it stands out like a neon sign as it floats along among a hatch of naturals. Nevertheless, the fish like it, as they do the Ginger Quill, which looks little less bogus than the former to my eyes.

These are only two of the classic examples which seem to explode the exact imitation theory. They are interesting because they both concern orange and a shade of this colour. In the last war the camouflage experts decided that of all the colours, orange was only second to yellow in its inability to merge into the background of the countryside; For this reason all objects designed to be visible from the air, such as ground signs and air-sea rescue equipment, were painted yellow or orange. It is not, therefore, strange that this bunch of orange feathers should be mistaken so readily for those delicate B.W.O. duns with their olive bodies and their delicate blue wings.

Some time ago I read a short account of a lecture delivered by some eminent professor of veterinary science, in which he stated that all fish were colour blind, and, therefore, quite incapable of deciding whether it was an Iron Blue or a Pale Watery that was offering itself for dinner. From my own observations and from some experiments I have carried out I can only think that the learned professor may, as often happens, have been misquoted. Nevertheless, in spite of all the research that has been undertaken in this field opinion seems to be equally divided on this most interesting subject.

We anglers hold the strongest views. Very deep rooted beliefs are held that not only are fish able to distinguish one colour from another, but possess most discriminating tastes in the matter of shade. This is obviously a good thing because how uninteresting would be our days by the river side, and how uninviting would be the tackle shop window, if all our flies and lures were of but one single colour.

After all, though none of us seems able to assess exactly what colour means to fish, innumerable scientific experiments seem to prove beyond doubt that under given conditions certain species of fish that have been tested do react to colour. It has also been proved beyond doubt that cartilaginous fish, such as sharks and dogfish, are completely blind to colour.

Experiments have shown us that aquarium fish tend to collect in the most brightly lit area and, if a spectrum is projected, they choose to gather into yellow and green bands. If the colours are extinguished one by one from the violet end, they move through the colours towards the red end of the tank.

However, when red alone remains they disperse. In a red light fish refuse all food, but seize it immediately a blue light is substituted for the red. After a sojourn in darkness, dace prefer red to blue, but after a spell in bright light their tastes are reversed.

Personally, I am quite convinced that trout have the ability to differentiate certain bright colours that are presented to them, but to go further than this is to tread on very dangerous ground, because so much depends on many difficult circumstances. Very obviously, any shade of colour is less visible when seen floating and silhouetted against bright sunlight than it would be if it was sub-surfaced and seen at the fish's eye level against a background of rocks or weed.

As far as their night colour vision goes, I have always felt that it is a question of 'are not all cats grey in the dark?' Admittedly, a white-winged sub-surfaced fly is obviously more visible than a black one in the late evening, but I feel it unfair to expect a trout to distinguish a Sherry Spinner from a Lunn's Particular of similar size when floating rapidly down stream over their noses and silhouetted against a dark sky. A very simple experiment I carried out would seem to prove this theory.

A fisherman friend of mine owns a delightful cottage on a southern country chalk stream, through whose ground runs a tributary of a famous river. Almost outside the back door, a small carrier feeds into a small artificial pool. In this live some half-dozen large and corpulent trout, whose main occupation in life is to beg for scraps of bread to be thrown to them. These customers were the perfect subjects for colour testing, and although the result of their reactions may be somewhat confusing they were nonetheless interesting.

The first test was carried out in a strong light but with no sun. They were offered small cubes of bread dyed laurel leaf green, daffodil yellow, butcher blue, blood red and royal purple. All these colours were as dark as they could be made by the use of normal cooking dyes. Having first stimulated their appetites with a couple of cubes of undyed bread, they were offered a blue. This they inspected closely and at length, but refused to take it. Next a yellow was inspected and again after several offerings one fish reluctantly accepted one piece. Orange and purple were inspected but refused but after close inspection the red was eaten on all occasions. The odd part about this test was that the green was eaten with even greater relish than the white.

Using the same coloured bread cubes at dusk the same evening, all colours were taken equally well except green and no amount of tempting would persuade them to go near this hitherto favourite colour.

In bright sunlight the next morning, using the same material, they refused all colours except the red which they took only after prolonged inspection. An interesting point, however, was that if the cubes were cut to only one-third their thickness, thus letting more light through, all colours except blue were eaten, I found that if the bread cubes were dyed in tones of less density, pink instead of red, etc., I found the reactions were the same as with the sliced cubes.

Now, although these tests were repeated under almost similar lighting conditions, and although the results were almost identical, they are obviously not conclusive. The fish were reacting to food floating in gin-clear water of no greater depth than two feet. The material fed to them below the surface might have produced a completely different result. So again might the results have varied if carried out in coloured water. Nevertheless, they did establish certain interesting facts.

In the first instance, it would seem that bright green and bright red changed their acceptability according to the lighting from the sky, but that if all the colours were reduced in depth, or if more light was admitted through the bright coloured bread being reduced in density, all colours with the excep-

tion of blue were eaten equally well. This would seem to argue that fish are colour conscious only where vivid colours are concerned and reach a point down the scale of colour depth where all look the same.

The one exception to this was blue. They were evidently conscious of this tint, even when the material was dyed so that the blue was of a light blue colour.

At dusk, as I expected, all colours were eaten, madly, except the green. Why this should be so is anyone's guess.

The more we read about the very interesting subject of colour blindness in living creatures the more we are faced with a mass of conflicting evidence and opinions. If fish, as my tests seem to show, are only capable of differentiating between bright colours, are not we dry fly purists wasting our time in being so particular about the choice of material used in our dry flies?

The more we think about this absorbing subject the more confused we become. Why, for instance, should the amateur fly dresser become so thrilled at having run to earth some precious Andalusian cock hackles and in the next breath enlarge on the merits of the new orange fluorescent body material with which he intends to tie some Orange Quills to imitate the B.W.O.

Can it be that we are all barking up the wrong tree by thinking that our man-made creations fool the fish into thinking they are real flies? Is there not some ground for believing that the fish selects the bogus from the real thing, not because of its similarity to the real, but because it looks slightly different and thus triggers off some reflex action which impels it to snap at it?

An Irish fishing companion of mine may have summed the situation up when, referring to a most successful Spent Gnat, he said: 'No fish could refuse your gnat: doesn't she sit on the water far better than them naturals?'

🍃 Some fly dressers, particularly those whose names are linked with a particular fly, rose quicker than the hungriest trout to any alteration of either colour, shape or material used in the original pattern.
🍃 Dick Walker, himself the creator of several patterns that have lasted the course – he would never publicise a fly until it had caught 50 fish – warned buyers of flies to look up the correct dressing before parting with their money.

THE IMPOSTERS
by RICHARD WALKER, *August 1977*

RUDYARD KIPLING wrote: 'If you can bear to hear the truth you've spoken, twisted by knaves to make a trap for fools . . .'

I am reminded of this when I see what happens to effective fly patterns that I, and others, have invented. They are described in books, and they crop up in tackle shops and tackle catalogues, bearing only a superficial resemblance to the originals.

About ten years ago, with helpful advice from Peter Thomas, I produced a fly called the Sweeney Todd. It is a most useful stillwater pattern, and if I had to be limited to a single pattern for reservoir trout fishing, I would choose it. The dressing is fairly simple; here it is:

ॐ *Hook*: Any size from 12 to two tandem size 6s; size 6 and 8 long-shank are perhaps the most useful sizes.

ॐ *Body*: Black floss, ribbed fine silver thread (oval tinsel). Just behind the wing roots, take two or three turns of magenta drf wool.

ॐ *Throat hackle*: A false hackle of crimson-dyed cook hackle fibres.

ॐ *Wing*: Black squirrel tail hairs.

ॐ *Tail*: None.

Now most of the books that describe the Sweeney Todd specify a magenta throat hackle instead of crimson. Many specify flat tinsel for the ribbing. And lately, the fly has started appearing in the tackle-shops with a red tail, which entirely defeats the object of putting magenta wool at the wing roots. So, in general, what is being described and sold as a Sweeney Todd, while it may catch fish, is certainly not the Sweeney Todd that Peter Thomas and I invented.

Tom Ivens' Jersey Herd is another example. The original pattern had an underbody of floss, built up to a fish shape and then covered with copper foil. I have never seen one in a shop that had a copper body. They all have gold bodies, and most of them do not have the underbody at all; just gold tinsel wound over a single layer of tying silk. Again, these things may catch fish, but they are not Jersey Herds.

My own Polystickle has suffered, too. It is rare indeed to find one in a shop in which the tying includes a spiral binding of black silk over a silvered hook-shank, or the alternative of silver tinsel in open spirals over a bronzed hook-shank, so that you get the appearance of a translucent tiny fish with its vertebrae showing through. And the tyers have now taken to making a tiny head no bigger than that of an ordinary fly, whereas one of the features of the original was a big, bold, built-up black head. As if that is not enough in the way of alteration, they have also decided to leave a tail twice as big as it ought to be, and to cut it forked. The original had a short tail, clipped square.

One of the minor break-throughs of my fly-tying career was the discovery that an artificial Daddy-long-legs should have its legs trailing backwards, not spread out all round. In other words, imitate the fly as you see it either on the wing or drowned in the water, not as it is when it sits on your window-ledge.

An artificial tied with trailing legs is at least ten times more likely to catch trout than one with its legs spread out. I have explained this in numerous articles and in a little book called *Fly Dressing Innovations* which contains a full description of my Daddy-long-legs, together with two pictures of it, one a colour photograph and the other a black and white sketch.

Despite this, people continue to sell artificial Daddies with spread-out legs. Of course, other people have produced their versions of an artificial Daddy, and if they want to get it wrong, they're fully entitled to do so; but if they do, I'd be obliged if they would avoid selling it as my pattern – which they very frequently do. If it is going to be sold as Dick Walker's pattern, it should have eight backward-trailing pheasant-tail fibre legs, each knotted twice. And the wings should slant back, too, not be set out at right-angles to the body like a spent Mayfly.

As for Mayfly nymphs, I shall never cease to wonder at the extraordinary things that are tied and sold under that name. Their inventors and their tyers cannot possibly ever have seen a real Mayfly nymph, which is a large creature, a good inch long, whose predominant colour is a very pale yellowish buff, almost ivory, with dark brownish markings and wing-cases. Most of the alleged imitations I see look like scaled-up live nymphs, and bear no resemblance to Mayfly nymphs at all.

I fish for grayling quite often in autumn and winter, mostly in Hampshire, and one of the most common flies on the chalk-streams in that county is the pale watery dun. Actually several species come under this heading, but one pattern of dry fly suffices for those that hatch in the part of the year when I am grayling-fishing.

I used to find the grayling difficult to catch during hatches of pale watery when I used the usual imitations, until I invented one of my own. It was tied with primrose silk, of which three turns were exposed at the rear end of the body, and varnished to give a semi-translucent amber appearance. The body itself was very pale greenish-white. It had so little green that you had to look carefully to see that any green was there at all.

Apart from flies tied by Miss Jackie Wakeford, I have never seen this pattern tied correctly. The exposed turns at the tail-end of the body are usually omitted, and the body is commonly bright green. As a matter of interest, I tried some of these wrong 'uns on the grayling, which said, 'We do not wish to know that; kindly leave the stage!' So here is a case where adulteration has made the pattern useless. Why? The fly was described in *Trout and Salmon*; it is in *Fly Dressing Innovations*. It is just as easy to tie it right as to tie it wrong. It costs no more, either.

Yet another pattern of mine that I have never seen tied correctly, except when I have tied it myself, is the hairwing Mrs Palmer. The original was tied thus:

- *Hook*: Size 6 or 8 long-shank.
- *Body*: White drf wool, ribbed fine silver thread, with a few turns of arc chrome drf wool just behind the wing root.
- *Throat hackle*: A bunch of white cock hackle fibres.
- *Wing*: Very pale primrose fine goat hair, twice the length of the hook.

- *Tail*: None.

This is a very useful pattern at times because it is attractive when retrieved very slowly, unlike many lure-type flies that need fast movement. It also does well in deeply-stained water.

I have never seen any but my own flies with wing hair of the right colour or length. It is usually bright yellow and no longer than the hook itself. And in a recently-published book, this fly has been given a tail, the body material changed to chenille, the ribbing changed to silver tinsel, the turns of arc chrome wool omitted, and the pattern described as having to be moved fast! I still remain credited with its invention, however!

It may be thought that my complaints are concerned largely with my own patterns. Not so; I have quoted these as examples because I know them so well. Others who devise flies suffer equally, if not more so. I can only suggest that anglers who wish to buy or tie the genuine article should beware of what is commonly on sale. Look up the original dressings and order from a professional fly-tyer if the local tackle-shop insists on offering unacceptable deviations.

• *Many of the flies we think of as being brand spanking new are often little more than ancient patterns which, apart from the substitution of new materials, are still those old favourites in a different guise.*

• *New patterns are, in truth, very few and far between. Buzzers, midge pupae and even the Black Lure – we've seen them all before.*

OLD FLIES IN NEW DRESSES
by CONRAD VOSS BARK, *March 1976*

MY OLD maternal grandfather, Willie Cox, of Bristol – a terrible old rascal he was, but a great fisherman – had a fly-box. I wish you could see it, but unfortunately it was, as they say, destroyed by enemy action, in 1940.

However, Willie Cox's fly-box was a treasure. In it were the flies he used to fish Blagdon, from when it was opened, in 1904, to the time of his death, sometime in the early '30s. It was a pretty good selection of the most popular reservoir flies and lures then in use; and some of them dating back to late Victorian times.

There was nothing very unusual about Willie Cox's flies. They were the kind that everybody, more or less, would be using on reservoirs 50 to 75 years ago. He was no innovator, apart from designing a minnow fly for use when bait-fishing was banned. His box,

therefore, was full of standard reservoir patterns for the period 1900 to 1930.

Compared with the literary output from chalk-stream fishermen at that time, which was enormous, little or nothing was written about reservoir fishing and reservoir flies. So most of the standard reservoir patterns are unknown to us, which is unfortunate, especially as some of them, at least, are widely used today under other names, while others have been lost and sometimes rediscovered by fly-tyers who think they have invented a new pattern.

There is little new in many of today's reservoir flies except in the materials used. Fluorescent materials and plastics hadn't been invented. Apart from that, many standard reservoir patterns of today have been in use in stillwater fishing for a very long time indeed.

I suspect their spider patterns –

the Black, Green, Blue Dun and Badger Hackle Spiders – have been used in stillwater fishing for at least 100 years, both on lochs and reservoirs. Willie Cox had a number of spiders in his box, including several with a black hackle and a peacock herl thorax – almost exactly the same to look at as the modern Black-and-Peacock Spider dressing.

The spiders were used during a hatch of midge, fished wet; and often as a team of spiders, with as many as seven or eight droppers on a single cast.

But patterns designed specifically to imitate the midge pupae were certainly in use at Blagdon in the 1920s. Whether or not they were created by the late Dr Bell, of Wrington, I do not know. Dr Bell created the famous Blagdon Buzzer pattern and several of these were in Willie Cox's fly-box. But Willie Cox also had one pattern more or less exactly the same as the modern pattern known as the Footballer. Whether this was his own creation or Dr Bell's, I don't know. I wish I did.

Now we come to lures. Willie Cox had a splendid collection of these. Mind you, in those days most of the lures in use on reservoirs were salmon flies. I am talking about big lures, 1½ inches or even 2 inches long. But Willie Cox had a number of lures dressed on thinner hooks and some on smaller hooks tied in tandem which I suppose we should call streamer flies. What he called them, I don't know.

Two of these I remember clearly – a long Black Lure and a Squirrel Tail. The Black Lure was dressed in tandem with a coloured hackle and several black feathers about 3 inches long. The Squirrel Tail was dressed on a long-shanked hook covered closely in some kind of silver foil. The squirrel tail fibres were undyed. The hackle varied – sometimes blue, sometimes orange.

I remember the Squirrel Tail because many years later I designed one of my own, only to remember that I was unconsciously cribbing from the pattern in Willie Cox's box. This does happen. The pattern is registered somewhere in the brain and then forgotten. But when you start tying flies it is remembered, sub-consciously perhaps, and comes alive again.

The rest of the flies in Willie Cox's box were all what we call traditional wet-fly patterns –

Butcher, Mallard and Claret, Mallard and Green, Peter Ross, and so on. But there were also a few oddities, such as beetles made out of some hard plaster, hand-coloured, which would sink like a stone; and fly-spoons, which were ordinary flies with a little silver-coloured spoon clipped on to a swivel at the front – certainly that would be feathered spinning – and things such as drone-flies and wasps and bees.

But I have left until last one of the delights of the collection. There were a few dry flies; several large Palmers, the Green Midge, and the Golden Dun Midge, which dates back, so far as I can tell, to Ronalds in the late 1830s. Very curious. The only pattern I cannot remember seeing is an ordinary pond or lake olive nymph. Why? Again, I don't know.

What is the point of all this? Why on earth bother with Willie Cox, who lived and died before most of us were born, or at least before some of us. I suppose the answer is that one does, or at least one can, learn a deal from history. And in fact Willie Cox has taught me a lot – just from looking at his fly-box all those years ago.

The first thing that one realises

– and I think with something of a shock – is that a lot of reservoir flies that we think of as modern are not. They are, shall we say, descendants from patterns which are at least 50 and in some cases more than 100 years old. Sometimes, of course, they make use of new materials. Sometimes there are subtle refinements. But that's about all.

And the second thing one realises is the need to be a little sceptical about the claims which are so often made nowadays that someone has invented a new fly or a new lure. There are new patterns – of course! – but they are few and far between.

Nor are we right in thinking that we have improved a great deal on the methods by which these patterns of the Victorian and Edwardian days were fished. Long-distance casting of lures did not start with the invention of the shooting-head. Willie Cox cast his squirrel tail and black lures with a heavy sinking line and a 16 foot greenheart rod which could put them 30–40 yards away. There are new things under the sun – indeed there are – but not so many as we sometimes are led to believe.

This is not to say we haven't made progress. Good heavens, no! We have nylon and fibre-glass and plastic lines and so many things that Willie Cox would have loved. How he would have loved them! And how he would have loved the variants of some of his own flies and lures. He would recognise them at once. And as for the skill of angling, that hasn't changed at all. I reckon that if Willie Cox came back to Blagdon today with his old 16 foot greenheart and his wicker creel and stocking waders he would do as well as some and very possibly better than most.

SO WHERE HAVE ALL THE OLD FLIES GONE?

by J. F. TODHUNTER, *February 1972*

RECENTLY, A friend of mine showed me his late father's salmon-fly boxes. His father had caught many salmon, in many rivers in Scotland, at different times in the season, before the last war. The contents of the boxes were a joy to look at. There were about a dozen, containing a wide range of different varieties of fly with both full and low-water dressings, professionally tied in sizes from about 9/0 to 8.

The varieties included Black Doctor, Blue Charm, Dunkeld, Durham Ranger, Dusty Miller, Green Highlander, Jock Scott, Mar Lodge, Shrimp, Silver Doctor, Thunder and Lightning, and Yellow Torrish, as well as a lesser number of others which I did not recognise. There was not a hairwing among them, and all were tied on single hooks. They represented all that was thought necessary to lure salmon, in many different rivers, at any time of the season from early spring to late autumn, in high or low water.

My friend has probably caught as many salmon as his father did, and I asked him to show me his own fly-boxes. He normally used only two. One of these contained, in a variety of sizes, Hairy Mary, Blue Charm, and Thunder and Lightning, all tied with hairwings, and some different patterns of shrimps. There was one variety of silver-bodied fly, a Silver Doctor, in two or three different sizes. All sizes from 6 downwards were tied on double hooks. There were also a few unnamed varieties, consisting mainly of black or dark hair-wings, with jungle cock cheeks. There were no specific low-water dressings.

The second box contained tube flies, ranging from 4 inch heavy, hairy horrors tied round 30 amp fuse wire to ¼ inch Stoat's Tails. Apart from a tippet here and there in the shrimps, a topping for a tail, and an ostrich herl for a butt, and some cheeks of jungle cock, there was not a feather in the collection.

Before going to Scotland to fish this year, I took a more detailed look into my own fly-boxes. Although I carry round an unnecess-ary number, I soon realised that all the flies which I thought might catch a fish (apart from tubes) had gravitated into one box. This con-tained, in a variety of sizes, Hairy Mary, Blue Charm, Thunder and Lightning and Jeannie, all of which, with the exception of the Thunder and Lightning, I had tied with hairwings. My box of tube flies held mainly Stoat's Tails, with some larger varieties of hair or mo-hair for heavier water. Apart from some yellow in the body of a Jean-nie, all the hairwinged flies have simple black bodies, ribbed with

gold or silver. These boxes of flies have served me well on at least half-a-dozen different rivers, in widely separated parts of Scotland.

Intrigued by this self-revelation, I asked a number of my acquaint-ances who fish many different Scottish waters, including Awe, Spey, Helmsdale, Brora, Thurso, Naver, Borgie and Nith. All agreed that the flies they used most were the Stoat's Tail and Hairy Mary, followed by the Blue Charm – and if tied with hair-wings, there is little difference be-tween the last two. My brief inves-tigation revealed that among my own acquaintances at any rate, most summer salmon are taken on simple black-bodied flies with minimally coloured hairwings, sometimes with jungle cock cheeks, and usually with a blue throat hackle.

What, you may ask, does this prove? Nothing for certain, but it is at least an indication that a salmon in the mood to take a fly is not very particular about the pat-tern, so long as size and presenta-tion are right. Forty years ago, salmon were lured by fully dressed, mixed wing flies; now they are just as easily lured by a simple black body, and a few strands of hair.

And what has become of the wonderful, built-wing creations, containing a great variety of exotic, and now unobtainable feathers?

A professional fly-tyer of my acquaintance told me that there is still a demand – but most tied are not for fishing! Many go to America, where they are kept in display cabinets, like butterflies. Others find themselves set under glass in souvenir table mats, or trays, or even on pins for decorating hats. Many contemporary, commercial fly-tyers can fill their whole time tying Hairy Marys, or Stoat's Tails, without ever bothering to learn to tie a really complex fly.

If their use for fishing continues to decline, there will, in time, be nobody left with the skill to produce a fully dressed Jock Scott, incorporating every one of the feathers and hackles in its formula, which is perhaps the supreme test of the fly-tyer's art. It would indeed be a sad day if this craft were to die out.

All fly fishers have flies in their boxes that hold memories. It could be one that led to the downfall of a momentous fish, or perhaps an oddball creation with no name that brings a memorable day back to life. They are usually old and tatty, but like an old hat will never be thrown away.

FIRESIDE FLIES

by MARK BEVAN, *April 1971*

I HAVE a rather unusual fly-box. Unusual in more ways than one.

In the first place, it is made of solid brass and with the amount of polishing it has had over the last half-century or so it shines like burnished gold. Stuck inside the lid is an ornate little card which reads:

With Best Wishes for
a Victorious New Year.
From the Princess Mary
and Friends at Home.
Christmas 1914.

Originally, it held cigarettes and chocolates and one like it was sent to every member of the B.E.F. in France. My father subsequently converted it to more peaceful, piscatorial purposes by sticking cork strips inside. He passed it on to me and it is now lined with some rather fetching sponge-rubber in an *eau-de-nil* shade and houses a small but select batch of 'old favourites' in various stages of undress and decay. I have it in front of me now.

Top left, I notice the strange ginger, buzzy, hackled affair tied on the banks of the Towy and given to me, many years ago, by a little bandy-legged, octogenarian Welshman (whose name I never knew). He not only gave me the fly, but also the most salutary lesson in the art of taking sea-trout in broad daylight that I can ever remember. Using the same pattern he had seven fish (to my one) in just over an hour, in low water and under a blazing July sun! It's quite unusable now. The barb went long ago and the shank is brittle with rust – but I shall never throw it away.

Then there's this one: a rather tatty-looking Mallard and Claret. The Claret is now definitely vintage and faded to a pale pink, while the Mallard is in an advanced stage of moult. But how could I possibly part with it when it brought me my very first salmon, in Ireland, as a boy – some 50 years ago? Admittedly, it was one of a leash of five trolled behind a gently paddled boat on a soft evening (and I was dozing at the time!). But, no matter, there it was, at last, hooked in the angle of that fierce jaw as Timmy Rahilly swept him aboard in the great, long-handled net that he kept in the bottom of his old boat. I can still hear one of his nine children rushing off to his cottage by the lakes as we landed, crying 'They have a fush, Granny – they have a fush!' and I see her now leaping barefoot, like a little fawn, over the tussocks of the bog. She's more than probably a grandmother herself by now.

And don't, please, laugh at this one! I know it looks like a small shaving brush with peacock herl bristles and the sort of monstrosity that any self-respecting fish would avoid like the plague (except perhaps one of those omnivorous pellet-fed fellows so popular nowadays). The 'iron' itself resembles, as much as anything, a large mackerel hook, but, despite its robust construction, it is clearly on the verge of complete

disintegration. It was never even attached to a cast, much less 'offered'.
Then why is it here?

Well, some 30 years ago, I had a
letter from my son (then about
eight years old) and at his prep.
school. I no longer have the letter,
but I can remember that after the
usual mis-spelt account of sporting
prowess and scholastic injustices
(coupled with the conventional
hints concerning pocket money) it
went on to say:

'I am sending you a "fly luer" I
have tied up for you. Mr Ellison
gave me the feathers and I found
the hook. Mr Ellison says it is a
"Somerset Terror" and most dedly
anywhere. Please use it and let me
know how many it gets.'

I have to confess to a good deal
of subsequent 'white lying' about
the prowess of that 'luer', but as
the inventor himself is now a
much better fisherman than I am,
perhaps it doesn't matter any more.
Of one thing I am certain, however, and that is that it will stay
enshrined in its faded magnificence
for the rest of my fishing days –
and possibly even longer.

One or two others I can't quite
place exactly. I know I put them in
this particular box as souvenirs of
some special occasion, but for the
life of me I can't remember precisely where or for what. Most
likely, this little black speck on a
size 18 (?) hook is the one responsible for the only river trout over
3 lb I ever took – and that on a
North Riding chalk-stream at 6
o'clock on a May morning nearly
a quarter of a century ago! I know
I tied on the smallest fly I'd ever
used and that it produced the largest trout I'd ever had. The theor-
ists may make something of this. I
never could.

At the other end of the scale is
this enormous double-hooked Mar
Lodge presented to me by the
young lady for whom I gaffed a
28 lb fresh-run Tay salmon – after
she had had it on for nearly two
hours and was tearfully praying
that someone would happen along.
Luckily for her, I did. Just as I
heaved it ashore the Mar Lodge
dropped out of its mouth! She insisted that I kept it and there and
then I stuck it in my hat, where it
braved the wind and weather for
several seasons before being pro-
moted to the 'special box'.

Nor am I quite certain about the
two Mayflies – both of the
Straddle-Bug variety – but I am

pretty sure they are preserved as the ignored memorials of a complete and utterly blank day when every fish in the river was taking the natural with senseless abandon! The same thing applies to the Lough Mask dapping fly. It is either a handsome fraud or I am no dapper! I did, in fact, do much better with an ordinary Zulu, but it is a reminder of those wild, windy days on the lough and those wild and tuneful nights in the bar.

Here they all are then – these and others. All sorts, shapes and sizes. Some barbless, blunt or broken. A few scarcely recognisable in

their old age, but all recalling, in one way or another, some day of triumph or disaster: all reminders of some dimly recollected incident or a half-forgotten foray of long ago.

I never was a one-fly-only man. Nowadays, I carry to the riverside at least three of those fancy aluminium boxes and am forever changing flies (generally as an excuse for a rest and a smoke!).

But this box is different. It only comes out in the winter – by the fireside. And when it does the spring seems just that bit nearer and the sound of the stream almost within hearing again.

❧ *Fishermen have always been fascinated by flies, but what about those milling masses of flies that are apparently obsessed by fishermen, and why do some anglers suffer more from their biting attentions than others?*

THOSE OTHER FLIES ...
by MARK BEVAN, *December 1971*

NOT EVERY fly-fisherman is an expert entomologist, but over the years, many of us have managed to glean a rough working knowledge of the subject. We are, for example, fascinated by the *Ephemeridae* – particularly that most showy and obvious example, the Mayfly (and hardly less, perhaps, by its even more useful relative the b-w.o.). Some of us refer pontifically to our old friend the large dark olive as *Baëtis Rhodani*; to the sedges as *Trichoptera*, to the alders as *Megaloptera* – and so on. It can be quite impressive.

We may not tie better imitations as a result of this apparent familiarity (and our pronunciation would probably raise a few scientific eyebrows), but the fact remains that a reasonable working knowledge of the genus and habits of the flies of stream and lake can be a useful asset to the serious fisherman. Ever since Dame Juliana Berners recommended that hackle of 'roddy wull', fishermen have been obsessed by flies – but what about all the legions of flies that are apparently obsessed by fishermen?

For some inexplicable reason I am one of those by whom every variety of fly seems to be fascinated. I cannot think that this is due to some unmentionable reason that even my best friends would hesitate to tell me about, but whatever the reason, by any river or lake I am readily identifiable from a distance as the central core of a whirling cloud of a winged insects which clearly regard me as a heaven-set riparian blood-donor.

More than once I have been forced to abandon the field and to retreat, punctured and itching, to the shelter of my car, there to survey the baffled attackers vainly assaulting the closed windows. It is at such times particularly that I am given to wonder why we spend so much time thinking about flies that may be acceptable to the fish and so little to those that plainly find the fisherman irresistible!

Nearly all these flying, biting, blood-thirsty nuisances are what is (laughably) called 'true' flies, or *Diptera*. In Britain alone nearly 5,000 species have been recorded – and a terrifying study they are.

The next time you swat a mosquito on your ear or flatten a gnat on your neck you may well be reducing (infinitesimally, alas) the order of *Culicidae* or even *Ceratopogonidae*, neither of which should, of course, be confused with the non-biting midges which (as every schoolboy knows) belong to the *Chironomidae*.

Then there are those particularly evil and persistent pests variously anathemised as horse flies, gad flies and clegs, none of which is likely to be less voracious if correctly addressed as *Tabanidae* – though to be able to identify one's enemy is (possibly) something. The list is, of course, endless: Fungus gnats, fever flies, stiletto flies, robber flies, assassin flies, hover flies and hundreds more – all dignified by unpronounceable Latin names and all determined, in one way or another, to harass the genus *Homo sapiens piscatoris* without mercy.

Not that the battle is entirely one-sided. Apart from the customary manual reprisals, various protectants and repellants are available. I have tried most of them and found some quite effective – temporarily. But for me, the cure (if you can call it that) is generally worse than the complaint. To fish smeared with some evil-smelling unguent is to put too high a price on even total immunity.

Far better, I think,
The sting than the stink!

There is, too, plenty of advice for the victim. Tobacco smoke is certainly a proved deterrent, and the chain-smoker coughing his way from pool to pool may well be relatively fly-free – but the price can be high, both medically and economically. In those lush southern valleys where the mosquitoes 'Come not as single spies, but in battalions', I know of fishermen who ply their skilful craft in headgear draped at the back (like members of the French Foreign Legion) with handkerchiefs steeped in ammonia. Alas, they can be spoken to only in a stiff following wind. I would rather be irritated than ostracised.

Another school of thought relies on 'colour', and a gentleman in Scotland once assured me solemnly that flies 'detest blue'. Perhaps so, but not all of us are prepared to fish all summer wearing a sort of sky-blue Balaclava helmet and matching mittens! In Yorkshire, the 'sprig-of-mint' school has its adherents, and a small bunch stuck in the cap over each ear is supposed to act like a charm.

Unfortunately, my attendant *Diptera* don't seem to have heard about these magical properties. Nor have I forgotten the occasion when I dropped in at the local on the way home, forgetting that I was still festooned with this particular greenery. The landlord (betraying a hitherto unexpected familiarity with the classics) enquired loudly, 'What'll it be, Bacchus?'

Frankly, I am baffled. I have tried everything. My haversack bulges with tubes, bottles, sprays and atomisers. I smoke, I calculate, approximately five fags per fish (interspersed, in particularly fly-ridden areas, with a pipe charged with a particularly noxious mixture). I exude a powerful odour of carbolic soap as a result of prepiscatorial bathings. I have camouflaged my more vulnerable parts with a variety of sweet scented herbs. I have peered through bee-keeper's gauze and fumbled in muslin mittens – but all to no avail. Still they come (as the hymn says) 'in clouds descending!'

Surely it is high time that our scientists abandoned their researches into the obliteration of comparatively minor predators like the cabbage root fly, the onion fly and the lesser boll weevil. Let them focus their microscopes on what the poet once called:

Those midges, gnats, those bugs,
  those flies,
That swatted wasp that never dies.

Fame, fortune and gratitude await the inventor of some odourless, greaseless, unobtrusive, concentrated and infallible fly repellant – but meanwhile the apostles of the artificial must, it seems, endure the natural as best they can.

There was an old music-hall ditty which used to ask, rather plaintively, 'Where do flies go in the winter time?' I never knew the answer to *that*, but I can assert, positively, where a great many of them congregate between April and October!

➤ *We've all met the man with the tattiest tackle; rod held together with tape lashings, a line fit only to tie up a row of raspberries, and a box crammed with flies with their best days and many wettings well behind them.*

➤ *But why are we always astounded when he manages to winkle out good fish that have turned their nebs up at our pristine creations? Could it just be that there's a good deal more to fishing than having all the right tackle?*

PADDY GETS HIS TROUT

by G. A. CHATTAWAY, *August 1971*

I FIRST met Paddy at a stone bridge over a tributary of the Shannon in Co. Roscommon. He was studying the water downstream; beside him was a local man who kept the village garage, some hundred yards away. It was obvious the two men had not met before.

Paddy was a large flabby man in his late fifties. He smoked incessantly. A florid, blotchy complexion belied his association with Irish whiskey. He wore a dark, shabby suit under which a roll-necked Aran sweater had stood the test of time, never having seen the inside of a wash-tub since the wool had left the sheep's back on the Connemara mountains.

The two men leaned in silence, looking at a slight bend in the clear limestone stream. It was early May, and the full glory of the Irish spring was emerging. A slight breeze ruffled the sedge and an overhanging hawthorn near the bend.

Paddy shifted slightly, puffing the cigarette dangling from his broad, chapped lips.

'Now, wouldn't that be a great spot for a good trout to lie?' he mused. A slight flush spread over the local garage man's face.

'I never did see a trout at all. Sure, 'tis full of pike. The lough is tik wid thim. Don't they come up the stream in t'ousands? Ravagin' ivery livin' ting.'

Paddy puffed his cigarette, blowing the ash carefully.

'I've seen divil a many foine trout come out of pike water. Isn't the Inny near Sheelin a great pike water? 'Tis full of trout, too, I've kilt miny a fish from it.'

The garage man stuck resolutely to his task.

'Me Mammy and Daddy were born in the Sheelins on either side of this stream. Nivir a divil of trout did they iver see.'

Paddy continued to contemplate the stream. A small hatch of iron blue duns appeared. One, emerging below the bridge, cast its nymphal case and, like a tiny sail-boat drifting in the breeze, slid quietly downstream. At the bend, an eddy caught it and for a moment the dun fluttered, but its wings were not quite dry enough for flight and instead the eddy carried it downstream along by the sedges. A boil appeared in the ruffled surface of the stream. It was hardly detectable but the fly had gone.

Nothing was said between the two men, still leaning heavily on the bridge, the garage man using the silence lest it betray his dark secret. Paddy's steady downstream gaze hardly flickered. But he had missed nothing.

''Tis a foine day,' said the garage man at last.

'A great day,' agreed Paddy.

The garage man shifted the talk.

'I saw ye park the car near the bridge. Isn't t'at a Dublin registration? Are ye from the City?'

'No. I'm from Westmeath,' said Paddy.

'Arragh, don't I know Mullingar well,' the garage man continued. 'Isn't t'at a great town for the pretty girls?'

''Tis even a better town for the fishin',' Paddy replied.

The garage man scowled, walked towards his garage, growling over his shoulder:

'Sure, I've little enough time for fishin'. Isn't it a game for a worm at one end and a mug at the ither?'

Paddy chuckled, and for the first time addressed me.

'Are ye a fisherman?' he asked. I nodded assent. Paddy continued.

'I've a feeling your man at the garage's a divil of a liar. Sure now, isn't it lucky that I niver travel anywhere without a rod in the car?'

Paddy opened the boot of his car, producing an ancient rod, an exquisite example of built-cane's finest era. A greased line was threaded through the rings, a fine cast attached – I could have sworn it was horsehair – and a firmly hackled Grey Duster selected from a massive leather fly wallet produced from an inside pocket.

Within minutes, Paddy had walked downstream well away from the stream, then stealthily he worked his way back upstream to within casting distance of the bend where the trout lay. He began to false cast, kneeling on one leg. To watch a master dry-fly fisherman at work is a joy for ever. Paddy was certainly that. I watched the final cast snake out, the fly itself gently parachuting on to the surface of the water a yard or so above the sedges.

A riffle in the water caught the fly and moved it away from the sedges. Paddy waited patiently until the fly had swum well downstream, lifted it clearly and false cast to dry his fly perfectly, making the fast cast again. This time he made a slight pass with his casting arm before the final delivery. This caused a loop in the fly-line as it touched down on the surface of the water. It had the desired effect, holding the fly into the sedges away from the riffle.

I was suddenly aware of another figure at the bridge by my side. The garage man had returned.

'The divil give him bad luck,' he muttered.

We both watched the fly swimming slowly along the sedges. Then came a swirl, and the fly had gone.

'I have him,' yelled Paddy, as he tightened on the fish. A stream of black oaths followed from the garage man. Paddy, unperturbed, battled the fish out, finally slipping the landing net under a magnificent brown trout, topping 3 lb.

The garage man was beside himself with rage.

'For two years I've been after that filla. And he gets him wid his second cast. Arragh, God has no justice.'

Paddy returned to the bridge, the trout still twitching in his landing-net, its deep golden sides, shading to the creamy buttermilk yellow of its belly. What a fish! The garage man inspected it, and I sensed that his grudge and rage were waning to admiration.

'Arragh, he's a great fish,' he sighed. 'I raised him a dozen times in t'ree seasons. And niver set the hook to him once.'

Paddy lit a cigarette and produced a hip-flask from his pocket.

'Thin we'd better wet the fish's head,' he said, passing the hip flask to the garage man. He took it and, with a great gulp, nodded at Paddy, saying, 'Slauncha!'

As the garage man's head went back to take another gulp, Paddy winked broadly at me and quickly put his index finger into the roll neck of his Aran sweater, momentarily exposing to me, but not to the garage man, the dog collar of a Catholic priest. Just as quickly, the roll neck was flicked into place again.

'Arragh,' said Paddy. 'He's a great fish. But like us all, wasn't he sure to make a mistake at some time or ither?'

❧ Just occasionally there is the day when everything goes to plan. The right flies are instinctively plucked from the rows in the box, the casting is fluid and the fish respond like they've rarely done before.

❧ But it's not always the action that makes the day. Sometimes the best and most memorable part is when you are making the slow, homeward plod.

WALKING BACK ...

by TOM ATKINSON, *July 1971*

ALTHOUGH THERE is still a good hour's fishing left before the light fails, you have decided to call it a day and are making your way slowly back to your car. Your bag is heavy, with the weight of two good brace, and you have returned five lesser fish. You are relaxed, pleasantly tired, well content.

You glance at your watch and nod with satisfaction. Yes, despite the deceptive promise of the evening rise, you have packed up in good time. A gentle plod back to the car, then off with the waders, sort out the gear and just time for one drink at the Wheatsheaf before setting out for home. Your tongue moves involuntarily over your lips at the thought, and now that you are no longer fishing, you notice how warm the evening has become. You begin to look about you, to take in details which earlier passed only half-noticed because of your concentration on the business in hand.

A thrush is calling '*Jump-to-it! Jump-to-it!*' from the top of a horse chestnut, and swifts, swallows and martins are swooping low over the meadows. You screw up your eyes against the sunlight, the better to enjoy their darting flight. Somewhere in the distance a cock pheasant shouts a warning.

Someone you do not recognise – a guest or a new member perhaps – is fishing Big Stump Pool. He is too intent on the business in hand to notice you as you detour across the field, but you mentally wish him well and hope that he gets into a fish or two. Your thoughts go back to your own first season and the difficulties and disappointments you suffered before you really came to terms with this tricky little river.

As you near the Plank Bridge a moorhen sounds her alarm note and two chicks move reluctantly over towards the reeds where she is lurking. Only two chicks? When you came this way a week ago there were at least five and you re-call that Hilton, the keeper, has been muttering darkly about find-ing mink tracks along the river. If there are mink about it looks like being a bad time for moorhens. The thought saddens you momen-tarily for you have a soft spot for the perky little water hen.

Further downstream a trout rises, and for a moment you toy with the idea of putting a fly over him. But no: you have had a good day – let someone else try for him. You pat appreciatively at the solid bulge of the four fish in your bag and think about standing yourself a double when you get to the Wheatsheaf. It really has been a very good day . . .

You slosh, heavy-footed, through the wet patch at the front of Long Meadow and a snipe takes off with a loud '*Scrape! Scrape!*' of alarm. In a twinkling the rod in your hand becomes a 12-bore and you watch the bird jink – right . . . left . . . and then right again, and as he

straightens out at extreme range you knock him down cleanly – in your mind's eye! – with the left barrel.

You chuckle at the conceit of it, because even when you were a good deal younger and shooting regularly you didn't bring that trick off very often. Nowadays, you are rather glad that with the passing of the years your interest in killing for sport has waned and that – apart from when it becomes necessary to drive the too-persistent wood-pigeons from the brussels sprouts – the shotgun remains in its case.

Bill Hardy, the treasurer, is fish-ing near the alders. He calls a greeting and you make your way over to him. He has been there for about 20 minutes and has just taken his first fish. So you chat cas-ually for a while about fish and fishing, and before you leave him he compliments you appropriately on your two brace. Good type, old Bill . . .

Now the sun is sliding more quickly down the western sky and its rays are warm on your face. You hitch your bag into a more comfortable position and your thoughts run on before you along the quiet road home. She who sends you fishing will be waiting, and she will know – even before the question has been asked – what sort of day you have had. Swiftly your favourite dish will appear and the four trout be displayed to best advantage. And when she asks you about the big one and just how and where you caught him, she won't be making small talk: she will really want to know.

You are crossing the last field now, the rough pasture. The grass swishes and taps against your waders and you notice that the buttercup petals are making a bright pattern on the damp rubber. At the gate you turn and look back, once more drinking in the familiar scene – the level meadows, the distant village and the clumps of trees marking the line of the river. Then, stiffly and rather clumsily, you climb over. For a while your footsteps are loud in the quiet lane and then, cool in the shade of the old barn, the car is waiting.

Sometimes the best part of the day is when you are just walking back . . .

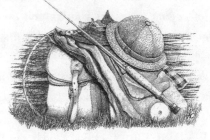

Chapter ten

THE GREAT RAINBOW SAGA

 The catching of massive rainbows in small, clear-water fisheries has become a specialised form of fly fishing calling for specially designed flies, the patience of a heron and a deepish pocket.
 By the mid-seventies the race was on for the first fishery to produce a twenty pounder, whoever took the prize being assured of a steady stream of paying customers knocking on the door.
 Then the bar was raised to 25 lb and, when that was beaten, up went the target by another 5 lb.
 Will tackle have to be radically changed to match the power of such monsters and is the ever-escalating race good for fishing?

'76 – YEAR OF THE 30lb RAINBOW?

by RICHARD WALKER, *January 1976*

FOR MANY years the British record for rainbow trout stood at 8 lb 8 oz, a fish caught at Blagdon, where it can still be seen in its glass case at the fishing lodge, together with the fly and the salmon-strength gut cast on which it was taken.

When Grafham Water opened in 1966, there was much specula-tion as to whether it would pro-duce a new record rainbow, but before it could do so, the small man-made trout fisheries, begin-ning with Packington, started a run of big fish, of which the latest and largest is Mr Julian Farmer's 14 lb 4 oz specimen.

Like his immediate predecessors, Mr Farmer is unlikely to retain his record for long. There can no longer be any doubt that rainbow trout can be produced in this country weighing nearer 30 lb than 20 lb. It has in fact been done, and I will risk predicting that it will not be long before the rainbow record stands at 30 lb or more.

Many anglers have expressed surprise at the rapid progress that has been made in producing rainbows with such greatly increased growth capability, since selective breeding with other kinds of livestock takes much longer to produce far less spectacular results. I will try to explain how it has been done.

In any species, there is considerable scope for variation. Except in the case of identical twins, no two individuals are alike. The species possesses what is known as a gene pool: that is, a wide range of inheritable characteristics. It is the aim of the breeder to combine in selected individuals the inherited and inheritable characteristics that he desires.

The greater the number of offspring from a pairing of two individuals from which he can select, the greater is his chance of finding, among those offspring, some individuals that have a very high proportion of the characteristics he

desires. In addition, the greater the number of pairings he can contrive, the greater is the number of desirable characteristics, from among the gene pool possessed by the species, that are likely to be found among the offspring from all the pairings.

When he is dealing with domestic mammals, where the number of pairs of animals available is somewhat limited, and the numbers produced at a birth are relatively small, it takes a long time to effect progress. Few cattle-breeders keep more than two or three bulls; a cow seldom produces more than one calf. Even in rabbit-breeding, of which I have had some experience, we have to think in terms of perhaps 20 pairings per year with four or five bucks, and litters averaging six or seven.

Consider now the possibilities with fish. It is easy to arrange 50 pairings between 50 cock and 50 hen rainbows; and each hen fish can produce upwards of 20,000 eggs. That produces a total of a million, and even allowing for a mortality as high as 90 per cent, leaving only 100,000 individuals from which to select, it becomes clear that the selective breeder of rainbow trout can progress towards his goal at an incomparably greater rate than the breeder of domestic livestock of other kinds.

Having produced a generation of such size, from which the most desirable individuals can be selected, these are used to produce the next generation, in which a high degree of uniformity can be expected, as well as a future true-breeding performance. The characteristics the breeder requires will be largely fixed in the strain.

If by these means two or more separate races, families, or strains – call them what you will – are produced, the fish-breeder may at any time select parent fish from different strains, all of which may have concentrations of desirable characteristics. By making these crosses, off-spring will be obtained that possess what is known as hybrid vigour, giving a further boost in the direction in which the breeder is working.

In adopting this procedure, the fish-breeder has to guard against fixing in his strain any undesirable characteristics. In practice, this means that nobody wants rainbows, however big, that cannot survive in angling waters, or which do not fight when hooked, or which are unpalatable, or lack resistance to disease or parasites.

Consequently, there is constant checking, in two ways. Individual fish are killed at regular intervals and dissected, and others are transferred to waters where anglers can seek to catch them. The information the fish-breeder obtains from these procedures guards against the likelihood of his producing a race of fish that is in any way unacceptable for the purpose of stocking sport fisheries.

In the past, one of the difficulties that was encountered in breeding very large rainbows was purely physical; handling and stripping fish of 20 lb or more is extremely difficult if those fish are conscious and struggling. The solution was found in the use of anaesthetics, and since breeding stock can now be spawned-out without stress, a much higher survival rate among parent fish becomes possible. That in turn means that a programme of progeny testing can be undertaken, and selection can be made not only in terms of desirable physical characteristics, but also in the ability to pass on these characteristics to succeeding generations.

The implication of all this to anglers is quite startling. Rainbow trout can be produced whose average weight is greater than that of Atlantic salmon. Perhaps more important, fish with much higher growth-rates can achieve whatever size is required in a much shorter time. While the food they consume is proportional to their size; the overhead costs must be reduced; and where fish are to be introduced into waters having rich feeding, their higher inherited growth capacity must result in faster growth and eventual greater size.

There is a further benefit to anglers from an established, true-breeding strain of rainbows. Those now being produced spawn between October and December, the same time of year as brown trout. No longer need we have to deal with gravid rainbows in April and ay; we can fix an open season that is equally suitable for both brown and rainbow trout.

It is a great mistake to suppose that the very big rainbows that are being produced are in any way inferior. I must confess that I have yet to deal, either piscatorially or gastronomically, with anything bigger than 9 lb; but I am well convinced that the bigger fish we

can expect will prove as hard to tempt, as easy to scare, and as difficult to bring to net as anyone could desire.

There is ample evidence to show that when trout are transferred from stewpond to angling waters, all they have learned in the stewpond, including familiarity with humans on the bank, is forgotten. There is a reversion to dependence upon instinct, and to selective feeding, within a very short time after release.

What influence the distinct possibility of hooking a 30 lb rainbow trout will have on the design of trout tackle remains to be seen, but there is one area in which the trend is predictable. The small flip-up landing net is entirely unsuitable! For myself, there is no problem; I devised a landing net capable of dealing with a 30 lb fish back in 1951, and proved its ability with a fish somewhat larger. I still have a net of the same type and size and look forward to the day when I have to use it for a rainbow trout.

HOW SHALL WE CATCH THOSE 30lb TROUT?

by RICHARD WALKER AND ALAN PEARSON, *April 1976*

RICHARD WALKER

Selective breeding of rainbow trout has produced fish nearer 30 lb than 20 lb, and there is every reason to expect that this season some anglers will be trying to catch rainbows of this order of size from angling waters.

Those who do have this opportunity will be faced with the problem of dealing with what might be described as salmon-sized fish on trout tackle, for while these huge rainbows may far exceed the ordinary run of stock-fish, they will be of similar age and feeding behaviour.

Most of us have been brought up with the notion that the larger a trout grows, the more predatory it becomes; that it changes its diet more and more from insects and crustacea to small fish and snails. This remains substantially true of brown trout, but it is not true of rainbows, however large.

It is true that rainbows will at times feed on small fish, usually coarse-fish fry; it is equally true that they can be caught on large lures, fished on strong leader points; but that applies to rainbows of all sizes.

Much more feeding, however, is done by rainbows of all sizes on comparatively small organisms and much of this feeding is selective. The richer the water, the more selective is feeding likely to be.

Let me emphasise that rainbows, however big, are not nearly so inclined to feed on small fish as is generally supposed. In the lakes at Avington are huge shoals of minnows; yet I have never seen trout attacking them, nor have I ever found a minnow in the stomach of a trout taken from these lakes. That these trout do at times eat minnows seems very likely; but it is certain that for most of the time they forgo the ever-present opportunity to do so.

Possibly for the same reason, large fish-imitating lures − Polystickles, Muddler Minnows, and other lures of that kind − are not very effective on the smaller man-made trout lakes into which outsize rainbows are likely to be introduced. I hasten to qualify that by saying that there are times when such lures do succeed, but an exaggerated opinion of their effectiveness is widely held because relatively few anglers select the right imitative pattern, and fish it correctly, when the trout are feeding selectively. Consequently, larger lures take a greater share of the big fish than they really deserve.

For some reason, anglers who would expect to have to choose the correct pattern of imitative fly to suit the preferences of the trout when fishing a river commonly rely on fancy flies when fishing lakes of all sizes. Traditional patterns, such as Peter Ross, Dunkeld, Butcher, and the like, remain in great demand, and as trout are by no means always feeding selectively, such patterns achieve sufficient success to maintain their popularity.

In the course of a day's fishing on a reservoir, or a large loch, these flies will be offered to large numbers of fish, whether the angler realises it or not. Among these large numbers are bound to be some fish that accept the traditional fancy flies. I fancy most anglers would be startled if they could know how many trout refuse them! Most anglers who fish Grafham fail to catch the bag limit

of eight fish. How many fish, I wonder, see their flies in a day? It must run into hundreds.

When we consider a small man-made lake of a few acres, where is hoped to catch a very large rainbow trout, we realise that we cannot expect to cover nearly so many trout in a day; and that selective feeding is much more common on such waters. If we are to make the best of our opportunities, we must pay more attention to imitative patterns.

These are often small. They range from things such as damsel nymphs and Mayfly nymphs, through shrimps of various sizes, down to ephemerid nymphs and midge pupae in sizes from 12 to 16: and they demand leader points appropriate to their size. You cannot fish a size 14 or 16 fly successfully on an 8 lb b/s leader.

But landing a trout of 10 lb or more on a size 14 fly and a leader whose wet strength is about 3 lb or less is a tricky proposition, especially if the water is weedy, or has rafts of algae floating on the surface. The fish, if alarmed, is liable to bolt at high speed, and to keep going for a long distance. At once we realise the advantage of a short fly-line; the drag of a full double-taper is enough to cause breakage, either of hook or leader, if that line is all drowned, even though the angler gives line freely. Matters are worsened if the line picks up floating weed.

A short fly line of 10–12 yards is therefore advantageous, but better still is the avoidance of the long, fast run whenever possible. This means concealment both before and after hooking the fish. If the trout cannot tell from which direction danger threatens, and if he is not subjected to undue pressure, he will usually swim around in a limited area, with perhaps some 'head-shaking' until he tires, whereupon pressure can be increased.

One of the unavoidable handicaps sometimes suffered is the well-meaning fellow-angler who comes thundering along the bank waving a landing-net, usually of inadequate size and handle length. A net with 28–30 inch arms and a 5 foot handle is what is needed for really big trout; and a dark brown or green mesh helps, too. The sort of net most trout fishers carry is inadequate for a fish 30 inches long.

It pays to slide the net stealthily into the water early in the fight; not infrequently the chance occurs to guide the fish over it with gentle side-strain long before it is exhausted. I have heard this condemned as unsportsmanlike; my attitude is, let guile and cunning prevail whenever possible. The angler who is connected with one of these monster fish is in enough difficulty without needing to encourage the fish to break the tackle.

The frequency with which I find flies other than my own in the mouths of trout, not all of them very big trout, reinforces my belief that breakage is very common, and I do my best to avoid it. The last fly I found sitting beside my own in a trout's mouth had 5 inches of nylon attached, with two wind knots in it; I expect it broke at a third. It pays to check for wind knots, and to remove and re-tie on the fly – and to do so often where outsize trout are likely to be encountered. It also pays to test every hook for strength and sharpness, and it is folly to fish more than one fly, even in open water. There is always the possibility that a second trout will grab a fly trailing from a hooked fish, especially when the angler is keeping out of sight.

These big trout present an interesting challenge, and while only a raw beginner or a fool judges the enjoyment of trout fishing by the size of the fish, there is no denying the excitement that a 'monster' hooked on ordinary trout tackle can provide. It is also very entertaining to be slicing the smoked side of such a fish while one's guests watch in eager anticipation.

ALAN PEARSON

More than a year ago I wrote a piece for *Trout and Salmon* entitled 'Somewhere, oversize rainbows . . .', which merely progressed along a line of thought originated by Richard Walker and dealt with my own researches into potential growth-rates of rainbow trout. In fact, I made so bold as to suggest that a growth in weight of 18 lb was feasible within 21 months, provided strict control of the environment was maintained – a notion howled to scorn as absurd by a number of people.

But was it so absurd? Was I so far wrong in my postulations? It seems not, because Sam Holland has now set the pot a bubbling once more with his remarkable Avington-strain rainbows (reported in the January *Trout and Salmon*), which have now achieved weights in excess of 30 lb at the four-year mark and are still growing! I should add that up to 20 lb of this weight has been added in less than eight months, and all in the form of solid, muscular flesh, not unhealthy fat. Mind you, Sam Holland has not been controlling his rearing environment to any great extent; he has relied upon combating the debasement of the genetic pool by selective breeding.

I suppose there are many people who will say that they are not interested in these super-large trout, that they do not wish to fish for them, and would not like to see them introduced into this or that fishery. Some of these people may be telling the truth, but I do hope that no-one is naive enough to ask what good these big trout are, because that ought to be obvious. These fish are highly efficient converters of protein to body weight, which is why they grow fast. They pass on similar characteristics to their progeny, and evidence so far available, completely irrefutable, is that each successive generation shows an improvement in strain and is larger and more powerful at any age than was the previous generation.

So now we come to the crux of the matter. Would you, as an angler, prefer that your trout of any given size were young, or old? If you have the option of catching 3 lb fish, would you prefer that they were 15 months out of the egg, or three years? If you think it does not matter, then you are missing a vital factor.

The cost of producing a trout to any given weight is a compound of feed cost and overheads. A more efficient feed-converter in effect may consume nearly as much protein as a poor converter to achieve the same weight, but is unlikely to do so. However, it spends much less time in the rearing ponds, and therefore attracts a significantly smaller proportion of all other overheads. Thus the total cost per unit is reduced, and this saving can be passed on to the purchaser without any diminution of profit to the producer. In other words, if one-year-old fish of a quick-growing strain are 14 inches long, there is no reason why these should not be offered at about the same price as one-year-olds of a slower-growing strain averaging 6 inches.

There would have to be some minor variations, of course, relative to different cost structures, but the principle remains the same. Unfortunately, economic law has now entered the arena, and because there is currently a shortage of trout which is likely to persist for at least one or two more seasons, the high demand for inadequate output is bound to result in price inflation. How much better, then, if such stock is available to go for the quickest-growing strains achieving takeable size in far less time.

Can you eat these big trout, should you be fortunate enough to catch one? Of course you can! Treat them like salmon in terms of preparation and cooking, and you may find them rather preferable to that fish. Or send them off to be smoked as salmon, when you will find that they surpass anything you have ever previously tasted.

I have been fortunate to be able to devote a good part of my time to the pursuit of large trout, both at home and abroad. I do not mean the worn-out old brook stock used in some fisheries, but strong, healthy young fish, full of fight, full of guile, and in full possession of all their fins. (In passing,

Richard Walker, many moons ago, posed the question – why are so many stock trout tail-less, and why do so many of them have button-like stubs instead of pectorals? All sorts of odd answers were given. The truth is that these symptoms, particularly stub pectorals, denote an earlier attack of furunculosis, or endemic furunculosis. Perhaps this explains why no one cared to give the true answer, although many knew it!)

To me, the great thrill is to fish in clear water, locate a trout visually, attempt to deduce upon what it is feeding, and lure it on a sound imitation. The ultimate thrill is to stalk the very largest trout, ignoring all its lesser brethren, unless it is necessary first to catch the smaller trout which often act as bodyguards and food-tasters.

Strange though it may seem, these large trout rarely seem to feed on smaller fish during daylight hours, and none of my double-figure trout – indeed, none of my trout over 7 lb – has contained a smaller fish of any description, although the water may have been thick with minnows or coarse-fish fry. Instead, they seem to cruise casually, but with great purpose, absorbing a particular insect as op-posed to a variety. Some of these insects are pretty small, as for instance those midge pupae which need to be tied down to size 16 or 18 for accurate imitation. And it is my experience that accuracy is essential, a marginal difference in size either way seeming to ensure that the offering is unacceptable. Of course, it is virtually impossible to fish a fly of this size on anything but a very fine leader. In fact, the hook pattern which I use has a slightly larger eye than normal, which enables me to use a nylon leader of about 4 lb b/s – and even that is perhaps a shade coarse for perfect presentation.

Provided the offering is acceptable, and the presentation impeccable, the large trout imbibes the fly in leisurely fashion, almost like a connoisseur of wine enjoying a rare old vintage. This eliminates the first major problem – that of the so-called smash take. Striking is as leisurely an affair as was the take, with the fine hook being pulled into the trout's mouth, rather than driven home. Then comes the hard bit!

It is my experience that double-figure trout normally behave like hooligans, causing a great deal of fuss and commotion. But provided the water is reasonably snag-free, that the tackle is well-balanced and all knots have been tested, a reasonably competent angler need not fear a break unless he makes a serious error of tactics.

Many people think that my favourite rod is too short, too weak, and my tackle generally too light. Whenever possible, usually quite frequently, when my back cast goes astray and lodges firmly in a tree, I offer my rod to these critics and invite them to pull for a break. The truth of the matter is that the break usually has to be induced by hand-lining, since there is an obvious limit to the pressure that can be applied, no matter how long or strong the arm of the angler. So, as long as one keeps cool, the odds are against the trout.

Not so in the case of those few big rainbows that fight a very different fight, boring deep and sullen, smashing their tails against the line and producing those dreaded heavy poundings of the tackle that all too soon begin to develop and exploit the potential weak spots. This sort of battle goes on for far too long, and the longer it lasts, the more likely it is that the angler will lose out. Knots and hook-holds can stand only so much of this sort of pressure. Even on heavier tackle, the hook pulls out when all else remains sound.

In the fisheries I enjoy most, the smaller lakes with crystal-clear water, lure-stripping is looked upon as being inappropriate. Nevertheless, I have resorted to this technique in larger or heavily-coloured waters, with some limited success. The take tends to be much more violent, and where the trout is very large – and they do run very large in, say, Ethiopia – there is grave risk of an immediate break, no matter how strong the tackle. Perhaps the difference is that the big trout imbibes nymphs and pupae in a relaxed, casual manner, but strikes viciously at the lure because it is an alien thing.

So far I have been discussing trout into the 'teens of pounds, but however do we cope with rainbows in excess of 20 lb or 30 lb, let along those that have the potential to top 60 lb? Much as I have faith in my light tackle, I begin to have doubts.

I remain firmly of the opinion that the way to hook these giants is to adhere to the tiny fly, but will such a hook retain its hold over the period of time that one is likely to spend playing the fish? And frankly, how much use would a

4 lb leader be in such a situation? There is the trap. One cannot present a small fly correctly on a heavy leader. It seems that we need a new material for leaders, infinitely stronger, thickness for thickness, than our present nylon monofilament. Has anyone any ideas?

&❧ *Will the time ever come when huge rainbows can be regularly expected at all but the smallest daily-stocked fisheries; and will their capture be more a credit to the fish farmer than to the angler?*

BILLY BUNTER RAINBOWS
by CONRAD VOSS BARK, *November 1976*

ANGLERS WHO have been hoping to catch 10–20 lb trout regularly as the result of the huge rainbows being bred at Avington Lakes, in Hampshire, are going to be disappointed. Fingerlings of the new Avington strain of rainbow trout will not grow any larger than any ordinary rainbow trout if they are stocked in waters where conditions are less than perfect for growth and development. They will not grow to 20 lb in weight without intensive feeding.

They are very good publicity value for commercial fisheries who stock a few 'Billy Bunter' fish for this purpose, but these would be far too costly and quite uneconomic to stock on the large water authority reservoirs.

The man who breeds them at Avington, Sam Holland, blames angling journalists for raising false hopes. He told me: 'The people who've written about these fish have got it all wrong. I'm not supplying big fish, I'm not talking about jumbo fish, what I'm doing is supplying cheap fish.'

Holland, now 51, retired from working on the American space research programme 10 years ago, came to England, and bought a fish farm in the water-meadows of Itchen Abbas, near Winchester, to develop his theories on selective breeding of trout.

In America, where the rainbow

is a wild fish, natural selection ensures the survival of the biggest and strongest. Holland believed that in England, where rainbows are artificially bred, fish farms were breeding smaller fish by matching any cock fish to any hen without discrimination about size of genetic history.

Holland started to discriminate. He found a new method of storing milt from the cock fish. He started breeding specially selected cock fish to specially selected hens, inbreeding them generation after generation to fix a new strain, as dog and cattle breeders have done.

It is anyone's guess how much the experiments cost him, but it was probably well over £150,000. He was not breeding jumbo fish for anglers to boast about. What he wanted was to get into the food market. To do that he wanted to produce a rainbow with a growth-rate twice as fast as that of the average stock rainbow – quick, cheap production of marketable fish.

He says: 'So far the results are small. We've only scratched the surface of what can be done and we've a long way to go, but now we have produced a rainbow of up to 3 lb in weight in one year, instead of the two years it took before, and the faster growth-rate means they are cheaper to produce.'

He quotes facts and figures.

The important side of his business is the mass food market. He already has a contract to supply Associated Fisheries with 250 tons of rainbows for 1977 and hopes to make it 1,000 tons by 1979. He is thinking in terms of producing hundreds of thousands of tons a year.

Against this background, this prospect of a mass market for rainbow fish-fingers, or something like that, supplying Billy Bunter trout for anglers is of little importance. What is important to him is supplying normal-sized rainbows at prices below the present market rate.

'For example,' he says, 'we've supplied 1 lb Avington rainbows to Datchet reservoir at 60p a fish delivered, whereas with an ordinary rainbow for the same price you get a fish of about 7–8 oz.

'We can produce good cheap fish in this country provided we breed them properly. From December to June this year (1976) I sold 11,500,000 eggs and fry. That's only a beginning.' He gives a grin, his eyes twinkle. 'There won't be much cod about soon, you know.'

The aim, as he emphasises again and again, is good, cheap fish for the market. The capture of huge carefully bred and carefully fed fish by anglers in the Avington lakes helped to create nationwide interest. 'A big one,' he says, 'is good publicity.'

It is also a problem, especially for anglers, for water authorities, fish farmers, and the owners of private lake fisheries. Intensive breeding and intensive feeding can certainly produce monster rainbows, but the requirements of the commercial food producers and of fly-fishermen do not always coincide. Large artificially produced rainbows of the 10–20 lb class can be curiously disappointing to catch and have little fight in them compared with their wild American ancestors.

It all depends what anglers want. Some private fisheries are already stocking one or two monster fish – not necessarily from Avington – in the hope that they will be captured by anglers after a British record. But one wonders what is the value of catching a 20-pounder (which is certainly possible) which has probably been stew-fed to within a pound or so of weight? Is the credit more to the fish farmer than to the angler?

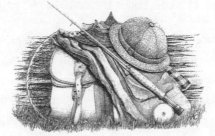

Chapter eleven

THE PRINCE OF FISH

❧ *The art of night fishing for sea trout was, with a few notable exceptions, in a state of arrested development for many years until the publication of a book which was to become the sea trout fisher's bible.*
❧ *Hugh Falkus's logical and almost clinical approach to night fishing inspired a whole new breed of sea trout fishers. Never before had the behaviour and lifestyle of the elusive fish been quite so well understood.*

THE BEHAVIOUR OF SALMON AND SEA TROUT

by HUGH FALKUS, *November 1961*

THE SEEMINGLY weird behaviour of salmon and sea trout has engaged the attention of many fishing writers. Not without reason – it is a fascinating problem. There is not one month of the year during which, in some river of the British Isles, salmon are not running: and few months which don't contain some movement of sea trout.

Why do these fish return to fresh water at such different times of the year, and after such varying periods at sea? Why do some salmon return in the early spring, to spend the long summer mouldering in the river, whereas some arrive in the late autumn just prior to spawning? Why do some kelts start their seaward journey as soon as spawning is finished, but others not until several months have elapsed?

It *seems* strange behaviour. But is it? Is it not, in fact, perfectly logical?

It is reasonable to suppose that

Nature should provide some means of protection against the mass extinction of a species. Were all fish to return during the same month, or after the same period spent at sea, some catastrophe might well wipe them out. As it is, those fish still at sea and destined to make their homecoming during a later month, or even another year, form an insurance against total loss, at least, for a number of years. And so with the return of the kelts. Should some meet with disaster, there are others to follow, and there are those that have gone ahead.

Whether this providence is accidental or otherwise is a purely metaphysical conjecture. Nevertheless, *something* induces the fish to abandon their ocean pastures at a particular time and enter the river – and later, return to sea again.

Have they any choice in the matter? Surely not. How many would prefer the ascetic river life to the rich feeding grounds of some distant sea; how many would choose to linger after spawning in such unsympathetic surroundings, if there were the option of immediate return to a vastly higher standard of living?

It is imperative for salmon and sea trout to migrate from the sea to fresh water, for their eggs cannot develop in saline solution. But the fish can enter the river only with the necessary osmotic changes required for survival in this new environment. And for the kelt's return journey, reversed changes must take place.

Could not this physiological change provide the answer? Is it not probable that intimations of this are the fish's cue to move?

It may be that the fluctuation in the appetite of migratory fish is explainable in terms of these variations in osmoregulation; the reluctance to take on the part of the running fish (until it stops to rest) and the symptoms of voracity displayed by the kelt.

It seems only natural. Salmon leave the sea with sufficient rations stored in their tissues to last them for 12 months, in addition to the food supply for their eggs. And it is interesting to reflect that the time of waiting endured by these early running fish probably seems long only to *us*. In pitying them, it is likely that we fall into the error of a 'pathetic fallacy'!

Be that as it may; few rivers, if any, can provide the meals to which the fish have been accustomed during their pelagic wanderings. If only from the point of view of supply and demand, it is clear that neither salmon nor sea trout can do much feeding while in the river. They can expect little in the way of food; certainly, they expend little enough energy in search of it. Nature has made their return to a (comparatively) barren river inevitable; equipped them to withstand a prolonged fast and, which is more, removed the *desire* for food. Intent only on a sufficiency of oxygen, they remain quietly in some comfortable lie, gradually edging up river as their ripening sexual urges take them onwards to fulfil the purpose of their migration.

This is not to say that they are incapable of deriving nourishment from the river, but feeding in anything like the style to which they have been accustomed is an impossibility.

For this reason, it seems probable that a migratory fish accepts our lure through habit. A feeding habit, or reflex, which may be stimulated by offering the fish a simulation of some prey on which – in conditions comparable to those prevailing at the time of fishing – he may have been feeding at some previous stages of his growth. So that correctness of presentation,

implicit in this, epitomises almost the whole of the salmon and sea trout fisherman's art.

But hungry fish? They are not concerned with food until their task of procreation is done and the physiological changes which follow prepare them – or some of them – for their return to the feeding grounds; and are responsible (probably) for replacing their lost appetites.

But not, of course, all at the same time. As we know, kelts don't go down river in a bunch; but in staggered order, much as they entered it. The policy of 'Divine Insurance' seems evident – as indeed it does before the fish ever enter salt water at all; for parr cannot leave the river until, among other changes, salt-secreting cells have developed in the gills. This may be delayed, so that some parr put to sea after, perhaps, two years; others, not until after three, four or even five years of river life.

Is all this really so puzzling? The movements of migratory fish appear odd when we ascribe psychological origins; but is it not far more likely that they are physiological?

From this viewpoint, salmon and sea trout behave, in their different ways, quite logically – which is of fundamental importance when we come to fish for them.

All too often they are described as being 'unpredictable'. This is nonsense. From a practical angle, analysis of their movements in the river indicates that they conform to clearly defined patterns of behaviour. It is, I suggest, the fisherman whose philosophy and technique are based on careful study of these patterns who is the most consistently successful.

❧ Tom Rawling recalls how Hugh Falkus's new book became his key to unlocking the sea-trout mystery.

SEA TROUT – THE BOOK
by TOM RAWLING, *September 1975*

I LONGED to start fishing, but although the sun had already slipped behind the Lakeland fells, I stayed hidden in the broom bushes. It was too early yet. I had a breathing space; time to enjoy the afterglow that etched the ridge against the western sky in front of me; time to listen to the music of the beck and tune in to my surroundings, and to sea-trout.

It was mid-June, almost the shortest night of the year. The river was low and, as my Polaroids had shown that afternoon, the main pools were holding very few fish. But in a bush-lined run just below the ford, through a gap in the alders I had glimpsed three or four square tails, tucked in by the bank where fast shallow water widened and deepened into a bay a few yards long.

Lying prone, I had watched with great desire those pearl-grey tails lazily fanning the clear water to send sunlight ripples over the stony bottom. Slowly, stealthily, I edged away – one frightened flick of the tails and they would vanish behind the roots of that young sycamore undercut by spates. No fly could tempt them there.

It was a fascinating challenge for

my first night of the season. To cover those fish correctly in that swift current, my fly – teal-and-blue Medicine No 4 low water hook – must sink at once and then swing across them a few inches under the surface. On a floating line it would merely skate over the lie. But a high-density line should do the trick. All this I had decided during my reconnaissance, when I had studied the lie and picked a landing-place for the fish I planned to catch. That upstream eddy would be deep enough to sink my net, and there was a gap in the overhanging branches where I would be able to raise my rod – just by that patch of shingle. I had memorised it all. Distances seem so different in the dark.

Now I was by the shingle, with my tackle ready. I believed that I could hook one of those fish, but I knew the night's fishing would be short. The sky was clear: in an hour or so the moon would be rising behind me – the worst possible situation for a night fly fisherman. My hope lay in the bushes and trees that guarded the run. They posed a desperate threat to any careless back-cast; but they would give me

cover and throw dark shadows across the water.

Brambles scraped my thornproof coat as I stepped down to the shingle. In the gathering dusk I could just make out the sycamore marking the bay where the sea-trout were lying. It was little more than an hour to moonrise, but I forced myself to wait for a few more minutes . . . until the distant bank dissolved into darkness.

I started to wade quietly downstream, working line out into the throat of the run. Then, with a gap behind me, I deliberately cast almost square, lengthening line a foot at a time, until I heard my lure patter on a leafy twig. It came free at a twitch. So, I had a length of line that just spanned the river, and I could confidently search the darkest shadows. I would need several arm's lengths more when I began to cast at an angle downstream, but I had a basis for trial – and error, perhaps? But the risk of overcasting had to be taken. My lure must land within a foot or so of the opposite bank.

I stripped in the line, letting the coils fall, and checked lure and leader by touch. Everything has to be perfect when the first casts are made over a sea-trout lie at dusk.

That enchanted hour as twilight thickens into darkness is often the most productive, and tonight the short spell before moonrise would give me the best – probably my only – chance to hook a fish. Any error could ruin that opportunity.

It was time to start in earnest. With the same length of line out, I shuffled further downstream, taking care not to splash in the shallow water (so much easier to wade quietly in deep water). Here at my back I had an unbroken bank of high bushes; I concentrated hard on every detail of my steeple cast, talking myself through it:

'Cock your right wrist forward on the rod handle. Dip the rod-tip to the water. Start to draw line smoothly with your left hand to full arm's-length – and lift. Reach for the sky. Right wrist solid, arm straight. Stop at the vertical, right wrist solid all the time. Pause. Drive forward and down, arm straight. Aim your thumb at a point just above the lie – and let the line in your left hand shoot away.'

The cast felt good – a clean cast, a straight line, kissing the stream.

Again, a longer line, moving a pace downriver as the fly landed – a trick to slow the lure as it swings. I took another yard from the reel and cast once more. The fly ought to be fishing the lie by now.

But no offer.

Not far enough across? I pulled more off the reel and cast again . . . There was a slow draw on the line . . . split-second thoughts as I raised the rod-point: 'Damn! I've overcast! That sycamore!' Then, suddenly, the rod bent and throbbed with a plunging fish.

His downstream rush ripped yards off the reel, well past the backing splice, before I heard a loud *splosh*. I reeled in, slowly, hoping he was on, but fearing the worst . . . then felt him again. With rod outstretched square across the river, I backed upstream, inviting him to follow. I used no direct pressure, only the belly of line. He came willingly enough, stemming the current, using up his strength. He was just where I wanted him, clear of far-side snags, and of the dangerous shallows at my feet.

When he'd passed me, I recovered

line and bent the rod. He ran again, but not far this time. He was tiring. The next walk brought him to the eddy, where he wallowed and showed his gleaming flank. I sank my big net deep; glanced up to check the clear space overhead; then raised my arm to slide him to the net. A quick lift and he was kicking in the meshes.

Back in the broom behind the shingle, torch in mouth, I admired my prize: a magnificent early season sea trout, upwards of 3 lb, still carrying sea-lice. My fly had fallen from its hold, as often happens with soft-mouthed fish fresh from the sea. Any slackening of the line as I'd played him and he'd have got away!

I checked my fly and leader, waiting a while to rest the run, smoking a cigarette, rationalising my addiction as a way of measuring five minutes.

But no longer than that! Already the glow of a rising moon was spreading across the sky. I should have to be quick if I wanted to hook another fish.

I stubbed out my cigarette and waded into the shadows still cast by the broom and alders.

As the moon rose in a cloudless sky above Raven Crag, and the river ran silver, I relaxed on the bank. With that spotlight behind me I could no longer hide from wary sea-trout. The all-too-short June night's sport was spent. The magic hour had passed. Indeed, what magic! From the grass at my feet, two fish flashed in the splendour of the moon.

But as I savoured my success, I found myself remembering the time when fish like these would have defeated me; when I didn't even appreciate the problems, let alone know how to solve them – those frustrating fishless nights before I had read Hugh Falkus's *Sea Trout Fishing*: the book that changed my whole approach.

The way I'd caught my brace from the run – my 'recce' and my wait for darkness – the strategy and tactics – my concentration, stealth and confidence – all the details of technique (I could list more than 20 items) – everything I did, was straight from the book that, back in 1962, convinced and captivated me and brought about my friendship with the author, too. He gave his book the sub-title: *A Guide to Success*, and that is exactly what I have found it to be, many many times.

Some people may consider two three-pounders nothing much to

shout about. I agree, if conditions are favourable and your water is full of fish. But in the exacting conditions I've just described, that brace of early sea-trout covered in sea-lice matched up to the true yardstick of success. I know that Hugh Falkus would have been satisfied to do as well. We've fished together many nights, in fair weather and foul. Some nights brought an easy harvest. Far more were challenging. Success was sweeter then, with every fish a hard-won triumph.

However difficult the conditions were, with the sole exception of coloured water, I have never known Hugh to fail on any night. I remember him telling me once: 'Catching sea-trout is like a conjuring trick – relatively simple once you know how the trick is done.' (He might have added that there's more than one trick, and that you have to know where and when to try them!) I know the trick now, though sometimes I foozle it – a careless cast perhaps. But on that June night, in the heavily-bushed run where the only practical cast was the steeple, I'd got it absolutely right. Just like the photographs in Hugh's book.

At this point, well-read anglers may protest that there are no illustrations of the steeple cast in their copies of *Sea Trout Fishing*. Quite right, there aren't. Not in the first edition, nor in its reprints. But they are in the second edition, which I have had the good fortune to read in manuscript and which is now with the printers.

But a 24-frame high-speed sequence of the steeple cast isn't the only new thing about the second edition. There is a wealth of new material. Most notable, I think, are the new chapters on stillwater and saltwater fishing. The latter includes a fascinating account of how, as a young man, Falkus made a sea-pool, out on the open shore far from a river mouth by clearing away a quarter of an acre of seaweed and constructing 'lies' with boulders. It took him days of hard labour – but what results!

He holds to his original tenets, but has enlarged them and widened his scope to cover all the methods he has used, by day or night, throughout the British Isles. Lures, tackle and techniques are described in great detail and illustrated with more than 100 photographs and drawings, all dovetailed into the text.

Readers of *Trout and Salmon*

were largely responsible for getting this new work written. In 1970 the magazine published an article of mine on the Falkus concept of sea-trout fishing. The enthusiastic flood of letters that reached Hugh persuaded him to write a second edition. (Antony Witherby, his publisher, had wanted it for years.)

Publication of the second edition will demonstrate, beyond doubt, that Hugh Falkus is a great original sea-trout fisherman; and will bring the recognition denied him by most reviewers of the first edition – they failed to understand his revolutionary concept, mistaking it for mere iconoclasm. But the only valid judges are anglers who have tried Falkus' methods for themselves. Many of them have written to Hugh to tell him of their success. He takes great satisfaction from their letters, for in the first edition he gave his reason for writing, thus: 'It is because for years I have seen so many fishermen fail – simply through missing opportunities of whose existence they seemed unaware – that this book is being written.'

A simple aim it seems. But consider these words of Schopenhauer: 'The man of talent is like the marksman who hits a mark the others cannot hit; the man of genius is like the marksman who hits a mark they cannot even see.'

Exactly so. Hugh Falkus has seen new marks and shown the rest of us how to hit them. Moreover, he writes with such lucidity, zest, and rare charm, that he has created not just the definitive book on sea-trout fishing, but a classic of angling literature.

> *Next is Tom Rawling's second article on the Hugh Falkus concept of sea-trout fishing.*

TECHNIQUES TO INDUCE
BIG FISH TO TAKE

by TOM RAWLING, *June 1970*

THE READER may object that my experience is mainly on one river and that the behaviour of sea trout in other rivers is quite different. But such first-class fishermen as Brigadier G. H. N. Wilson, Dr Jimmy Skene, Mr Michael Marshall, and others, have told me of their success with Falkus methods on other rivers – Border Esk, Cumberland Derwent, Irt, Lancashire Leven, Lune, Crake, Cothi, Towy and Torridge.

It may be claimed that Falkus methods do not work on all rivers; but they certainly work on all rivers where Falkus and his friends have had the chance to use them. And by 'work', I mean not only catch fish, but succeed when traditional methods have failed!

When considering these apparent differences in sea-trout behaviour in various rivers, it is important to remember that the behaviour I am discussing is elicited in response to certain types of lures presented in certain ways. The type of stimulus, the method of fishing, is of crucial importance.

I would suggest that the fisherman for whom Falkus's methods do not work has probably applied them without conviction. He has failed to understand, or has not accepted the whole approach from which the methods spring.

A fisherman's approach to sea-trout fishing is determined by his conception of sea-trout behaviour; in particular, by his acceptance or rejection of the hypothesis that sea-trout feed in freshwater.

As a consequence of their belief in fresh water feeding, most anglers fish for sea trout as if they were brown trout, with flies that are considered to be representations of insects found in that particular river. Many of the 'flies' are clearly small-fish imitations, though this is not always admitted.

Both these types of 'flies' are usually fished on a 'floating' line just under the surface, as in traditional wet-fly fishing, with success from dusk until midnight, or so. When the fish go 'down', the conventional explanation is given –

significantly, in brown-trout terms. The 'rise' is over, the fish are 'off', and the fisherman might as well go home to bed. It may be that some thoughtful anglers have realised that nymphs and small fish are not always found just under the surface, and that sea trout might be 'feeding' deep, but F. W. Holiday roundly declares: 'Almost all fly fishing for sea-trout is now (1960) done with a greased or floating line and this is the only method which will be discussed.'

Only Bluett, of the recognised sea-trout authors I have read, discusses sunk-line fishing, although he does it with purist reluctance. My reading of his books leads me to think that though he was a good fisherman and an alert observer, he was blinkered by his belief that sea trout, when in rivers, behave exactly like brown trout.

So, to put it very briefly, the upshot of the belief in 'feeding in freshwater' is that fishermen give up at midnight, or before, when they consider sea trout have stopped feeding.

Now to Falkus, who affirms that sea trout in freshwater do not feed in the accepted sense of the word, i.e. because they are hungry and search for food. He has unrivalled opportunities to observe sea trout (and salmon) every day they are in the river. He is a highly-skilled observer, with an international reputation 'for the television films he has made in the field of bird, animal, and fish behaviour. Writing in *Anglers' Annual 1966*, he states his case, with characteristic force and lucidity. I quote a key passage:

'I do not suggest that *no* sea-trout ever takes food. No, no. But there is a very important distinction between "taking food" and "feeding" . . .

'In some rivers sea-trout will take a certain amount of food, if it is available. In others, nothing at all. But sea-trout have no need of food. Like salmon, they are equipped by nature to withstand a prolonged fast while in fresh water; and although their behaviour may vary according to their environment, and although, in consequence, some may avail themselves of occasional snacks, very few, if any, sea-trout can reasonably be termed *feeding* fish.

'Several hundreds of adult sea-trout (I am not referring anywhere in this article to herling, or immature sea-trout), come into my cottage every summer, some fresh from the sea, some after varying periods of river life. We examine the stomach contents of a great many of these fish. And what do we find?

'Nothing.

'Well – that statement is not *quite* in accordance with the facts. In the 350-odd adult sea-trout examined last year, five items of food were found: three fly larvae, one caterpillar, and remains of one unidentifiable creepie-crawlie. No fish contained more than one item. So that out of 350 fish, only five had any-thing at all in-side them. And as

that can be taken as being representative of food I have found in sea-trout over the years, you will understand why I base my fishing philosophy on the idea of "habit"!'

So much for Falkus. Now for my own experience. Every day of my holiday, I make a 'recce' of the river. Except during a spate, the water is crystal clear. The grey-green shingle bottom is lined with sized ranks of sea trout (and here and there a salmon – you can see the concave tail fin in this transpar-ent water). It is wonderfully excit-ing and instructive to peer through the alders at this great flotilla. Some fish bear scars and can be re-cognised as individuals – almost old friends, at the end of a fort-night! Occasionally, a fish will flash its side or move a few yards, but soon it glides back into station.

Insects on the water are almost entirely ignored. So, too, are ex-perimental offerings of worms and maggots. Occasionally, if the watcher persists, a salmon or sea trout can be tempted to intercept one of these many offerings – as it can an artificial lure. But such fish are rare exceptions. How dif-ferent from the hungry parr and brown trout, snapping at all that comes their way. *They* are feeding. But the sea trout and salmon lie motionless, save for a lazy fanning of the tail.

The sea trout are not feeding, yet they take a lure. Sometimes, es-pecially when the 'offers' are very tentative, I have wondered if the fish were merely investigating this strange object moving across their field of vision. Be that as it may, however, Falkus suggests that although it declines in strength as time passes, the *habit* of sea-feeding persists in freshwater. Hence, sea trout can be stimulated to take a lure that gives the impression of a creature on which they have recently fed in the sea – usually an imitation of a fish. And so, for most of his fishing he uses *lures*, and these vary in length from between 1¼ and 3¼ inches.

In the early part of the night, he fishes these lures near the surface (common ground here, at least about depth), but after midnight when the fish go 'down' (and even before, on the nights when the fish are never 'up'), Falkus does not allow himself to be persuaded that the sea trout are not 'feeding', and that, therefore, he might just as well stop trying to catch them. On the contrary, he continues to fish. And with mainly sunk-line techniques he is not only able to *induce* sea trout to take, but frequently to catch the biggest fish of the night. I have seen him do it, many times.

MOON TIDES AND SEA TROUT
by DAVID PILKINGTON, *June 1987*

WE HAD fished hard all day in the hot July sun, with just two small sea-trout to show for our efforts. The salmon had eluded us, and now, as the shadows lengthened, we were taking down the rods. The tide, which had been absent since morning, was slowly pushing up into the first run below the tail of the weirpool. We had covered this water thoroughly during the day, and had seen hardly a sea-trout. The whisky bottle was passed around, and as I paused to savour the moment, out of the corner of my eye I saw a little flash of silver in the far corner of the weir. I focused carefully, and immediately saw another, then another. 'The sea-trout are running! Look at the weir!' I shouted.

It was a sight I shall never forget, and it held us spellbound for the next hour. Whisky, wives and work were all forgotten as fish after fish came skipping and dancing through the white water, up over the weir and away. Most of them were small school peal from a few ounces to 1½ lb, with some larger fish and one or two shining, silver grilse. They were belting over that weir as if there were no tomorrow, and a little thought will explain why.

The weir in question was Gunnislake, on the Tamar, right down where fresh and tidal water come together. The tide was a big spring, 5.8 metres or so, and a tide of this magnitude raises the pool below the weir by more than 2 feet. This reduces the jump over the weir, virtually halving the vertical distance, and the salmon and sea-trout certainly know all about it. The weir is served by two quite adequate fish-passes, but on the day in question the river was carrying a fair volume of water for mid-summer, reducing the significance of the two flows from the fish-passes, so the fish were jumping fairly evenly along the 50 yards or so of the crest of the weir.

The interesting point was that, throughout the day, the weirpool had seemed to be holding only small numbers of salmon and sea-trout, and probably was. I had deliberately taken a trout rod, with a long, fine leader and tiny black flies, which I knew could be deadly for sea-trout by day down in the tidal water, and had received scant response from the fish. Few had even followed the tiny flies, and I resigned myself, rather sadly, to the fact that, despite the time of year, sea-trout were pretty scarce. Then came the magical transformation, from a river apparently sleeping to one that was, quite literally, alive with leaping, flashing, silver fish.

But this dramatic and profound influence is no magic, though it certainly seemed like it that day; it is something that happens day in and day out, with the activities and movements of the sea-trout inexplicably linked to the constant rhythms and pulses of tide and moon. In view of this vital influence, it is surprising that few writers give the tide and the moon the credence they deserve. Instead of considering the fundamentals, they go off at a tangent about line-density and fly-pattern.

I have found that the moon particularly influences my catches of sea-trout, with virtually all my best bags coming a day or two before, or up to a week after, the full moon. Yet even today, many anglers consider the full moon to be the death-knell for night fly fishing, and I cannot for the life of me understand why.

For a start, the increased light

makes movement along the river-bank so much easier and safer. More significantly, the moon affects the tides, and from the peak of the spring tides, fresh fish will come shooting upriver, ready takers and superb fighters. The waters I fish are mainly well up-river, but the speed with which sea-trout run, even in low water, is astonishing, and if I know they are taking Gunnislake weir, I fish with great confidence for the next few nights.

But there are a few things an angler should remember when he is fishing under a big moon. One of the main reasons for night fishing is to avoid spooking the fish, but there is no better way of alarming them than for an angler's moon-shadow to fall across the river. I behave just as I do in the daytime, keeping low, crouching behind bushes, and generally doing every-thing possible to keep out of sight. The sea-trout are certainly less spooky by night, but that is no ex-cuse for a casual approach.

Fortunately, much of the water I fish can be covered from the north-ern side of the river, thus avoiding any moon-shadow on the water. This does not mean that it is per-missible to stand out in the full glare of the light, however, and I remain careful at all times. One of the best beats can be fished only from the southern bank, and this presents serious problems, particularly since the pool, rather untypically for the West Country, has wide-open spaces along its banks. Here it is vital to be aware, in advance, of the exact location of the moonrise.

Divine providence has decreed that the full moon will rise after the sun has set, and that each day thereafter the slightly smaller moon will rise progressively later. This happy state of affairs can be used to great advantage. A few days after the full moon I can start in dark-ness proper, and fish thoroughly all the open sections in complete safety. Then, around midnight, the slightly dented moon lifts above Dartmoor, sending a watery light down the valley. I can still fish a few more places until, as the moon swings clear of the wooded hill be-hind me, I seek refuge in a tunnel of alders, where I can fish until dawn if need be. This sort of knowledge of a water comes only with time and careful observation, but the lessons, once learned, are priceless.

The late rising of the moon a few nights past the full has been responsible for me losing an awful lot of sleep. At other times of the moon's cycle the night becomes progressively darker, and I often pack up after a couple of hours, by which time it is often quite dark, morale has sunk, and the fish seem to have gone off. If at this point the first glimmer of extra light comes pushing gently from the east, I often get a second wind and launch into the attack with renewed vigour. The moon stimulates both fisherman and fish, often with fatal consequences for the latter.

I find that during the very light nights sea-trout will often take much smaller flies than usual. My most killing fly, overall, is a large black hairy thing, a Black Bumble, tied on Partridge lure hooks in sizes 6 and 4. I usually have something lighter and brighter on the dropper, a Peter Ross or an Alexandra about size 8. This smaller fish takes a high proportion of fish in the moonlight.

The importance of size was brought home to me dramatically quite early in my night-fishing career. I was using my usual big black fly, solo, due to the fear of nocturnal tangles, which are a little less prevalent these days. My companion was quite new to night fishing, but I could hear him having some action down at the pool tail while my stance further upstream was proving quiet. When we met at midnight, the full August moon was shining high and bright. My companion had five fine sea-trout to my one, and I asked to see his fly. It was a Peter Ross, no bigger than an 8 and rather tattered. I changed immediately to a similar fly, and we fished on up the beat, pool by pool, with the moon-shine making it almost as bright as day. It would have been possible to read newsprint at 3 a.m.!

When eventually we made our way up the hill to the car, the score had evened to nine sea-trout each, with two good brownies, a dace and a grayling thrown in for good measure! Of those 22 fish, 21 had taken the size 8 fly. I have found it worth going even smaller on occasions, particularly late in the season. Indeed, experimentation with fly-size is always worthwhile in the constantly varying conditions of light, water colour, time of year and freshness of fish.

Tidal influence is of greatest interest to those who fish on the lower beats, since an influx of fresh fish can be virtually guaranteed after each high tide. How long after obviously depends on the distance from the head of the tide. A few years ago I was privileged to fish for late-run salmon on the Plym, where my host assured me that with high tide at noon, we would see fresh fish by 3 p.m. Although I did hook a fish in the morning, sure enough it was well into the afternoon when salmon started showing consistently, and every one was bright silver.

Rather like the fish, anglers appeared everywhere, some taking fish from the most hazardous of stances on this steep, narrow river. I managed only a brief encounter with one fish which let go of the Mepps after a few seconds, but I shall long recall the sight of those deep-shouldered shining fish head-and-tailing in the swirling current, all of them straight from the tide.

If the water being fished is actually tidal, intimate knowledge of the tide's behaviour is vital. Sea-trout (and salmon) are generally best fished for in freshwater flows, which will return to normal at different times, depending on the position along the river and the height of the individual tide. Gunnislake weir is actually above the influence of the lower neap tides and can be fished regardless, but on springs the water will fill in and stand for two hours either side of high water − and not the time forecast for Plymouth Sound, but a clear hour later.

Fishing in that hallowed water below the weir one magical evening several years ago, I took fish after fish, and lost three times as many owing to their freshness. Sport was unbelievably good right up to the moment the tide eased itself into the weirpool. But once that tide came, I could not touch another fish. As I slipped away into the darkness, I had the satisfaction of knowing that the sea-trout, too, were slipping away as the tide filled in below the weir, up over the weir and away into the vastness of the river system.

❧ *To fish for sea trout in a bible-black night with only the flitting bats for company is to enter another world, one filled with hitherto inexperienced race memories when fearful things happened to those foolish enough to venture away from the fireside.*

❧ *Eyesight becomes eagle-sharp and a scuttling mouse sounds like a stalking tiger about to leap. And then there are those nights of farce . . .*

THINGS WHICH GO BUMP IN THE NIGHT . . .

by BARRY LLOYD, *June 1978*

SLOWLY I fished down through the pool in the darkness. The only sounds were those of tinkling water in the run just upstream and the 'whoosh' of the line travelling to and fro. Occasionally a sea-trout launched itself out of the depths, a whirring of a mighty tail for warning, the splash as it plunged back into the water. In front of me a high, steep, tree-clad slope ran down to the water's edge enclosing the pool within its protective shadow.

A deep sense of contentment filled me on this most perfect of fishing nights as I felt my way cautiously step by step down the pool. The charm and every characteristic of the place were embedded in my mind, for I could see little of my surroundings.

Suddenly a horrendous bellow shattered the night air and was still reverberating across the valley as something thundered its way down the banking opposite, crashing through small trees and bushes rolling and thrashing in a rapid descent that ended with an enormous splash.

A deathly silence ensued – except for the thudding of my heart. Wiping the spray from my face, I gingerly held out a torch in a less-than-steady hand. At the end of the shaft of light a pair of large eyes glowed back at me. With another bellow the clumsy cow swam ashore, leaving a shaken sea-trout fisherman once again to the solitude of the pool by night.

Little incidents such as these add a certain dash of piquancy which makes sea-trout fishing a fascinating sport for many, yet, undoubtedly, not all anglers feel this way; when dusk falls the latter tend to make their way home, leaving the fishing to others. This vague uneasiness experienced by such fishermen with the approach of darkness is present to a greater or lesser extent in most of us. Possibly it is the vestigial remnants of a fear engendered in primitive man who had no protection – except the seclusion of his dwelling – against creatures which roamed abroad at night.

Hollywood has made fortunes by playing on these apprehensions of ours and giving us vicarious thrills by means of haunted castles, swirling mists, vampire bats, and hooting owls. People with too vivid imaginations may find it impossible to relax and enjoy the solitude of the river at night, and fears are compounded for those unfamiliar with the countryside and its associated noises.

The sudden consumptive cough just behind you is easily recognised for what it is by those in the know – cows often seem to have this irritating coughing habit – but others may suspect Frankenstein is standing there waiting impatiently until they've finished the forward cast.

You may pooh-pooh the whole idea as fanciful nonsense, but first ask yourself two questions when there is nobody but yourself around to hear the answers: Are you quite happy to fish all night completely on your own, or do you often pack up after an hour or so with some excuse? Second, are you more relaxed when fishing with an open field at your back or surrounded by a dense, silent wood?

I think most honest anglers would have to admit to a certain uneasiness at times and, if we analyse our motives, perhaps there is a sense of *machismo* in overcoming this which may add to the satisfaction and enjoyment of night fishing.

Now all this plays only a minor part in our fishing, but it is as well to recognise that it might be there and may surface from time to time. Once, on a dark night when walking through some woods which separated one pool from another, my mind was engrossed as usual in the problem of what fly to try next. Halfway through the wood I felt a strange sensation on the back of my neck. I put up a hand and discovered that the hairs on the nape of my neck were standing on end. At that moment I realised that I was very apprehensive indeed – what about I'd not the faintest idea, but I was almost running by the time the end of the wood was reached.

What makes the whole episode so incomprehensible is that I'd walked through the wood hundreds of times before and knew every inch of the way, so much so that I didn't even need a torch. Feeling suitably ashamed of myself, the next night I deliberately walked through again, and this time experienced not the slightest qualm. So it has been ever since. I cannot give a logical explanation for my feelings, but I'm more understanding now of those who give sea-trout fishing a miss after dark.

Undoubtedly the companionship of a friend is a help to those who suffer from this unease, as they can then relax and enjoy their fishing, but a word of warning is necessary here regarding such companions if you are not to make the mistake that I once did. I invited my fiancée along one evening to allay any future suspicions of untruth when saying that I was going fishing at such a strange hour.

As dusk fell, I could sense an air of uneasiness about her and this was heightened when bats began to flicker a few feet overhead on their nightly pursuit of insects. The sudden screech of an owl from directly above her in a tree was the final straw and she fled back to the security of the car with visions of becoming the bride of Dracula. This was so nearly the end of a beautiful friendship, but my wife prefers to take my word for it when I now say I'm going sea-trout fishing.

To the experienced sea-trout fisher, the sight of bats coming out in search of their evening meal is a welcome one as it usually means that conditions are right for the fish to become active. Even bats – furry little creatures – have sinister connotations, but I'd never made their close acquaintance until one night last season.

I was playing a fish which had taken the point-fly when, without warning, the fight became different in a puzzling way. As I drew the fish nearer the net, I could just discern in the dusk something caught around the dropper fly. Netting the fish, I turned the torchlight on to this strange object and I was surprised to see a very angry bat which was hooked in the chest and a wing – they usually enfold their prey this way.

There I was with, in one hand, a net containing an agitated fish, the rod keeping up the tension in the other and a furious bat fluttering up and down in front of my nose. The ridiculous contortions to solve this problem were blessedly hid by the darkness from my companion upstream, but I'll never forget the fierce click of teeth on to the artery forceps as I attempted to loosen the hook.

That swirling mist, which sends a chill down the spines of addicts of late-night movies, is ominous for sea-trout fishers too – not in a ghostly sense, but for the abrupt cessation of sport which accompanies the sudden drop in temperature as the white fog rolls down off the meadows to blanket the river. I can remember only one occasion when sea-trout took well under such conditions, and another time when brown trout busily kept on taking spent spinners so that I had to strike whenever I heard an ill-mannered slurping noise from the general direction of my dry fly.

When things do go awry at night we usually have only ourselves to blame and not the supernatural. It is surprising how few anglers undertake the most elementary precaution of even a superficial daylight reconnaissance. It is easy for familiarity to lead to complacency, and yet things may have altered since our last visit to the river. A spate may have brought down a submerged tree trunk, or washed away part of a shingle spit. Who hasn't experienced that sinking feeling that comes when placing a foot and finding the river-bed no longer there? Wringing out trousers while standing on the bank bare-legged and with shirt-tail flapping is a chastening experience, especially as a sneaky breeze always seems to spring up just about then. Reconnaissance should not be confined to the actual river – the bank, too, should be explored. Then, when you set off in hot pursuit of a fish determined to take your fly back to sea, it's reassuring to know that your thundering along in the dark will not end in a dawn search-party finding you inextricably impaled on a barbed-wire fence.

Some hazards cannot be foreseen, as an acquaintance of mine found to his cost when striding over a small bush while following a powerful fish. The 'bush' rose between his legs with an alarmed bleating, and the startled angler was deposited on his back further on down the field.

Some hazards are human in origin. On one river in Wales there are two delightful characters, Thomas and his arch-rival 'Morgan the fish' – both sea-trout enthusiasts. One night Thomas left the pub at closing time as was his custom and, on arriving at a favourite pool, found Morgan the fish was 'trespassing' from the far bank. Naturally indignant that a fellow angler could sink so low as to take advantage of another's thirst, Thomas crept down through the bushes and, unseen in the dark, splashed one hand about in the water while pursing his lips and making repeated otter-like calls.

Soon blasphemous comments on otters in general, and one in particular, floated across the night air and 'Morgan the fish' was heard to wind in his line and stump away down-river in disgust.

An hour later he returned that way to find Thomas fishing the pool. On informing him that it was a waste of time due to there being an otter about, Morgan was surprised to be shown a nice, freshly-caught 5 lb sea-trout lying on the bank. The ear-to-ear grin splitting Thomas's rubicund face gave the game away, but Morgan the fish manfully forbore from making any comment and quietly went his way.

Soon Thomas decided to pack up for the night and, on walking back to where he had left the fish, was horrified to find only the head and tail remaining, the two parts being connected by the glistening bones of the skeleton.

A howl of wrath rent the night after he espied a little note pinned to the tail and which said: 'That otter I heard probably did this – Morgan the fish.'

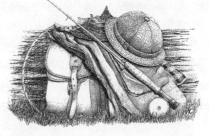

Chapter twelve

TO PUT OR TO TAKE?

⊷ Apart from returning a fish that is gravid or out of condition many anglers are convinced that to put back their captures is bad for both fish and fishery. Others are equally keen to point out that game fish, particularly those not stocked, are precious and should be returned at every opportunity.

WHO NEEDS BARBED HOOKS?
by JOHN GODDARD, *March 1985*

IT IS NOW well over ten years since I have used a hook with a barb on it for fresh water fishing. In this period I have been extolling the virtues of using barbless hooks when I could and would like to think I have helped influence the growing number of fishermen that have switched to them. There is little doubt that the numbers are now rapidly increasing, and most admit they are only sorry they did not change over years ago.

It is most encouraging to note that today apart from fly fishermen, many coarse anglers have also changed to barbless hooks, particu-larly match fishermen, although in their case they may have an ulterior motive. In matches speed is of the essence, and it was eventually realised a hook without a barb could be removed in a fraction of the time that it took to remove one with a barb. Whatever the reason I am only too delighted that this change has taken place.

I remember only too well many years ago when I used to do a lot of coarse fishing, I used to be shocked at the condition of most roach or dace I caught in rivers that were popular match venues. Mouths that were ripped and cut, others raw with fungus growing and some with missing lips that had been ripped off by the match fisherman in his haste to remove the hook. Surely these facts alone must be the biggest indictment against the use of barbed hooks, as no matter how carefully a barbed hook is removed some damage is inevitable leaving a wound that will in most cases attract some form of infection. I understand that since the introduction of barbless hooks in match fishing circles the condition of fish in match venues has vastly improved. If you doubt the damage a barb does to the mouth of a fish I suggest the next time you remove one you examine the exit point carefully. I am sure that if you are conservation minded you will seriously consider changing.

On trout fishing waters where the rules do not permit the return of fish the change to barbless hooks may seem somewhat frivolous, but in fact nothing could be further from the truth. It is now rapidly becoming accepted that far fewer fish are likely to be lost when using a barbless hook. As I have pointed out many times, unless it hits bone a barbless hook will always penetrate up to the bend, unlike a hook with a barb, where the barb itself will often prevent penetration. When this happens three things are likely to happen; either the hook will become dislodged, it will if a little soft open up at the bend, or if over tempered or if the barb has been cut too deeply break off at the point. These three hazards which result in the loss of a lot of fish are more or less eliminated when using barbless hooks. Furthermore, contrary to popular belief a barbless hook definitely does not fall out when a fish jumps or is given a lot of slack line.

On those waters where it is desirable to return undersize fish or where catch and release is not frowned upon trout can be easily and quickly released without removing them from the water. This factor alone is of great importance as the removal of a fish from its natural environment together with possible rough handling can often be injurious.

Barbless hooks are now widely used by fly fishermen in the U.S.A. and many different patterns of barbless trout hooks are available to them. Unfortunately at the moment they do not seem to be generally available over here, although it is possible now to order specially from a limited selection from Partridge of Redditch and possibly one or two other manufacturers. However the fact that barbless hooks may be difficult to locate at the moment should not deter anglers as the barb on standard hooks can be simply and quickly flattened, with a small pair of flat nosed model maker's pliers. I normally do this after I have tied the fly onto the leader and it only takes a couple of seconds.

In the U.S.A. over the past decade or so considerable scientific research has been commissioned into various aspects of trout behaviour, including specific research into the use of barbless hooks. Initial research seemed to indicate that barbed hooks were more damaging to trout than barbless ones.

However, further research seems to have proved otherwise as now on many catch and release fisheries in the States I understand you are not allowed to use a hook with a barb on it. American State Fishery Departments are now very conservation minded and I am therefore absolutely certain that they would not have introduced

such a rule without being certain it was in the best interests of the trout.

In view of the above it is very sad to note that in a recent article in another fishing journal one of our leading big trout experts stated that in his opinion barbless hooks were actually harmful. The main point of the case he put forward was that a hook without a barb will penetrate far deeper – down into the area where some nerve endings exist thereby causing more pain to the trout and possible infection when it pierces the true flesh. First of all I should like to know if this is just a theory or if it is based on scientific facts. If the latter I should like to know what his references were. In any case I find it very difficult to accept that the small hooks used by fly fishers in most catch and release situations could possibly cause such effects. Perhaps the author of this article only uses very large hooks. If this is the case then this may add a little plausibility to his opinion as the distance from the point to the bend on a hook size 8 or larger is quite considerable.

THE KILLING MUST STOP

by JOHN GODDARD, *April 1985*

DURING RECENT visits to North America I have been surprised at the rapid growth of 'no-kill fisheries', as they are often called in the States. In many areas such fisheries are now more popular than stretches on which no catch-limits exist. It is a little difficult to understand why they have become so popular, but from my conversations with anglers over there, it seems it is partly due to the fact that most American anglers are more conservation-minded than we are, and because most catch-and-release stretches hold a heavier head of trout, including many larger specimens commonly referred to as 'lunkers'.

Over the last half-century many new products and trends from the U.S.A. have eventually become popular over here. Is this likely to happen with catch-and-release? Opinion among trout fishermen seems very divided. A few fishery-owners have experimented with catch-and-release fishing, and while some are still operating such fisheries, others have given up.

Why should there be such a di-vision of opinion, and why are so many fishery-owners and managers reluctant to give it serious consideration? The main reason is probably that little or no scientific research has been carried out over here and so little positive information is available. However, considerable research has been done in the U.S.A., and it is due largely to the favourable results of such scientific studies that this form of fishing is now so popular and widespread in North America.

From my own research in the U.K., it seems that most fishery owners are opposed for two main reasons: first, that a large percentage of trout will die after being hooked and returned; second, that trout after being hooked once or twice will become impossible to catch.

Both research and practical fishing experiments in the States seem to prove beyond doubt that these fears are groundless. The weight of research over the past 20 years shows that less than 6 per cent of trout returned die as a result of being hooked on a single-hook fly. Likewise, research over the same period shows that trout do not become too difficult to catch as a result of constant hooking. In one experiment, several tagged fish were caught four or five times in a controlled period. In another study, on one stretch of the Yellowstone River in Montana, it was established that most trout are caught and returned at least five times in each 12-month period.

The success of catch-and-release in the States can be gauged from the results achieved in the Yellowstone National Park. Records kept by the park authorities show that more anglers are now fishing than ever before, and it has now become one of the most popular venues for fly-fishermen in America. The park covers several hundred square miles and contains a host of rivers, ponds and lakes, and although only a small proportion of this water is catch-and-release, more than 90 per cent of all trout caught in the park are now being returned. Records show also that on the non-kill stretch of the Yellowstone River, the angling pressure is extremely heavy, coping with nearly 4,000 angler days per mile of river per season, which means approximately 20 fly-fishers per day on every mile of river throughout the season. Despite this

pressure, the fishing is still excellent. The park authorities now seem to favour the use of barbless hooks, while they are also against the use of landing-nets as they feel physical damage to the trout from struggling in the net can result in increased mortality.

I am now in favour of catch-and-release over here on certain waters, provided that barbless hooks are obligatory and that no fish is handled or taken out of the water for the hook to be removed. This last is unnecessary with barbless hooks anyway. I would also suggest that on such waters fishermen should be advised that any trout deeply hooked in the gullet, gill arches or tongue should be immediately removed and killed, as any trout so hooked is most unlikely to survive.

Apart from all the research conducted in America on catch-and-release, other experiments have been carried out, and I am sure fishery managers and owners, as well as fly-fishers, will be interested to hear of one such experiment carried out on the Madison River from 1967 to 1971. This research was undertaken to show the effect of the stocking of catchable trout. The results are most interesting.

The study was conducted on the Varney section of the Madison and on the lower section of O'Dell Creek. During 1967 to 1969 the Varney section was stocked with catchable rainbows and the wild trout populations of brown trout and rainbows were estimated, as a result of tagging and netting, at 295 per mile. By the fall of 1971, after two years without stocking, the number of catchable trout to the mile had increased to 833, or by 180 per cent. In O'Dell Creek, where no stocking was done from 1963 to 1969, the average population of wild trout during the period was 354 per mile. By 1971, after two years of stocking catchable rainbows, the population decreased by 49 per cent, to 182 per mile.

This study shows that when hatchery-reared rainbow trout are added to self-sustaining wild trout populations, the wild trout decrease dramatically within the first two years after stocking starts.

Many years ago, when the River Test was stocked mainly with brown trout, there was also a thriving population of wild brown trout. Today, wild brown trout on the Test are a rarity. I had attributed this to increasing pollution, but perhaps it is due also to the present heavy stocking with large rainbows. This started several years ago, when it became inadvisable to stock with brown trout for fear of spreading UDN, which affected them but not rainbows.

The American studies seem to indicate that it might be possible to preserve good brown trout fishing on many of our rivers without the need to stock them, particularly if catch-and-release rules were adopted. Fisheries would be much cheaper to run without the cost of stocking, and part of the saving could be passed on to the fly-fisher fishing the water. I have a suspicion that the first fishery-owner to offer such a deal would not suffer from lack of applicants. On the other hand, many owners may feel it is too bold a step to take initially. If so, a compromise could be offered in the form of reduced stocking with a brace or less per visit to be taken, and thereafter catch-and-release.

Another alternative to stocking

rivers with mature fish is to stock heavily with fingerlings, or even yearlings, each season to supplement the stocks of wild trout. This is a longer-term plan as it will be two, possibly three, seasons before the survivors of the initial stocking attain a worthwhile size. In this period it will be necessary either severely to restrict fishing or to allow catch-and-release only. Each angler could be restricted to, say, one trout per day, and catch-and-release could be encouraged.

I know of one stretch of river in this country where this policy has been successfully adopted. It was implemented about eight years ago, and now the syndicate that runs the fishery has a superb wild-trout fishery, producing a reasonable number of trout in excess of 3 lb each season. There are no rules, and although catch-and-release with barbless hooks is encouraged, the rods are at liberty to kill the occasional brace for the table, and everyone is happy. This is as it should be. I deplore the present approach to trout fishing in this country where the current disease of 'limititus' is unfortunately encouraged by many of our angling writers.

*But what effect does an often prolonged tussle have on a fish?
Does the memory disappear in seconds or is the trauma so long lasting
as to damage its future?*

THE MENTALITY OF TROUT

by ERIC HORSFALL TURNER, *December 1971*

THE FIRST fishing I had on Two Lakes was in its early days. The creator of this superb area of stillwater, Alex Behrendt, told me that it was his definite rule to have all caught trout, regardless of size, killed and kept by the angler. It gave him a measure of amusement when I showed him my catch at the end of the day. Three trout were towards or over the 3 lb weight in each case. The other two were small 8 inch types, only an ounce or two in weight.

The reason for his insistence on removal of all caught trout was simple. It was based on mankind's biological ignorance. He said that return of a caught trout could well mean that the tough handling ended its maturing in the normal way. He made no contention that his impression was correct on this possibility; but his considerable numbers of stock trout in the nearby ponds made it easy to ensure replacement of all fish caught from the seven lakes in the area. There was no reason, in such circumstances, to take a chance on permitting the presence of trout that had deteriorated in nature.

This rule was, without question, a very sensible one. The only danger is that a percentage of controllers of trout-fishing facilities may assume that such a ruling was based on known biological facts. Let us now turn to one or two practical experiences which question the nature of such an assumption.

In youthful days, my weekly salary was two pennies a week. The tackle this bought was of very poor quality. On a cold day in early March I went up the local river with an uncle who was staying with us in the mountains. The water was heavily clouded after the recent rainstorms. The only means of catching the plentiful trout of the river was bait fishing with the worm. We started our fishing 100 yards apart. In a matter of 20 minutes I had hooked three trout, as I thought, and all had broken the hooks off the wretched leader.

My uncle was a great Yorkshire fisherman who had spent plenty of his time with the great J. H. R. Bazley. I called to him. He joined me in a few minutes with a couple of good trout in his creel. He listened to my story of the three trout that had broken my rotten leader, and put me a good leader on with its correct hook. Then he did a quick cast into the gently running water where the trout had beaten me. His rod was soon heavily bent. A few minutes later a 1 ½ lb trout came to net. Its mouth contained four hooks. Three were those I had lost; the fourth was the one presented by my uncle.

During two of my hookings, this trout had fought against my rod for a minute before breaking off; and it may well be assumed that its grab of the fourth passing worm meant that it had chewed the earlier worms with satisfaction, despite their awkward behaviour. Could it be contended that the hookings had serious effect on the nature of the trout, or on its future way of feeding? This is a definite query. The experience also explodes any contention that the hooking of such a fish imposes cruelty by mankind. This has been vindicated by a further incident during the early part of this year.

The local morland trout stream has collected excessive numbers of grayling. We take out as many as possible during the winter. Fly fishing can be an effective means as the cooling weather puts trout off the surface takes; but as the floods and extreme cold comes, there are no more dimples by the grayling. We then turn to the gilt-tail worm as bait because it seems to have very limited appeal to trout compared with maggot and ground-baiting tactics.

Last February the gilt-tail had taken three or four good grayling during the first half-hour of fishing. Then the float sank again. The rod bent heavily after the strike. A few minutes later the hooked fish came alongside the bank, in the shallow. It was a trout of about 2 lb with a singular white mark on the left side of its head. A twist or two of the hook, with the trout still in the shallow, released the fish to swim on its way. Examination of the hook showed that some damage had been caused to it by the careless pulls from the tough mouth.

A few minutes later a new hook was on the leader. The same type bait was added and the line went out from the same stance. The float soon disappeared. Once again, the strike showed that there was a heavy fish on the line. I hoped it was not another trout. This time the fight was not worth the name. The fish came steadily to the bank side. It was the same trout with the white marking on the head. Whether its gentle release after the previous hard fight had inclined it to come in gently, or whether the fight had exhausted its energy, is guesswork. The material point is that the first fight had not ended its intended inclination to grab at anything edible as the requirement of its advancing life.

How, after these experiences, can the hooking of a trout show cruelty? The probable fact is that the mouth of a fish has much the same nature as the finger-nails of mankind, and there is no appreciable feel of the drive-in of the hook point.

The main possible effect on the maturing future of the fish is its intensive anxiety during the fight for freedom. It must be borne in mind, moreover, that there is no similarity between the mental and memory natures of fish when these are compared with those of the human being. In other words, the scares of the fight may disappear in seconds from the mentality of fish. Why, in such circumstances, should there be upheaval of the normal life development of a fish by its bringing to the bank by the angler?

Factual research into this questionable situation may be rather lengthy. The obvious method would be to get an angler to catch two or three trout, varying in size from 6 inches to 12 inches, from a normal stock-pond. These caught fish, trout in particular, could then be given the usual marking and put back. The markings would arrange that they be left in the pond for the remainder of their lives; and, from time to time, their development could be examined.

It might well take as long as three years to make a definite decision on the effect of the catch and return on trout development; and this could for that matter apply to most types of fish. Such a research would be of considerable value in the sense that the factual findings would give reliable guidance to the most sensible way of dealing with caught trout of any size.

Doubts About Catch And Release

by Geoffrey Bucknall, *February 1971*

'Put-and-take' is modern stocking policy on many trout fisheries, both river and stillwater, where trout caught are continually replaced by fresh fish. Its purpose is to allow for a more intensive fishing programme. As the demand for fly fishing increases and fishery costs rise, it becomes a virtual necessity, and, as such, is beyond criticism.

It also has decided advantages, in overcoming the trouble and cost of managing natural reproduction, and the raising and wintering of indigenous trout. It allows selectivity of healthy fast-growing strains of trout, which, since they are intended to be caught soon after introduction, need not be related in size and number to the available food supply. A fishery that would not naturally support good trout can yet be a successful trout fishery on a 'put-and-take' basis.

It might seem unwise to have reservations, yet I feel that some of the results of continually injecting fresh fish into a fishery are harmful. Although the fish are easier to catch, they lack 'wildness'. This 'wildness' is easier understood by what it is not. The trout are easier to catch simply because they have been in the water too short a period of time to develop both a natural wariness and normal feeding reaction to the native fauna. As a result of 'easy fishing', we have many anglers who expect fish in return for money spent. I think we should expect to buy fishing, a subtle difference. Ideally, the fish should be neither easy to catch, nor impossible, but if we were all thrown back on really wild trout we should feel very aggrieved.

The more dangerous aspect is of the change in the feeding habits of the trout upon which our traditional standards of deception by imitation are founded. Having watched carefully trout introduced into a lake, it struck me that 'preoccupied' feeding behaviour didn't develop until the fish had been in the water for some months. Without a good degree of preoccupied feeding, the whole foundation of the artificial fly is eroded, and with it much of the pleasure of tying a fly to deceive a trout.

The 'put-and-take' policy is mostly founded on the fast-growing rainbow trout. This fish is otherwise not entirely suitable in many respects of fishery policy. It rarely survives two years after introduction, and even in its second year, on lake and river alike, it survives in a keltish condition, though apparently it seldom reproduces itself in Britain. No scientific study has ever been made of the rainbow in British conditions. It is more susceptible to eye fluke and fungus attack, though more resistant to UDN than the brownie. My view is that UDN is a normal rainbow disease, that the disease was introduced here by the species, and that its apparent immunity is simply due to antigenicity for this reason.

While the rainbow is a free-riser, it is only after a long period of acclimatisation that it feeds with preoccupation. On the Test, for example, when the fish are not apparently feeding, we know we can lure a rainbow up to a most unlikely fly, which would be rare with a brown trout. It serves the 'put-and-take' stocking policy admirably, but in chalk-streams I wonder why it is favoured for dry-fly water where its early lack of preoccupation and its habit of swinging about in the stream make it hardly an ideal subject?

Now 'put-and-take' is a fact of life and we cannot turn back the clock. This past year I had some hand in the formation of a small lake fishery and I considered what could be done to alleviate some of the harmful effects, even if it did mean a somewhat slower development of the sport. First, it does seem poor sportsmanship to inject continual supplies of fresh stew fish during the fishing, many of which are taken almost immediately before they have dispersed. The answer is to have the bulk of the trout stocked as early as possible and to reduce the bag limit during

the acclimatisation period. Thus we restricted the rods to three fish per day in April and May, rising to five for the rest of the season when the fish had dispersed and become infinitely more wary. This was explained to members, who accepted it.

Even so, during a fishing period the stocks diminish quickly and must be replaced. Believing that rainbows need the longer acclimatisation period, we put these in during early March with the bulk of stock fish, following with one seasonal stocking of smaller brownies in June – fish which our members were asked to return if undersized or giving themselves up in great numbers from their bridgehead areas. The brownies did disperse and acclimatise fairly quickly, and by August were rising freely to natural fly while proving teasing to the artificial.

These brownies are intended to winter through to provide a future stock of wild fish, because many brown trout can live and grow for many years in lakes. Given a flow of water over the gravel beds at stream outlets and inlets, there will even be some natural reproduction. Even the rainbow is 'silly' for only a number of weeks after introduction, and towards the end of the season the fish stocked in March had grown very hard to tempt, even with the lure. Lure fishing has its place, but the aim must be to prevent it from dominating absolutely the fly fishing method, so the development of a near-to-natural population of fish is intended to balance up the use of dry fly and nymph to preoccupied feeding. The predominance of the brown trout supports this policy.

My private nightmare has been that an almost entirely artificial fishery will become the norm, where the angler will weigh his sport only in terms of fish-return for money. I believe that intelligent management can mitigate the pressures on our sport so that we can provide more trout fishing while keeping it within the essential spirit of hunting a truly wild quarry. If I knew that a trout I had caught was fresh from the stew pond, associated man with the arrival of food, and took my fly for a food-pellet, I should be somewhat put-out. That's an exaggeration perhaps, but just how long does that tame conditioning take to expire? Some experts say a fortnight. In rainbows I put it at two to three months, less for native brownies.

What it comes down to in the end is that the fly fisherman wants to be proud of his catch, and fishery policy should be directed to that.

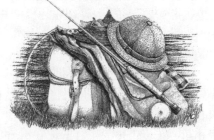

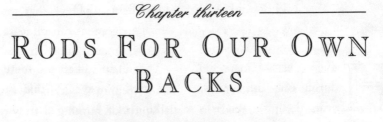

Chapter thirteen

RODS FOR OUR OWN BACKS

🦪 *I spent hours looking at that rod in the tackle-shop window. Eventually, after months of delivering newspapers, it was mine. Fashioned from greenheart, it cost a few pennies over a white crackling fiver, the first I had ever seen.*

🦪 *Lacking the bus fare back to my home in the Welsh hills I walked the eight miles clutching the rod that was to winkle out brown trout on flies tied from instructions in the back of* The Compleat Angler, *sea trout on the worm in a brown flood, and the occasional salmon taken when the keeper had retired to the pub for his evening pint.*

🦪 *With money, I blush to admit, coming from the sale of those fish, then came a built cane Alcocks Sapper, which I still treat to an annual outing.*

🦪 *My first glass rod, a solid wrist-aching affair with bright steel rings, broke on its first outing. That was over forty years ago, but those old boyhood rods are still more precious than any of the state-of-the-art carbon-fibre jobs which I cannot help regarding as being purely impersonal, yet admittedly wonderful casting tools.*

🦪 *Many gamefishers progressed through a similar genesis, making the often bitter debates which have raged throughout* Trout and Salmon's *forty years over the value of 'new fangled' rods, lines and reels all that more understandable.*

THE GLASS FIBRE ROD

by IAN CALCOTT, *June 1957*

HAVING BEEN marketed during only the last few years the glass rod is a relatively new development in the fishing tackle industry. In that time, however, it has made a considerable impact on the angling public and glass has joined built cane, greenheart and steel as one of the major rod building materials.

Two forms of glass rods are available – hollow and solid. Solid glass is the heavier, stronger and slightly cheaper of the two.

The term 'glass' is rather misleading when used in reference to rods. The glass rod is in fact made from fibres drawn from molten glass which are, in some cases, so thin that they are almost invisible.

The fibres are perfectly round and able to resist temperatures up to 1,000 degrees F. They are treated chemically before being held together by a plastic bonding agent.

Various techniques are used by different manufacturers in the building of solid or hollow glass rods, but the same microscopic filaments are used in both constructions.

The main difference between the two, however, is that in the making of a hollow glass rod the fibres are woven into a glass cloth. This cloth is chemically treated and then rolled on steel shafts, known as mandrels, to the correct taper before being baked in an oven. Following this baking the glass blank is sandpapered and varnished and is ready for assembly.

Two procedures exist in the manufacture of solid glass rods. Some firms taper the yarn before it is impregnated with resin and then molded, while others gather the yarn, impregnate it with resin, mold it and then grind the block to the desired taper.

The actual glass content of rods varies from as much as 75 per cent, to as little as 35 per cent. Lower quality rods have a very low glass content while a small diameter blank has a high glass content to give it additional backbone.

Thus it will be seen that glass rods have a considerable percentage of plastic and it is this material that really alters the quality and character of a rod for while the glass has great strength and elasticity the fatigue life of the bonding agent is not as great.

As a result, and contrary to common belief, glass rods can take a set or permanent bend.

Normally even the stiffest of fights will make no difference to a good quality glass rod and constant casting, too, should not harm it. But if the rod is put to a severe and prolonged stress a set is possible. One advantage of the glass rod is its ability to withstand high or low temperatures without suffering any ill effects.

The construction of the glass rod shows certain similarities to the building of a cane rod in that baking constitutes a major part of the operation, but when action and feel of both types are considered the similarity ends.

Practically every glass fly rod I have handled has been much too soft for good casting. Some have been decidedly floppy. In my estimation a glass fly rod cannot compare in action with a built cane weapon of the same length.

There must surely be some good glass fly rods available, but I have yet to see one. To my mind they just do not have the backbone of a good cane rod. I have not yet had the opportunity of trying a glass

salmon fly rod for Spey casting, but there is, I feel, some hope for them in that direction. Built cane rods are, of course, much used for Spey casting, but the twisting action of the cast tends to open up the cane. A glass rod would be able to stand the twist and would certainly not break so readily as greenheart.

Glass spinning rods, however, are a different proposition. I have in my possession an eight foot hollow glass salmon spinning rod which was bought with certain feelings of trepidation. But it has acquitted itself admirably. The feel in use is delightful; the action is stiff without being like a broomhandle – a fault of many stout cane rods. It is still as straight as it was the day I purchased it; it is exceptionally light – under 8 ounces; and is capable of handling any salmon.

Yet again, I have handled several solid glass spinning rods which were very soft. One tackle dealer showed me an American model and touched the off-set handle with the tip without using much strain at all.

To summarise: glass rods have exceedingly high tensile and compressive strengths, are extremely elastic and have an almost infinite fatigue life, but generally speaking cannot compare in action to a good built cane rod. While good glass spinning rods can be obtained the problem of the glass fly rod is not so easy to solve.

But surely if the manufacturers are able to build suitable glass spinning rods they can find a way of making a useful fly rod which will compare with a built cane model.

THOUGHTS ON TROUT RODS
by JACK WINNARD, *January 1962*

IT SURPRISES me that many experienced trout fishermen fish for small trout (average about 8 oz to 12 oz) with a rod which is stiff and more suited to dealing with sea trout and large brownies of 2 to 3 lb weight.

I remember that when I bought my first trout fly rod I knew nothing about fly fishing and had to be guided by the advice of the manager of a tackle firm. He enquired where I fished and supplied me with a beautiful fly rod, still after some 15 years of hard use and one renovation, an excellent rod. I now use it solely for sea-trout fishing at night and it really murders a five-pound fish. It killed three salmon one afternoon in a really

bowling water without any trouble. To use this as I did for many years on 8 oz trout was depriving me of much pleasure and many fish into the bargain.

To me it seems that many so-called trout fly rods are modelled on rods designed for fishing the chalk streams of Southern England where large trout are the rule rather than the exception. They are no doubt excellent for the chalk streams but an abomination on many of our northern rivers.

When a small trout, and by small I mean anything up to 12 oz, is played on one of these powerful rods, the fish has not enough weight to bend the rod sufficiently to take line, and the result is a flurry on the surface and a flapping and splashing all the way to the net. The only thing to do in such a situation is to get the fish out as quickly as possible because the longer it flaps, the greater the possibility of the hook coming away. And the disturbance must be frightening to other trout. This is all very well if one requires fish only, but what thrills are missed. Another fault with these powerful rods is that in the event of striking too hard, the fine cast point is easily broken.

A friend of mine was fishing with an original dry fly he had designed for coloured water. I doubt if there is another like it in existence. He came to me to tell me that he had been broken by a big fish. A day later I caught this fish, with his fly embedded in its jaw. It was just over six inches long. I am sure that had he been using a less powerful rod, the give in the tip would have absorbed the excess power of the strike. This particular angler had a general fault of striking too hard and lost many fish through doing this. Since changing his 'poker' for a more fairy-like wand he has lost far fewer fish at the strike.

There are very few trout rods in my opinion which are ideal for small trout. Generally speaking the average trout angler is not a purist. He fishes the method that takes his fancy; sometimes it will be wet fly, sometimes dry fly. And not all anglers go out sufficiently often to justify both a wet and dry fly rod, nor can all afford the luxury of two rods. The thing to do is to choose a rod which will serve for both methods of fly fishing.

A phrase often appears in fishing tackle catalogues: 'Medium-actioned for wet or dry fly.' So far as I am concerned these rods are a little too stiff for an ideal wet-fly rod. The phrase, 'Inclined stiffish for dry fly, usually means that once again for me the rod is too stiff for a dual-purpose rod.

When one thinks of past anglers fishing with horsehair casts, one realises that the rods they used in those days must have been very different from our modern rods. In the evolution of our modern rods, many advances have been made regarding weight, strength, durability and materials used; but some of the more delightful properties of these old-fashioned rods have been lost on the way. Old illustrations of rods show them to be of great length, and this is one of the properties to have been lost.

As one who never fishes a chalk stream this loss in length is alarming. An 8 foot 6 inch rod may be all very well when one covers a rising fish, but when one often has to hang a top dropper on the far side of a run, or float a dry fly on the other side of fast water, such a rod is too short. And if one fishes upstream, the fishing distance of each cast is small. The same fault is found when lake fishing.

I would not like to fish with a 12 or 13 foot rod for trout no matter how gentle the action, but a 10 foot rod to me is approaching the ideal length.

My ideal rod would also have plenty of 'give,' so that even when a half-pound trout was hooked, the rod would bend and allow the fish to keep below the surface and take line. If a trout should be lightly hooked, it stands a much better chance of coming to the net on such a rod than one of these 'poker' rods. One of the greatest pleasures for me is the playing of a trout. That doesn't mean that I like playing a fish for an excessively long time. On the contrary, I try to bring a trout to the net as soon as I possibly can. But there is no doubt that the softer the rod, the more pleasure I obtain from playing small trout. After all it is no more incongruous to fish for small brownies with an 8 foot 6 inch poker than it is to fish for salmon with tunny tackle.

The next trout rod I buy will be soft to medium in action. I find it easier to fish dry fly with a soft-actioned rod than I do to fish a wet fly with a stiff action.

The rod I want must be at least 10 feet in length, light, but not powerful. I hope I can find one!

  That well-made built-cane fly rods would have no place in modern game fishing was a fear which, happily for their many enthusiasts, has proved to be groundless.

GLASS OR CANE?

letter from FRANK HEWITT, *June 1957*

IF I WERE still in the split-cane, rod-making business, which I was for many years, I do not think I should be particularly upset by R. Barraud's statement that the days of the first-class, built-cane fishing rod are numbered. This would be principally because I would know that such a statement would induce an equal and opposite reaction from those who are still split-cane minded, and to some degree still disappointed in the rods which glass techniques have provided.

When he goes on to imply that sawing the cane strips before milling is a relatively new development, I am sure he is flogging a pretty ancient horse, since I very much doubt if any but a very tiny proportion of split cane produced in the last 30 years has been made by any other method. Furthermore, a skilled sawbench hand is always able to detect crossgrain and reject unsuitable material.

I doubt if anyone was very successful in using a 60 degree since, although this was theoretically perfect, the outside appearance of cane so made was not acceptable. Consequently, the practical limit of perfection in this respect was usually 59.8, or something in that order. Contrary to what Mr Barraud says, this did not affect the labour or skill. It was purely a matter of the angles at which the cutters were ground.

There is, of course, no shortage of the genuine Tonkin cane, except in so far that obtaining anything at all from China, where the best Tonkins grow like weeds, is obviously difficult. The difficulties are now, however, insurmountable. American split-cane makers have been the hardest hit for political reasons, as they had to make do with Formosan cane, but most split-cane makers in England are still getting adequate supplies of the genuine China cane.

I think all anglers will await the developments of new materials, such as carbon, with great interest, but for many years yet I am sure that the specialised, split-cane rod builder who knows his business will continue to find a ready market for his products.

❧ *In 1957, mention was made of a new fly line destined to oust for ever the old silk lines. Nothing was more certain to arouse the anger of* Trout and Salmon *readers who, at first, regarded the new plastic affairs as being little more than a nine-day wonder.*

BUBBLE LINES

by EDGAR ROCHE-KELLY, *July 1959*

EVERY ANGLER who goes after the big lake trout with the dry fly will remember an occasion when, on some lovely calm evening, he has manoeuvred his boat quietly into the vicinity of a really outsize trout well on the feed and has laid out his spent gnat or big sedge on the probable course of the fish which was steadily 'mopping' down the natural flies.

If it was the angler's lucky evening, the fish may have turned towards his fly fairly quickly. But more often than not, he will have had to shift the boat several times and make a number of casts before that wonderful moment when his fly disappeared in a heavy swirl.

And then, horror of horrors, he found himself dragging up two or three yards of his heavy tapered line which had sunk quietly near the boat while he was watching the approach of the fish to his fly. And by the time he did manage to connect with the distant fly, friend trout had let go at his leisure and had moved elsewhere for a softer morsel.

No matter how carefully you may clean and grease your line, there are certain conditions of rather scummy water where surface tension seems almost non-existent and the wretched line persists in sinking at just the wrong moment.

The problem was one to which I had devoted much thought and many experiments but it was not until the advent of the American bubble lines about two years ago, that I found the long-sought remedy. Like most experienced anglers, I tend to be conservative, but, having examined the first lot of these lines which came to Ireland, I decided to give one a trial.

J. R. Harris kindly selected a heavy double-taper to balance my old 'Knockabout' rod, and I used it throughout that season with the utmost satisfaction.

It seems quite impossible to sink the line and greasing is unnecessary. It casts and shoots line at least as well as an equivalent dressed silk line and it does not appear to require drying after use. I have used it extensively on Lough Sheelin and Lough Mask during the past two seasons and have killed a number of good trout up to seven pounds and on no occasion has the line failed to float, no matter how long I left it on the water.

In the first season the line was used only for trout fishing but during the second spring I decided to try it for salmon on the Boyne using the greased line technique, and here too, it was a complete success. It seems to me that it is perfect for the job. There is no preliminary cleaning and greasing of the line, always an irritation especially when fishing time is short, and it floats beautifully even in the roughest water.

Mending the cast is simplicity itself even with a light rod and the line does not become waterlogged during a long struggle with a heavy fish. I killed a number of spring fish using it with the trout rod and also with a heavier salmon rod.

A friend who is the proprietor of what is probably the best fishery on the Boyne and who is a most experienced salmon angler, began to use these lines about the same time as myself and he tells me that he thinks they float almost too well for greased line work on big water. He has adopted the expedient of splicing a yard or two of ordinary dressed silk line to the end of the 'bubble' line and fishes this ungreased, getting very good results.

In the version of these lines which is available in Ireland, each end of the tapered line contains a small metal ring which is built into the line itself and apparently intended for attachment of the cast. In my case I cut this off at once as I preferred to attach the line to the cast by means of a knot (conservatism again!). But it should be quite possible to attach the salmon cast to the ring in accordance with the American practice and then to nip on to the ring a grain of split shot of suitable size to achieve the desired degree of sinking. Incidentally, the makers state that these rings and their attachment to the lines have been tested up to quite considerable breaking strains.

I would suggest that before purchasing one of these lines, it should, if at all possible, be tried on the rod for which it is intended as it is rather difficult to judge their weights over the counter. There is a considerable variation in the relative diameters as compared with similar dressed silk lines to which most of us are accustomed. The bubble line for any given diameter is much lighter. The only snag I have encountered is that of price. It is fairly high, due no doubt, to a combination of import duty and the unfavourable exchange rate vis-à-vis the dollar. But in spite of this, I hope to acquire another one of these lines this year and it will be a lighter one to be used exclusively for trout fishing. I will reserve my first and well tested line for greased line salmon work.

No doubt too, it will not be long before some enterprising British manufacturer will tackle the question of manufacture. But in the meantime, even at their present prices, these lines seem to fill a long felt angling want.

BUBBLE LINES
letter from M. POTTER-MOORE, November 1959

I WAS very interested in a recent article by Mr Roche-Kelly, concerning the use of Bubble Lines.

I am a keen fisher for sea trout on the Torridge, and have always been interested in the comparatively small numbers caught, bearing in mind the thousands of fresh fish which, undoubtedly, enter our river from June onwards. I was, therefore, doubly interested when I met a fisherman who had caught several dozen good fish over a few weeks.

He asked me if I had ten minutes to spare and he would show me. He took me to the tail of a pool, around 9 p.m., where I have several times fished before with remarkably little success. He took two peal of around 1 ¼ lb in the first few minutes.

His secret was that he got his fly, almost any reasonable fly, right down to the fish, by using gut casts. I changed instantly to gut, and with my fly deeply sunk, took two fish of 4 ½ and 2 ½ lb the next evening.

Nevertheless, my troubles were not over, as very soon I found the grease from my line worked on to the cast, the fly did not sink deep enough, and I stopped catching sea trout. I solved the grease question, by buying a Bubble Line for nearly £5.

On its case it is described as 'non-sinkable.' Let me say straight away, that I have used this beautiful smooth line, size HEH, on still, gently flowing and faster water, and in every case it has sunk like a stone after two or three casts. The line is now being returned to the manufacturers for their comments, which I am sure will be nothing like my own!

I note, however, that your contributor used a line of a heavy double taper, and when selecting my lighter line, I noticed that the lighter lines were quite different in colour, texture and material to the heavier lines. I was tempted to buy one of the darker, heavier lines, but they were quite rough to the touch, whereas the light trout lines were dead smooth and beautifully finished with a high polish.

I should, therefore, be interested to hear the experiences of other readers who may have tried these lines. It may well be that they forgot to put the bubbles in, when they made my line!

CAN TROUT SPIT OR BLOW?
letter from HARRY BROSCOMBE, *September 1964*

I WAS very interested to read the contribution made in the October issue by our good friend Frank Sawyer on the above subject and his reference to Dermot Wilson's observations on the same thing.

Their opinions about this I find rather surprising for surely the descriptive word is neither spit nor blow but should be eject.

The writer has had many opportunities of observing trout feeding and ejecting any item which did not appeal to their palate. This is done quite simply by a contraction of the gills to the side of the head which causes a forward propulsion of water from the throat end of the mouth out through the lips. The water automatically carries the unwanted item out with it into the stream.

This is the reason why, assuming we strike correctly, the majority of our fish are hooked in the lip before the fly has passed out of the mouth.

❧ Hot on the heels of the introduction of a plastic line to replace the oiled silk followed the suggestion that there were definite advantages in fishing with a white fly line instead of the traditional green.
❧ And so were sown the seeds of a still to be resolved argument.

Fishing A White Line

by Eric Taverner, *January 1957*

I READ recently of an angler, who described himself as having poor eyesight, using a white line when he fished a floating fly. He found that when it was lying on the surface of the water it was easy to see and that in a ruffle it enabled him to fix the exact position of the fly. He was quite satisfied that the line so placed did not scare the fish.

If a line is floating properly it is invisible from below the surface, except when it enters the personal window of a given fish. In practice it may just penetrate at one or two short sections of its length, but no more than the general buoyancy of the line will support. Its colour, therefore, is of no account in terms of visibility. The most that can be seen from below of the presence of a line on top of the water (in the Area of Total Reflection) is the depression caused by its weight bearing upon the elastic skin of the surface. This long narrow ridge is unlikely to be constant in size or occurrence.

As far as aquatic vision is concerned, the opacity of a line is far more important than its superficial colour. A white line will look as dark as will an olive one, when viewed from below. Under special conditions there may be a minute amount of illumination received by the inferior surface of a line; and this will have been reflected from below. This transient coloration will be accepted more readily by a white line than by an olive one; but the cryptic effect, that is the degree of camouflage achieved, will depend on the depth of water. The greater the distance between reflector and receptive surface, the weaker the light received. The lateral illumination of a floating line is, also, insignificant in quantity and importance. There is no question here of any obliterative shading, as described by Thayer.

Now the explanation suggested as to why trout were not scared by a floating white line is that a white belly in a fish and the whiteness in such a line, when viewed from below, confer on either invisibility. Here, surely, is a fallacy. It is obvious that an object floating or submerged, when viewed vertically, is seen merely as a silhouette. A pike, for example, looking upwards toward the belly of its two areas merged jointly into a back-prey, sees it not as a pale-coloured surface, indistinguishable from the sky, but as an opaque object outlined against a light background. So indeed will a white line appear from below.

Thayer's Theory of Obliterative Shading sets out to explain the protective value of permanent pigmentation in all fishes, namely, a dark dorsal region and white, ivory or silver on the belly; while the flanks show a gradation in colour and tone from dark to light. Even the Nile catfish, which swims upside down, conforms to this scheme, having a dark belly and a pale-coloured back.

Thus a fish seen from its own level exhibits a pale under-side slightly modulated in colour or tone by reflection, and an upper surface so strongly illuminated by top light that the two regions of the body approximate to each other in appearance.

If the horizontal background against which a fish is seen is the sea or the waters of a large clear lake, it will tend to melt into it. If it does not thus become invisible, at least its shape will be obliterated to some extent. In a river, however, less protection is afforded, as the background will never entirely lack colour and contrast.

Reduced visibility is secured, not through the paleness of the belly of a fish, but through the upper side being so strongly lit by top light, that the ground is similar enough in tone to suggest that the fish is not there. But in the case of even a submerged line the only part to be directly illuminated is the top; and in a white line that will remain white. This aspect of a floating line can never be seen by a fish.

There are, however, conditions under which it is desirable to fish a sunk fly for salmon or in night fishing for trout, and it is important to make the line go down as far as is practicable. By day the line then swims through an area of diffused light, reflected by an infinite number of minute particles in the body of the water, and though it is still opaque it is illuminated differentially.

It is a matter for speculation whether, indeed, a submerged white line, owing to its ability to pick up environmental colouring may be no more visible to a fish than an olive one. It might even be less so. How a fish reacts to it at night is difficult to say with any confidence. Reflected light as well as direct illumination from above are absent, and it would therefore appear very dark. It could hardly have the attractive power of tinsel on the body of a fly, for that is a true mirror; and the advertising value of such a fly rests largely upon its contrasts. Morning and evening twilights may, however, create conditions that are not so favourable. In brief, I would not choose a white line for evening or night fishing, if I had another

available. Only extended experiments will establish the truth.

Many anglers must have observed the strong shadow thrown on to the river-bed by a line on the surface or just beneath it, a shadow many times broader than the object projecting it. But I have never seen this shadow frighten a fish. Probably, it is taken for the shadow of grass, twig or other trash going down on the current. If a fish will stand the shadow it will surely tolerate the presence of a line, no matter what the colour may be.

In conclusion, there is nothing detrimental to sport in the use of a floating white line nor, as far as can be judged, when it is sunk. As visual advantage to the angler ceases as soon as a white line goes under the surface, its use then cannot be justified until we know more about how fish react to it, especially at night.

A COLOURED FLY-LINE DEBATE
letter from T. B. THOMAS, September 1979

AS CERTAINLY the first person ever to use white fly-lines, perhaps I may comment on this matter? When, in 1947, Milward's started experi-

ments with Terylene lines, we found it was a most difficult material to dye. The first spinning lines we made were, therefore, white. The first white Terylene line ever used was by Colonel Roy Harrison, who promptly caught a 32-pounder almost with his first cast, on the Wye.

When we progressed to fly-lines, we found that oil dressings would not adhere to Terylene and nylon and we therefore developed a colourless plastic. Again, because of the dyeing difficulties, the first prototypes we tried were white. I found them delightful to use. At that time I had some correspondence with Esmond Drury, whom I had known for some years. He had had similar ideas, so I was very happy to send him some lines, and even happier, since I had long reckoned he was one of the best trout and salmon anglers in the country, to learn he was similarly enthusiastic. Since that time I cannot prove I have caught more fish on white lines, but I certainly haven't caught fewer.

I have doubts about the effect of flash on fish. The only subject to do with angling on which I have no doubts is the frightening effect of shadow. Those reservoir fishermen, whose lines are more in the air than in the water, disturb a big area of water. But the proof of the pudding is in the eating: white floating fly-lines greatly outsell those of other colours.

On another matter, I agree with the points made by Tony George on the matter of the Usk in the 1860s and 70s, except his belief that the method used was sunk line. Before the successful development of the oil-dressed line around 1880, lines were of horse hair and would not sink deeply. The fly had to be fished high in the water. Wood, like Rodin, did not invent; he discovered.

letter from A. A. SIPSON, *July 1981*

I HAVE followed the debate relating to the disturbing effect of white fly-lines with great interest (Richard Walker – May issue and earlier correspondence). One aspect which appears to have been patently overlooked is the fact that 'flash' is usually transmitted from polished or glossy objects. Therefore, while accepting that a white fly-line may be the worst offender – since the deflected sunlight is enhanced by the white background – polished lines of other colours can also produce the effect.

The similar problem encountered with the gloss varnish on fishing rods is avoided by the recommended solution of coating the rod with a matt varnish!

Opinions expressed in discussion on the correct casting stance appear academic to me; it is only in ideal conditions (for example, on a casting platform or on flat, open ground on a windless day) that a classic stance can be maintained. Usually, the angler has to modify his footing according to the environmental conditions to be overcome at the fisheries; the concrete apron at a reservoir is an extreme, but not unusual, example.

letter from A. TOMKINS, *January 1975*

I HAVE only just ended my second season as a very mediocre (or unlucky!) trout angler, but may I nevertheless offer my opinions in the controversy over the colour of fly-lines?

The main point, I gather, is whether or not light-coloured fly-lines scare fish. It has been my experience that even my ultra-fine 2 lb b.s. points have scared fish if placed anywhere in their range of vision (frequently accomplished with my indifferent casting techniques). I am sure that the anglers who proclaim the virtues of dark-coloured lines catch little more than those expounding light lines.

If the argument is that light lines are more easily seen waving about in the air, then I do not see how this can be proved by looking up at a static line from beneath a glass-bottomed bucket.

In all, I think it is the best anglers, and the anglers fortunate enough to be in the right place at the right time, who catch the most, regardless of the colour of their line.

letter from W. G. MCPHERSON, *October 1975*

I DO NOT think it matters what colour a fly-line is, from the trout's point of view. Over the years untold thousands of trout have been caught on the top fly of the wet fly fisherman's cast, which is 3 feet from the line. Now either the trout did not see the line, or it saw the line and was not bothered by it.

An angler fishing with a fly some 9 feet from the line should therefore feel with some confidence that it is not the colour of his line which prevents him taking fish, though that line be white, black or tartan.

I present the tartan idea to the line-makers free. Why not have our fly-lines in our clan tartan? This should be a hot seller in the USA. My own clan would have a choice – I rather fancy the dress tartan, a theme mostly in black and white. If I receive a complimentary one, I undertake to fish with nothing else.

As regards the adipose fin in fish, I side with Royalty in thinking it is now merely a relic, a useless appendage – nay, worse than useless in some cases, for I caught my best salmon by means of it, in the Spey. Pleasant it is to sin in good company!

I do not think the adipose fins is a means of storing up fat against lean times. The whole thing would be but a poor mouthful. Of course, when a trout gets thin it gets thin all over, including the adipose fin. One may as well say that the cheeks of a stout person were his food reserves – and see how they disappear in ill-health or short rations!

letter from RICHARD DERRINGTON, *September 1981*

PLEASE EXCUSE my naivety on the subject, but it does seem to me that the protracted correspondence on the colour of floating fly-lines is among the most futile ever.

In the cases where a fish really is scared off by a line, it is much more likely to be the 'driver' who is at fault. A line of any colour will cause a fast-moving and, therefore, maybe dangerous shadow when false cast in bright sunlight; and the colour won't affect the wake caused by an excessively speedy retrieve.

Perhaps the proof that this argument, though interesting, can have no positive conclusion, is that so many people can write with such conviction from totally opposing viewpoints.

❧ *If nothing else came of it, the sparring between the white line and plastic line camps served to mask the coming into regular use on game rivers of the fixed-spool reel. The accusation that they made bait fishing for trout too easy was followed by a strong suggestion that they should be banned altogether as being unsporting.*

INVENTION OF THE DEVIL?

by JACK WINNARD, *September 1962*

THERE IS little doubt that fishing, both for salmon and trout, is on the decline and has been declining alarmingly for the past twenty years. This decline cannot be laid at the feet of any one factor, rather it is the sum total of several.

We are all well aware of the fact that drainage authorities are rushing the water off the fells and fields back to the sea as quickly as they possibly can. Of the little left, water authorities (for the sake of cheap water) are abstracting it not from where it can do the least harm to the rivers (the lower reaches) but from the head-waters. Thus the shortage is felt throughout the entire river system. In addition to this, various sources pollute what little remains.

The effect of these depredations on the breeding stock can only be imagined, in fact they must be imagined as there is no way in which the damage can be measured. So we are left with a much-reduced volume and flow of water. This has a bearing on the amount of food in the river and consequently on the stock of trout and parr that it will support; a number far smaller than a hundred years ago. Due to the siltation of redds caused by the increased erosion from 'better drainage', the spawning qualities of the becks are also decreasing with consequent disastrous effect on stocks.

All these factors we must accept and leave to the appropriate authorities where they exist to combat. Another factor contributing to the decline of sport is the vastly increased number of anglers. In short there are more and more anglers to fish less and less water. Another factor closely coupled with this is the improvement in tackle. Less than a hundred years ago the trout fisherman fished with a horsehair cast, often without a reel; tackle which would permit no mistakes. With the advent of split cane rods, longer and more accurate casting has become possible; the horsehair has been replaced first by gut and then by nylon. Very efficient reels have also been developed. All these improvements in tackle make an angler's efficiency greater and reduce the amount of skill necessary to catch a fish. Consequently it is easier to catch the fewer remaining trout.

One of the greatest 'improvements' has been the development of Illingworth's fixed-spool principle. This, coupled with the reliability of nylon monofilament line, has done more to cause the decline in angling, particularly in trout fishing, than any other so-called 'improvement'. Were it possible for an authority to autocratically ban the use of the fixed-spool reel, I would be its most ardent supporter. Perhaps the salmon angler who fishes a small bait in small rivers in summer can put forward a good case for its use, but so far as I am concerned this case is far out-weighed by its evils.

I suppose every angler who goes fishing, does so because he enjoys some aspect of the sport. With some it is the peace and solitude of the country itself, with others the test of skill, pitting wits against the fish. Some go who have no appreciation of the finer arts involved; they go purely to kill fish; in fact they might be fishmongers. Into this last category I would place those anglers who spin a natural minnow for trout. The only skill required is to be able to cast a minnow fairly accurately and wind it back again. The trout will do the rest.

There is no doubt that this is a deadly method of catching brownies. Any novice who equips himself with the correct tackle and receives a minimum of tuition and advice can take trout after trout, and good ones, too, from the fast water of many rivers. Particularly is this so in the early part of the season. In such ways the trout stocks are thinned down almost as soon as a season opens.

Where is the pleasure in playing a small trout choked with hooks, on a fixed-spool reel with a slipping clutch? The damage done to immature trout extracting two or three trebles embedded in its mouth is such that the poor thing is almost sure to die.

A form of taking trout that has had the skill taken out of it by this infernal machine is upstream worming. Seldom do anglers fish in this pleasant manner now, using a long supple fly rod and carefully toughened worms. It apparently takes too much trouble to cast accurately and sufficiently gently to be able to keep the worm on the hook. The modern way is to use a fixed-spool reel with a 2 lb b.s. line so that with one or two small split shot and a small worm the angler can cast accurately and retrieve the bait easily. Once again more trout are being taken which would otherwise have been safe from all but those who had taken the trouble to acquire the necessary skill.

I have often come across anglers with, literally, a bagful of trout. They have quite unashamedly taken these on the threadline reel which instrument is making angling far too easy for too many. This is, of course, having disastrous effects on trout stocks all over the country and it is something that we as anglers can control by doing our utmost to ban the use of these reels for trout.

No doubt if all game clubs passed by-laws prohibiting its use they would upset a proportion of their members, but I am sure that all true anglers would wholeheartedly welcome such a ban.